**CAPITALISM
KILLED
THE
MIDDLE CLASS**

CAPITALISM KILLED THE MIDDLE CLASS

25 Ways the System is Rigged Against You

Dan McCrory

Copyright © 2019 by Dan McCrory.

Library of Congress Control Number:		2019901936
ISBN:	Hardcover	978-1-7960-1588-1
	Softcover	978-1-7960-1587-4
	eBook	978-1-7960-1586-7

All rights reserved. No part of this book may be reproduced or transmitted in any form or by any means, electronic or mechanical, including photocopying, recording, or by any information storage and retrieval system, without permission in writing from the copyright owner.

Any people depicted in stock imagery provided by Getty Images are models, and such images are being used for illustrative purposes only.
Certain stock imagery © Getty Images.

Print information available on the last page.

Rev. date: 03/07/2019

To order additional copies of this book, contact:
Xlibris
1-888-795-4274
www.Xlibris.com
Orders@Xlibris.com
784781

CONTENTS

Why I Wrote This Book..vii
Chapter 1   An Introduction..1
Chapter 2   Fair Trade vs. Free Trade...13
Chapter 3   Capitalism ≠ Democracy and the Occupy Movement..27
Chapter 4   ALEC, the Powell Manifesto and the Heritage Institution..41
Chapter 5   What's wrong with a two party system?.....................69
Chapter 6   What About a Labor Party?..85
Chapter 7   We the People: Abdicating Oversight of our Political Systems and our Politicians...97
Chapter 8   The Vanishing Middle Class.......................................113
Chapter 9   The Workplace Balance of Power..............................121
Chapter 10 Who's Telling Our Story? Media Consolidation 133
Chapter 11 The American Caste System 149
Chapter 12 Government As Protector..159
Chapter 13 Pension Raiders and Deadbeats..................................173
Chapter 14 Unions as Appeasement?..183
Chapter 15 Soldiers of Fortune 500s 195
Chapter 16 Third World Incursion: Bring Back Our Jobs!..........211
Chapter 17 Bankers, Stockbrokers and Money 223
Chapter 18 The Gig Economy 237
Chapter 19 Environment vs. Economy...247
Chapter 20 Education: Right or Privilege? 259
Chapter 21 No Justice! No Peace! 275
Chapter 22 Healthcare Haves and Have-nots 289
Chapter 23 Housing and Homelessness..305
Chapter 24 Death and Taxes 319
Chapter 25 Evolution Or Revolution? 329

References 347
Biography...359

Why I Wrote This Book

"Capitalism has defeated communism. It is now well on its way to defeating democracy." David Korten

"...when the United States is a service and information economy; when nearly all the manufacturing industries have slipped away to other countries; when awesome technological powers are in the hands of a very few, and no one representing the public interest can even grasp the issues; when the people have lost the ability to set their own agendas or knowledgeably question those in authority; when, clutching our crystals and nervously consulting our horoscopes, our critical faculties in decline, unable to distinguish between what feels good and what's true, we slide, almost without noticing, back into superstition and darkness..."
— Carl Sagan,
The Demon-Haunted World: Science as a Candle in the Dark

"The evils of capitalism are as real as the evils of militarism and evils of racism."
— Martin Luther King, Jr.

I have visited family members and many of the friends I had in high school and have been shocked at the plights of many of them: no pension, ill health, facing the prospect of a very bumpy ride into old age and premature death. I am one of the lucky ones. No matter how much I denigrate corporations – and my former employer AT&T specifically -- I have to give the company credit for providing me with a stable income and benefits, the opportunity for education and advancement, and some ability to steer my destiny though, of course, most of those benefits were bargained for with my union, the Communications Workers of America. This book is for those I'd like to help but can't, because helping them could upset my own shaky stand on the thin ice of Middle-Class existence.

The word "capitalism" in the title is shorthand for what some call "crony capitalism," an economy in which businesses thrive not as a result of risk taken for them, but rather, as a return on money amassed through a nexus between a business class and the political class. Crony capitalism is the result of corporate greed. Corporations aren't people, though, no matter what the Supreme Court has ruled. Corporates CEOs and their boards of directors have created this atmosphere of greed. The oft-quoted line from the film *Wall Street* as uttered by the character Gordon Gecko was "Greed is good." We know it's not; it's the road to ruin for us and our country.

And though my title refers to the Middle Class, I admit it's a marketing ploy to reach as many as I can because that title includes the 26 percent of US households that make over than $100,000 per year. The U.S. Census Bureau reported that the average median income was $59,036 per household in 2016. According to a study by the Pew Research Center, around 42 percent of households are the true middle class. They earn between $35,000 and $100,000 a year. If you're in this range, welcome! You've arrived!

A little more than 26 percent of households earn more than $100,000 a year. The Pew study considers households making at least $133,032 annually as the high-income group. The Census Bureau considers high-income households to be the 12.3 percent who earn over $150,000. Some who make $150,000 a year consider themselves middle class and an argument can be made in such high-cost areas like Silicon Valley and Manhattan. According to a website called thebalance.com:

> Most politicians label high-income households as the 6.1 percent who make over $200,000. Both President Obama and President Trump used $200,000 as the minimum for their high-income tax rates.

Those of us who teeter on the edge of our class know who we are: we sometimes juggle bills because of other unexpected expenses. As the saying goes, "I used to live paycheck to paycheck. Now I live direct deposit to direct deposit." This book is for us.

Much like the *Communist Manifesto* by Karl Marx, this book is an analysis of the plight of the working class, but it's a ringside seat to an economy that shifted from a promising future to broken promises. We'll examine without many, if any, charts and graphs of the ongoing exploitation and subjugation of white-collar and blue-collar union and non-union middle-class workers. We'll look at the tools and methods Corporate America aka Multinational Corporations use to keep workers in line while increasing productivity and profits.

With 37+ years in the corporate environment and as a leader in the labor movement for over 25 years, I have experienced firsthand a range of corporate culture from warm and fuzzy business/labor partnerships to authoritarian "do it or else" dictums. This book is an emotional response to those changes and is not meant to be a definitive analysis that could be provided by an economist or statistician. They may have lived it, as I have; they may have a broader base of knowledge to explain what happened, but my experiences in a changing telecommunications environment, first as a worker, then as an informed political and labor activist, and finally as a political candidate, put me on the front lines of those changes. This book was written for working folks – union and non-union, for labor leaders, students and teachers, family and friends, and the elite who may or may not wonder how the other 99 percent live.

We'll look at the movement of jobs, downsizings, and layoffs, the advent of permanent replacement workers, the shifting of health care costs, pension raids, the bait and switch of 401(k)s, and the new corporate global perspective that leaves patriotism at the airport.

We'll examine the "Occupy" movement worldwide, all the populist conversations about income inequality and how these actions have impacted capitalism, if at all.

And finally, we'll look at a possible plan of action that will involve unions, co-ops, and workers everywhere.

I'm telling this story because what happened to the telecommunications industry, and when it happened, are indicative of what occurred throughout the country, maybe with a tad more intensity: the abrupt changes in the industry, the slashing of employees as SBC in Texas culled the herd, and the current ongoing descent into hell as SBC aka AT&T aka DirecTV aka Comcast attempts to jettison the regulated side of the business. It's all part and parcel of the devastation of the workforce that began in the seventies and continues today.

I'm telling this story because I was there: as a working stiff, as a union activist and leader and as a political activist working within the Democratic Party and finally as a candidate for public office. I have lobbied elected officials from School Board to Congress, and I refuse to give into desperation. I have included in this book a little bit of history both personal and political, a smorgasbord of food for thought and a few possible solutions. This story will be told from the worker's point of view to show how these economic actions and theories impact us down here at the bottom.

More a how-done-it than a who-done-it, I hope by the final chapter that it's evident to everyone on both sides of the aisle how this "mystery" unfolded, who's behind it, and our complicity in our present predicament.

You will find some biases, and there's a definite message here for my union brothers and sisters. I'm an unabashed fan of the working stiff. From fast food workers to firefighters, I support the fight for quality of life. And I believe unions and the labor movement are the ONLY collective voice for working people and very possibly, the middle class' salvation.

Does the labor movement have problems? Yes and I'll address some of them here.

And listen up white folks: whatever has been done to us on behalf of oligarchies and rich people, our brothers and sisters of color have experienced much, much worse. There is such a thing as white privilege; we start out a rung or two higher even if we're dirt poor. Want to test that theory? You and a black or brown friend buy a phone case and walk out of the store with no receipt in evidence.

I don't pretend to have all the answers. There are clever folks out there coming up with new approaches on an almost-daily basis. I'm putting many of the ideas that have intrigued me and some context in this one place so you, dear reader, don't have to scour the Internet or your local library, as I have. We need to work *together* to ensure the prosperity of us all.

I have written this book for the same reason I first got involved as a union steward, a union leader, a candidate: the need to play a part in my own destiny and to make a difference in the lives of working people. I hope you do, too. If not, then please pass this book along to someone you know who wants to help me spring this trap in which we find ourselves. If I can inspire one person, the time and energy I put into producing this book will have been worth it.

CAVEAT: I have been asked by my European consultants that I make clear to all reading this book that this is the *American* story. Though many of the conditions and rigged systems are prevalent in the EU, our cousins are dealing with these issues in their own unique fashion.

In solidarity,
Dan McCrory

PS Just when I had it all figured out, along comes billionaire businessman and celebrity Donald Trump to win the electoral college and thus the election with a populist message that promised everybody everything. His win has rocked a stable political environment on both sides of the aisle. In fact, Campaign 2016 may end up being labeled The Year It All Fell Apart.

This book is dedicated to my "church," the House of Labor, and the working women and men who deserve all the dignity and respect we can give them. I owe a big THANK YOU to those who believed in me and my mission: my wife, Terri Haley, Matthew and Mikaela Collerd, Ralph Miller, Beverley Brakeman, Steve and Irene Cook for both a financial contribution and valuable proofreading, Mark Dudzic, Robert Gaskill, Dr. Loraine Lundquist, Kristi Czajkowski, Teresa Chung, Debra Kozikowski, and Marilyn Grunwald. I also want to thank my very special Beta reader Lisa Tze Polo, a kind, nurturing soul and dedicated nurse who inspired me to keep going. I also want to thank those who provided feedback and allowed me to interview them including Larry Gross, Terry Wren, Farid Khavari, Robert Gaskill, Gary Phillips, Noah Karvelis and my global union brothers in Finland and Switzerland. To all my political friends and labor brother and sisters: I wrote from my heart. If I have offended you, mea culpa. To future generations: This book is for you.

Dan McCrory
December, 2018

Chapter 1 Introduction

Chapter 1

An Introduction

"Since we cannot know all that there is to be known about anything, we ought to know a little about everything." Blaise Pascal

"An oligarchy of private capital cannot be effectively checked – because under existing conditions, private capitalists inevitably control, directly or indirectly, the main sources of information." Albert Einstein

"If you steal from one author, it's plagiarism; if you steal from many, it's research." Wilson Mizner

It was raining that day in December 2002. Residents of Santa Clarita Valley, California, were soaked to the skin within seconds under the open sky and so were we: 35 of labor's most dedicated activists wiping our glasses and wringing out our union t-shirts. The slogans on our picket signs ran down the poster board making them illegible. The AT&T golf tournament was rained out. No big-name golfers, no media would be showing up to take note of our protest.

I had just been elected as President of the Communications Workers of America Local 9503, and I saw the Writing on the Wall. Work performance pressures were mounting. Our members were getting summarily fired for petty issues that had formerly earned them a slap on the wrist. Employees were headed toward a big blowout against management; I was afraid they would fire the wrong guy, the one with a cache of firearms at home.

Hence the protest. Despite an empty parking lot we still managed to anger Chuck Smith, the corporation's VP in charge of the golf tournament. The only outcome we saw from our four-hour ordeal was a little vengeance from AT&T: they were hiring anywhere but in my local's jurisdiction. I was informed I could fix the situation. "You need to tell Chuck you're sorry," a high-ranking manager told me. I apologized in the only way that I could without choking on my words: I was sorry, I said, for actions by the company that had led to my decision to protest. It mollified his ego; work again flowed into 9503's turf.

Thank God I was wrong about the level of angst on the shop floor! In retrospect, I realized that the rank-and-file wasn't up in arms and the status quo prevailed because the members didn't share my perspective, they couldn't see the big bleak panorama that I could from my seat of responsibility. They didn't realize that AT&T was not just harassing folks in their department; it was happening company-wide.

As a new CWA local president, I also walked into the largest layoff southern California had ever encountered in the telecommunications industry with jobs disappearing in California and reappearing in Right-to-Work, Texas, headquarters for our parent company SBC, a corporation that morphed into the *New and Improved* (leaner and meaner) AT&T. And, of course, there were the thousands of tech support jobs in India and the Philippines.

How did my union members get to this point? The telecommunications industry was changing rapidly. First, there was the breakup of the Ma Bell monopoly in 1984 that dismantled the oligarchy that had stifled competition and innovation for almost a century while providing slow and steady growth on the stock market and a safe womb-like environment for employees. Now, in the 21st century, management crowed almost daily that their market was shifting away from POTS, Plain Ol' Telephone Service, the wire-line business overseen and scrutinized and regulated by commissions both state and federal, to mobile service. Now everybody had a phone and took it with them. The family had either pulled the plug on the home phone or kept it in the corner for emergencies, gathering dust, voicemails ignored.

Breaking up is hard to do.

By court order, the old AT&T was chopped up into seven regional Bell companies. On December 31, 1983, I worked for AT&T, as did everyone in my 8-story building. On January 1, 1984, I no longer worked for AT&T; I was now an employee of Pacific Bell. Our building was split. Assets, including employees, were clearly divided. My friends who remained with AT&T continued working in half the building while we toiled away on our own respective floors.

Mere months later my friends and former co-workers at the old AT&T were introduced to the concept of downsizing, a fancy corporate term used alternately with "rightsizing," to show that balancing the work and the workforce meant consolidation of responsibilities, and apparently sometimes meant that an employee had to follow their work to another floor or across the country.

Thanks to union negotiations, not corporate largesse, there was relocation pay, or jobs available for local transfer, often at a lower pay scale, and there was always "voluntary termination" for those who didn't want to uproot their families or couldn't subsist on a substantial cut in pay. Without a union, as we saw in other industries, there were no options.

Henry Ford didn't like unions, but he did say, "Make the best quality of goods possible at the lowest cost possible, paying the highest wages possible."

What is capitalism? Do capitalism and democracy go hand in hand or can one exist without the other?

Capitalism is our system of trade and, if conducted in a fair and equitable manner, reaps benefits for all concerned. But all the trade agreements bargained so far have lacked sufficient labor and environmental protections.

There are other forms of capitalism, incorporating checks and balances, that could rein in the excesses of our "marketing arm," the unfettered relentless pursuit of growth and market share prevalent in a capitalistic society, while adhering to the tenets and values that make us a democratic nation envied by many around the world. Most of us were raised to believe that if we struggled hard enough and played by the rules, we could get ahead and earn our part of the American Dream. We were also taught that it was better to be poor and noble than rich and heartless. There are invisible forces at play: merciless, unforgiving, unrelenting in their pursuit of total control. "Absolute power corrupts absolutely." A friend shared the refrain she heard from her sorority sisters and fraternity brothers, future CEOs and corporate board members, at her alma mater: "At other colleges were taught how the world is run; at Harvard, we're taught how to run the world."

Is it any wonder that people think the system is gamed against them? If we weren't spoon-fed our news and our daily diet of reality shows and sitcoms, would we sit idly by while our food and environment are polluted, our schools are underfunded, CEOs rake off millions in profit and buy elections, and our children shell out hundreds of thousands for student loans they'll never be able to pay off?

The following is an actual conversation I had online in late 2012 and reveals the pretty typical customary arguments and vitriol people on both sides of the spectrum continue to trot out to explain their viewpoint in rude, sometimes crude, terms. In terms of the Trump era of outright hostility and lies, this conversation years later feels almost polite!

Paul identified himself as Thinking Conservative: Here is the gist of our conversation.

PAUL

> *Public service unions and their bosses are pitting the everyday taxpayer's needs against the needs of the union members AND their bosses!*

Who are the Public Sector Unions striking against?
Yes, the very same people who are paying their wages!
The arrogance is unbelievable!

Should teachers receive a good wage? Absolutely, unless it deprives the taxpayer of living a "decent" life, void of life's necessities.
That goes for Firemen, policemen and all public sector union members.
Who determines a good wage?
Certainly not a union boss who shares in the bounty.

How about common sense?
A wage is offered--if acceptable, take the job. If unacceptable, look elsewhere.
If no takers, add incentives till a compromise is reached.
Politicians (school boards) and taxpayers will come to acceptable terms.
Public Sector Unions should be abolished! Yesterday!

ME

Is that how you would have wished to get your job? Take what scraps they offer because there are too many unemployed willing to take your place for even less?

Yes, some pompous jerks do too little and make too much, but most of them are Corporate CEOs! I worked in the private sector for over 30 years, including as a union leader for 12. I have known lots of public sector union leaders. Who bargains these contracts? In a negotiation, one side does not typically roll over for the other. A union is an advocate and collective voice for employees, and their job is to get the best contract for their members. Both sides supposedly bargain in good faith, and the union in either the private or public sector does not want to bankrupt the employer; without a steady stream of revenue, neither side wins. By the way, the union gets a small percentage for bargaining the contract. In CWA dues were $2^{1/4}$ hours pay per month.

We are in this predicament because companies aren't adding jobs; they're slashing them! The jobs that are out there pay a fraction of what an employee may have earned in the past. Without those good-paying jobs, fewer taxes are flowing into the coffers that fund our city, state and federal budgets - including pensions bargained in good faith. Take away the wages/jobs of those public employees, and there is even less funding for government!

Strikes are always a last-ditch effort. What else can a worker do to provide some leverage at the bargaining table other than withhold their hard work? "The arrogance is unbelievable" that you don't think that people at the bottom shouldn't have the same right to negotiate the best wages and benefits the market will bear. You shouldn't be saying "we should take that away from them." You should be saying, "We deserve that too!"

Corporations are trying to get you to look the other way rather than realize their hands are in your pockets. They used to invest in their communities, especially when corporations weren't faceless bureaucracies. They used to pay their fair share of taxes. Now they hide their money in the Caymans. Did you know GE and Bank of America paid NO taxes last year?

Keep getting distracted by their little puppet shows while they ship even more jobs out of our country because, after all, a service-type economy can be sent overseas at the flip of a switch. YOU and I are part of the 99 percent and we should be watching each other's backs rather than fighting THEIR fight!

PAUL

When employers can figure out how many new employees they can "afford" to hire, they will hire. Are they all "ignorant Obama haters" who are cutting off their noses in order to spite their face? They're not interested in "profit"? (Whoops, I used a dirty word).

"A union is an advocate and collective voice for employees, and their job is to get the best contract for their members." I got that, but for Public Sector Unions, who is providing the funds to get the best contract?

"negotiate the best wages and benefits the market will bear." The taxpayer is the market!

I'm well aware of the Corporations that do not pay Federal Taxes along with the 50% of American citizens who pay NO federal taxes!

The liberal cry of "Keep voting for me, and I'll continue to raise taxes on the people who make our country prosperous and give you all the "goodies" that their taxes will provide" is resonating across the land.

Forget the book idea. Karl Marx incorporated all of your ideas, in a number of volumes, many years ago. Why not try reading a few?

ME

"Forget the book idea." Karl Marx figured all the workers would be up in arms by now over the exploitation across the planet by multinational corporations instead of sitting glassy-eyed in front of the TV. I'm not parroting Marx in my book; I'm sharing my legitimate points of view as someone who has lived on the front lines of the economy. I have just as much right as you to say what's right and what's wrong with our economy and the way we treat working people.

I don't advocate for a big government, just one big enough to make sure none of us falls through the holes in our social net, i.e., the working poor, the disabled, etc. We as a nation need to realize, as we once did, that to be a great country we need to lift all boats, not just those who were born into privilege.

I agree about market forces, and I think unions should be one of them. I have been out of work for a year and still paid my taxes. It's a bit strange to compare corporate welfare and corporations who make billions in profit with the working poor who paid no taxes because they didn't make enough to live on!

"If Obama is reelected, maybe we should all join a union and work as government employees?" You're half right. For most workers to have a collective voice on issues like wages, hours, and working conditions, unions are the only game in town. Unions brought you 40-hour workweeks, paid vacations, healthcare, the 8-hour day, and more. FDR, our greatest president, recognized the value that unions bring to the marketplace and during his time the government put lots of people back to work following the Depression and after the war.

"...negotiate the best wages and benefits the market will bear." (my quote)

"The taxpayer is the market!" (your quote)

Those public workers who received those wages and benefits are ALSO taxpayers, an item that gets overlooked in the conversation. The average public worker is not getting rich at work or in retirement.

"The liberal cry of 'Keep voting for me, and I'll continue to raise taxes on the people who make our country prosperous and give you all the "goodies" that their taxes will provide,' is resonating across the land."

Really? Where did you hear that? Oh, right. Fox News.

I HAVE read a few books with big words and no pictures, but as a proud member of the National Writers Union, I know I have MY story to tell! By the way, profit is not a bad word, but GREED is! I wasn't laid off because I wasn't doing a great job; the idiots in Corporate in Texas said the work could be done by two fewer employees, a decision based on a cookie-cutter approach to business that may work in a rural setting but doesn't in an urban environment. They want to keep shaving off people who remember when we were treated like family rather than a redundant tool. They tell the bean counters how many people they want to get rid of and the accountants generate the numbers that justify the layoffs and keep the profit margin so upper management gets their bonuses. It's not even about the stockholders. They want stockholders to shut up and hand over the money. Stockholders try to introduce ways to keep an eye on their boards, and those boards will have NONE of it. And who decides how much money they and the CEO makes? Why, their frat brothers from Harvard, Yale, etc. The cards are stacked against us, and they want to keep all the little people in their proper place. WAKE UP!

Back to public unions: If the public unions are bankrupting us, then who gave away the bank? Nobody! Some projections maybe painted a rosy picture based on how the economy was doing at the time. If, as you say, "this too shall pass," then what the hell are we arguing about?

Maybe the problem isn't that you're not reading any books, you're just reading ones that perpetuate myths that reinforce your own ideology. Read some of Reich's stuff, though I'm still mad at him for the whole NAFTA debacle. Stop goose-stepping along with the Republican Party and think, man!

(Insert sound of crickets here. Paul had left the conversation…)

The media, often referred to as the "liberal media" by the Right, is anything but liberal. I pointed out to my late father-in-law Herb, an avid Fox News viewer, that *non-American* Rupert Murdoch and his corporation were there to provoke, to manufacture conflict because, as any writer will tell you, without conflict there is no story. (Oops! Murdoch became a naturalized citizen in 1985 to meet the legal requirement for U.S. television station ownership.) The true moniker for these "news" networks would be "corporate media" because they have a product to sell and ratings determine standings in the public consciousness and often don't reflect fair and balanced reporting. I told Herb that Murdoch and his ilk were laughing all the way to the bank while the American public's discourse grew from bickering and name calling to threats and a more divisive, dangerous country. Herb was a thinker, and he saw the truth in my argument; we carefully weaned him and his wife Shirley off Fox and onto the less provocative but still sensationalistic CNN.

Why do we subject our news organizations to the same infotainment criteria like market share, car chases, and PR fluff about the newest action thriller that pervades our sitcoms, dramas and reality programs? That's a subject for another book! Still, I will try to address this and answer the question: if corporations are ripping us off and the media isn't covering it, is it really happening?

There's a lot of ground to cover in the continuing fleecing of the Middle Class. I'll try to present a balance, but I've made up my mind about what's going on, and I think *my* job is to point the way to a better day.

As I wrote this there was hope on the horizon: Bernie Sanders, an independent US Senator from Vermont who was inspiring youth and shaking up the status quo, but former first lady and former Secretary of State Hillary Clinton was predicted to glide into the Oval Office. On the other side, we had a dozen candidates. One was a wealthy businessman who's an iconoclast in his own right, a man who was ruled unelectable and ridiculed for even launching a campaign: Donald J. Trump. If either Trump or Sanders was elected President, I wrote before the election, our country could sail into uncharted waters. Or not. The ship of state has a way of righting itself.

In a later chapter, I'll take a second look at Campaign 2016 and examine its impact on our nation and the middle class.

For now, let's climb into our time machine and figure out how we got here: stagnant wages, dwindling benefits, a proliferation of right-to-work states, worker fighting worker.

Chapter 2

Fair Trade vs. Free Trade

"Over the last 40 years, the largest corporations in this country have closed thousands of factories in the United States and outsourced millions of American jobs to low-wage countries overseas. That is why we need a new trade policy..." Bernie Sanders, Senator, Vermont and Presidential Candidate

"Five million U.S. manufacturing jobs have been offshored since 2000." CNN

"There is no such thing as a free market. There has never been – at least since the transition from hunter-gatherer to agriculture. Maybe not even then." Brian Kohler, IndustriALL Global Union

In the dusty Mexican town of Aguascalientes, there's a long white building that seems to stretch along the highway for miles. This plant assembles Nissan Sentras and other Nissan models. There's a private gated community for Japanese workers. The Mexican workers' living conditions are sparse and a lot further down the road, but they don't need to worry about the commute. Vans come by and pick them up on a continual basis because the factory runs 24/7.

The North American Free Trade Agreement (NAFTA) was signed into law in 1992 by a Democratic president, Bill Clinton, former governor of the right-to-work state of Arkansas. While President Clinton was the most pro-worker, pro-middle class president since Jimmy Carter, both paled in comparison to Franklin Delano Roosevelt. Both Carter and Clinton hailed from the south where organized labor had failed many years before in its mission to unionize workers en masse. Organized labor continues to ignore the south to the detriment of all workers, though that may be changing. The efforts of the UAW may also be a case of too little, too late.

NAFTA, an agreement between the United States, Canada and Mexico, guaranteed that goods would flow freely without tariffs among those three countries. It was touted as a way to create jobs and a thriving middle class in Mexico, which proponents promised would consequently dry up the flow of illegal immigrants over the southern borders of the United States.

US labor leaders had already witnessed the gutting of American manufacturing jobs with the Reagan administration's blessings on a move to Mexican maquiladora plants on the other side of the Rio Grande. The maquiladoras were Corporate America's experiment in the exportation of jobs in the interest of "free enterprise." We all watched as workers in this country lined up for unemployment while workers in Mexico were exploited and their environment ravaged. Mexican workers were paid much less, and continue to make less, than their American counterparts because, after all, that was part of the incentive for American corporations to move their plants there. The wages Mexican workers made did little to alleviate their impoverished lives. Mexico's environmental laws were ignored, and factory wastes spewed into the air and seeped into the land and water supplies. Pollution ignored the border and affected citizens on both sides of the Rio Grande.

President Ronald Reagan deserves the blame for what the maquiladoras wrought. Reagan, once president of the Screen Actors Guild, got swept up in the anti-Communist fervor of the McCarthy years and decided to try politics. His rant against the Evil Empire served him well throughout his career. He wreaked havoc as California's governor when he closed all the mental hospitals, creating a burgeoning homeless population that still roam the streets today. "Compassionate" conservatism was born.

Organized labor got an early taste of his priorities as President in 1981 when he summarily fired 11,000 of the nation's air traffic controllers. They had struck over the issue of flight safety. In a letter sent to PATCO, the air traffic controllers union, Reagan promised to help them after he was elected if they would help him get to the White House. After the election on August 4, 1981, he came on tough and said if the strikers didn't return to work, they were all fired, and the union was fined $1 million a day for every day the strike dragged on. Those who honored the strike and stayed out were permanently banned. Airport towers were immediately staffed with 3,000 supervisors who joined the 2,000 controllers who had returned to work and 900 military controllers. In a short amount of time, about 80 percent of flights had resumed. 11,000 air traffic controllers were the first wave of union workers who found themselves "permanently replaced."

After that, it was whatever business wanted versus the working man and woman. Economists point to that time in history as the start of a long decline of the worth of the Middle Class as wages stagnated and stayed flat for the next 40 years. Union density dropped from 12 percent to 9 percent as manufacturing jobs and other work were sent offshore. Big business and the Reagan White House had found a loophole in labor law that put striking workers on the street, not fired for union activities, but again, simply "permanently replaced."

NAFTA in the early 90s only exacerbated the problems created by the maquiladoras. Suddenly the movement of work was not only tolerated, but was also encouraged through tax incentives, and not just for large corporations like Zenith and General Motors. Many mid-sized corporations, too, wanted to maximize profits while driving down their labor costs. It became a race to the bottom. Initially, figures pointed to 700,000 lost jobs, with many more lost through a ripple effect on peripheral businesses – the coffee shop down the street, the gas station, the bank – all those who depended on the spending power of those 700,000 in their communities, including local and state governments coffers that were suddenly looking at budget shortfalls.

Despite legislation designed to minimize the impact on American workers by providing funds for retraining in the new service economy, workers found themselves unable to maintain the middle-class lifestyle to which they had become accustomed. The jobs they found paid substantially less than the manufacturing sector. They became the working poor, sometimes taking a second job when they could to make ends meet. Millions lost homes, and that resultant ripple effect on peripheral businesses devastated others who weren't able to point to a direct link between the local plant closure and their loss of meaningful income. They weren't eligible for retraining.

Enter Wal-mart. Like President Bill Clinton, the corporation came out of right-to-work Arkansas. Stores sprang up in devastated areas, employing displaced workers and former mom-and-pop business owners, and offered low priced American products. Wal-mart continued the devastation of local businesses by undercutting their prices, creating a one-stop shop for everything from tires to groceries. More on Wal-mart in another chapter.

What could have prevented the loss of good manufacturing jobs? President Clinton and his administration said at the time that NAFTA would "lift all boats," meaning that our companies could now sell goods at a competitive rate to our business partners on the other side of our nation's borders. Jobs created in Mexico would create a thriving, growing middle class eager to buy those goods.

Many saw the inevitable conclusion. There was a substantial hue and cry from organized labor as the first manufacturing jobs moved to Mexico and there was a later attempt to imbue NAFTA with worker protections. But other than protecting the output of some textile industries for a short time in order to protect business rather than workers and allocating retraining dollars for displaced workers, there were no worker protections. As 1996 presidential candidate Ross Perot stated, there was "a giant sucking sound" as jobs moved rapidly from the US to Mexico. And as jobs left the United States for Mexico and beyond, the trend picked up pace with 5.5 million fewer factory jobs today than in July 2000 - and 12 million fewer than in 1990.

Jeff Faux took a long look back in a paper he authored, "NAFTA's Impact on U.S. Workers" for the Economic Policy Institute, a pro-labor think tank in Washington:

> The inevitable result was to undercut workers' living standards all across North America. Wages and benefits have fallen behind worker productivity in all three countries. Moreover, despite declining wages in the United States, the gap between the typical American and typical Mexican worker in manufacturing remains the same. Even after adjusting for differences in living costs, Mexican workers continue to make about 30% of the wages of workers in the United States. Thus, NAFTA is both symbol and substance of the global "race to the bottom."

Did workers and organized labor complain enough when good-paying manufacturing jobs were leaving the country? As a force, a movement, within this country, some would say workers should have banded together and marched on Washington to say, "Stop!" Organized labor and workers, in general, stood in the way of "progress" and were labeled protectionists, obstructionists, and isolationists. There was talk at the time that labor would pull its support from those in Congress who had voted for NAFTA, but many of those same elected officials had fought with organized labor on other battles. The "line in the sand" that politicians weren't supposed to cross was ignored as more trade agreements were passed without protections for labor or the environment. I served on jury duty not long after the vote on NAFTA and found myself sitting with California Congressman Howard Berman as we both waited to be called for a panel. "How could you vote for that bill?" I asked him.

"It will create jobs. You'll see," he assured me.

"I hope you're right."

He wasn't. Presidents invoke Party loyalty when they attempt to pass controversial legislation, and they expect members of their Party to get on board. That's how we get laws that thwart the will of the majority because, after all, they know better than we do.

The Obama administration stated that the problems with NAFTA were because "labor provisions were not included in the core of the agreement. Rather, they were in a side agreement, virtually all of the provisions of which were not subject to any enforcement mechanism."

President Obama signed three free trade agreements during his two terms in the White House and even though then-UAW President Bob King managed to get US autoworker protection into the United States-Korea Free Trade Agreement (KORUS FTA), labor, for the most part, felt the agreement, indeed every trade agreement so far, was bad for working folks in the United States.

President King was lured into supporting the agreement because, as he stated, "The UAW was at the table every step of the way."

Currently, the U.S. has free trade agreements (FTA's) with twenty countries: Australia, Bahrain, Canada, Chile, Colombia, Costa Rica, Dominican Republic, El Salvador and Guatemala, Honduras, Israel, Jordan, Korea, Mexico, Morocco, Nicaragua, Oman, Panama, Peru and Singapore as well as Trade and Investment Framework Agreements (TIFA) with many countries in Africa, and bilateral trade treaties (BIT) with Uruguay and Rwanda. Before the presidential election, two Trade monsters were rearing their heads: the 12-nation Trans-Pacific Partnership, an agreement opponents were calling NAFTA on steroids and T-TIP, a trade agreement with the European Union.

So who's looking out for Americans? That job belongs to the Office of the United States Trade Representative (USTR), which is, according to the website "responsible for developing, negotiating and coordinating U.S. international trade and investment policy.

Established in 1962, the Office of the United States Trade Representative provides trade policy leadership and negotiating expertise in areas including bilateral, regional and multilateral trade and investment issues, expansion of market access for American goods and services, negotiations affecting U.S. import policies, oversight of U.S. preference programs, trade-related intellectual property protection issues and World Trade Organization (WTO) issues. USTR is part of the Executive Office of the President and the head of USTR, the U.S. Trade Representative, is a Cabinet member who serves as the principal trade advisor, negotiator, and spokesperson on trade issues."

The Office of the United States Trade Representative also participates in negotiating Trade in Service Agreements (TiSA), umbrella-like free trade agreements focused on "promoting fair and open competition across a broad spectrum of service sectors." According to the USTR, there are presently twenty-three economies participating in TiSA negotiations, representing roughly three-quarters of the world's $30 trillion services market. With every $1 billion in services exports supporting an estimated 5,900 U.S. jobs, says the Trade Representative's office, promoting the expansion of services trade globally will pay dividends for the United States. If that's true, why are all the support services and call center jobs in other countries? In an agreement the Communications Workers of America signed with AT&T in 2004, thousands of call center jobs were to return to the U.S. I don't know if that ever happened, but I do know how often the heavily accented voice on the other end doesn't understand cultural references and claims his name is "Bob."

Then there are the Trade and Investment Framework Agreements (TIFA). These agreements, which include a large swath of Africa, China, and much of the Middle East, are in place to allow "the United States and our TIFA partners [to] consult on a wide range of issues related to trade and investment. Topics for consultation and possible further cooperation include market access issues, labor, the environment, protection and enforcement of intellectual property rights, and, in appropriate cases, capacity building." Capacity building to me means teaching third-world countries how to market their resources and, ultimately, forces them to buy into the capitalist way of dealing with the rest of the world. That leaves these poorer regions susceptible to exploitation by multinational corporations and more "opportunity" for their citizens.

The United States Trade Representative also deals in Bilateral Investment Treaties (BITS), of which there are 42, representing 39 countries, currently in existence. According to the USTR website, "A Bilateral Investment Treaty is designed to ensure that U.S. investors receive national or most favored nation treatment (whichever is better) in the other signatory country. It protects U.S. investors against performance requirements, restrictions on transfers and arbitrary expropriation. BITs set forth procedures for the settlement of disputes. By providing a more open and secure environment for investment, they also promote private sector development."

All of these agreements are meant to adhere to Trade Promotion Authority (TPA), "laws to guide both Democratic and Republican Administrations in pursuing trade agreements that support U.S. jobs, eliminating barriers in foreign markets and establishing rules to stop unfair trade," according to the USTR website.

There's also talk to get rid of the "country of origin" stickers on products coming into this country, probably to hide the number of imports that are undercutting American businesses, everything from Colombian roses to Chinese steel. In this case, Congress voted in 2015 to remove country-of-origin labels on beef and pork sold in the U.S., citing a claim by the World Trade Organization that labels discriminate against meat imports. The Trump administration has no plan to include labeling in NAFTA renegotiations. According to Food Safety News, mandatory labeling led to "wasted taxpayer dollars, job losses, and economic harm to rural communities." That's the sound of Big Business pretending to care.

The Catholic Church, not known to weigh in on such matters, has issued an encyclical where Pope Francis has pointed out our complicity of ignorance and lays the fault of our current fiscal predicament at the wolves' doors:

> "...Some people continue to defend trickle-down theories which assume that economic growth, encouraged by a free market, will inevitably succeed in bringing about greater justice and inclusiveness in the world. This opinion, which has never been confirmed by the facts, expresses a crude and naïve trust in the goodness of those wielding economic

power and in the sacralized workings of the prevailing economic system. Meanwhile, the excluded are still waiting."

These agreements are based on corporate greed. Domestically union contracts are undermined as the public at large points the finger at so-called greedy union members for having negotiated decent pay and benefits in good faith. Corporations have perfected "divide and conquer" to the detriment of working people around the globe. As Mexico is declared "too expensive" an environment for manufacturing, jobs move to China and Qatar where workers are paid pennies a day and are grateful for any type of income.

Of course, there's a race to the bottom happening within the borders of this country. The bottom is only as low as the federal minimum wage and occurs in right-to-work states, mostly in the south. We will talk about that exodus of jobs and its effects in another chapter. The following resolution was passed by the California Democratic Party.

TRANS-PACIFIC PARTNERSHIP

Resolution 13-07.11

WHEREAS, the trade agreement known as Trans-Pacific Partnership is being negotiated in secret, and opponents in the labor and environmental communities argue that it would give new enforceable monopolistic rights and privileges to multi-national corporations, and establish limits on sovereign governments' ability to regulate corporations' actions, including but not limited to the areas of intellectual and copyright provisions, prices, labor practices, environmental impacts, disclosure requirements, and safety issues and

WHEREAS, according to public documents from the US Trade Representative, this agreement would allow multi-national corporations to sue governments through international tribunals, staffed by private sector attorneys, which could force governments to pay compensation to corporations and investors if the challenged policies are deemed to hinder investors' future profits, even if those corporations are not abiding by the countries' laws and regulations and

WHEREAS, past trade agreements have had a detrimental impact on jobs and wages, the environment, and fair, equitable trade, this agreement goes beyond what has been done before, and should not be pursued

THEREFORE BE IT RESOLVED, that the California Democratic Party calls for withdrawal from Trans-Pacific Partnership negotiations, and calls for a new, more transparent paradigm for trade negotiations

THEREFORE BE IT FURTHER RESOLVED, that the California Democratic Party forward copies of this resolution to President Obama, the Office of U. S. Trade Representatives, Governor Jerry Brown, Speaker John A. Perez, Senate President pro Tempore Darrell Steinberg, Speaker of the House John Boehner and Senate Majority Leader Harry Reid.

[Amended with the consent of the author]
Authored by Susie Shannon, AD 50, Dorothy Reik, AD 50, Adrienne Burk, AD46

***

Adopted by the California Democratic Party At its July 2013 Executive Board Meeting

TPP was expected to pass, though an actual vote was to be postponed until the lame duck session following the 2016 election. The agreement, if it had passed, would have devastated good jobs with decent wages as another sell out to corporate interests. After his election as president, Donald Trump signed an executive order that officially killed the agreement, though the deal's critics were clearly in the majority. Those of us who view all trade agreements with healthy criticism were momentarily confused by his actions. Sure, he had promised to kill it once in office, but it must have given his wealthy friends some pause.

The Democratic nominee, Hillary Clinton, had spoken in favor of TPP until she wasn't, calling it the "gold standard" of trade agreements. During the election, she said she was against it. Many see it as a change of heart borne from Progressive pressure and the campaign of Vermont

Senator Bernie Sanders. Clinton's pick for running mate, Virginia Senator Tim Kaine, had also very recently praised TPP.

According to the *Washington Post,* he was promoting TPP until the day before he was chosen to run for VP. "I see much in it to like," he said. "I think it's an upgrade of labor standards, I think it's an upgrade of environmental standards, I think it's an upgrade of intellectual-property protections." But the Senator seemed to have a change of heart after discussing it with Clinton. "He agreed with her judgment that it fell short" on protecting wages and national security, a Clinton aide said. Post-election, pundits think TPP may have lost her the election.

Donald Trump also promised he would renegotiate NAFTA. When air conditioner giant Carrier announced they were moving a plant and 1100 jobs from Indiana to Mexico, the president-elect negotiated a less-than-stellar deal to save those manufacturing jobs: the company was offered $7 million in tax breaks and other incentives to stay. Of course, Carrier was looking at saving $65 million by hiring Mexican workers where the minimum wage is $4 a day.

Trump, the jobs president, at Day 120 was remarkably inconsistent. TPP was dead, NAFTA still has not been renegotiated and Carrier still laid off 1,400 with jobs headed south of the border. Meanwhile, crops in the central valley of California died without sufficient seasonal immigrant labor.

As we were going to press, President Trump announced a new agreement that would redefine elements of NAFTA. The White House is calling the pact the US, Mexico, Canada Agreement or USMCA.

UAW President Gary Jones Issues Statement on USMCA Announcement

"For a quarter century, NAFTA has been disastrous for working people in the U.S., Canada, and Mexico and a gift to corporations offshoring good U.S. jobs. The true test of a new NAFTA agreement will be in whether it protects and enhances opportunities for the U.S. workforce and leads to higher wages and benefits for UAW members and manufacturing workers who have suffered for far too long. We think the idea and concept of the USMCA could have the potential to provide some needed relief for America's working families.

Numerous details still need to be reviewed and resolved before making a final judgment on this agreement. New protections for working families and the closing of some loopholes for global companies seeking to ship jobs overseas are a step in the right direction but there is more work to do. We need to be assured that Mexico is going to fix weak labor laws and enforce new worker protections. We do not know what the USTR (the office of the US Trade Representative) and Congress will do to make sure the words in the agreement are carried out. We need to review and resolve the details of the agreement when they are available to be sure that this agreement truly ends NAFTA's legacy of shuttered factories and low wages.

Given the history of loopholes in NAFTA, the UAW will withhold final judgment until all the pieces are put in place in order to determine whether this agreement will protect our UAW jobs and the living standards of all Americans."

The agreement does look attractive to domestic auto manufacturers and UAW rank and file. The U.S. Trade Representative states that one of the goals of the agreement is "to drive higher wages by requiring that 40-45 percent of auto content be made by workers earning at least $16 USD per hour."

Other goals in the agreement seem to protect the American auto industry:

- Help to preserve and re-shore vehicle and parts production in the United States.
- Transform supply chains to use more United States content, especially content that is key to future automobile production and high-paying jobs.
- Close gaps in the current NAFTA agreement that incentivized low wages in automobile and parts production.

The AFL-CIO has weighed in on its website on the overall tone of the agreement as written so far: "If the labor rules and enforcement system is left as it is in the text that we have reviewed, without other measures, the overall labor package could fall short of what is needed to create real change for working families." In a strong rebuke to both major parties, the organization seems to be hoping for the best, but preparing for the worst: "We have learned through 25 years of experience that it is simply too easy for trading partners and firms that outsource to violate labor obligations and for U.S. administrations, both Democratic and Republican, to do nothing."

Many of the issues remain to be negotiated.

Is Capitalism a force for good or evil? Is Capitalism, like fire, a force that depends on who sits on the board? Can Capitalism exist without a democratic foundation? Was Calvin Coolidge accurate when he stated, "The chief business of the American people is business?" Interestingly, he made that comment in a speech about the role of the press in free-market democracies. We'll cover that in a later chapter.

Chapter 3

Capitalism ≠ Democracy and the Occupy Movement

"The combination of economic and political power in the same hands is a sure recipe for tyranny." Rose and Milton Friedman in "Free to Choose"

"The chief business of the American people is business. They are profoundly concerned with producing, buying, selling, investing and prospering in the world. I am strongly of the opinion that the great majority of people will always find these the moving impulses of our life." President Calvin Coolidge

The Occupy Movement surprised a lot of people though some of us not so much. Ever since I grew aware of the world around me, this imbalance between the "haves" and the "have-nots" and its impact on the American way of life, I've wondered how long it would take for the American public to wake up and take notice. Sometimes I wondered if it would ever happen.

This is it I thought when the maquiladoras were proposed and then built across the border, laying the groundwork for NAFTA. Many of our jobs headed to the other side of the Rio Grande. There were a few conferences to examine the effects, especially from organized labor, but it seemed at the time that unions were afraid to raise too much of a fuss under Ronald Reagan because we weren't sure how far he'd go to bend us in his attempt to break us.

This is it I thought when Bill Clinton was elected. Suddenly the Dems had the reins of power, and we were all "thinking about tomorrow." We should have dreaded tomorrow because the North American Free Trade Agreement (NAFTA) was introduced by our "friends" in the Clinton administration. Big business was getting its way now with both parties. In fact, a proposed Labor Party arose for a short time. "Business has two parties," they said. "How about one for us?" But it was a case of too little, too late. Before labor in the private sector had dwindled, labor may have been able to mount a strong third party, but money had pervaded the system so fully unions couldn't amass the fortunes large enough to enter the ring with the Big Boys.

This is it I thought when I was elected as a union local president in 2002. I was going to educate and engage my members in the political process and get them involved, make a difference, *blah, blah, blah.* With 40% of my members staunch Republicans, I was a little afraid I'd inadvertently unleash the other side of the aisle. It didn't help that there were skunks in the woodpile among my Executive Board gunning for my job. In budget considerations, dealing with a company in downsize mode, my political agenda was reduced to woulda, shoulda, coulda.

This is it I cried to the skies when Barack Obama, a seemingly progressive candidate, was elected in 2008. He brought up a lot of issues that Dems could get behind. He talked about the inequalities inherent in the political system. He promised to close Gitmo, end the wars and bring about a wave of prosperity. But when our whole economic system seemed on the cusp of collapse, he brought the foxes into the hen house: a whole handful of former stockbrokers and bankers who could save the day.

We know the rest: Lehman Brothers were allowed to go under, but AIG was deemed "too big to fail." A couple of the Big Three automakers, Chrysler and GM, teetered until the government bailed them out with low-interest loans. Those actions probably saved one million autoworker jobs and a million more that relied on the auto industry.

I know this is it. Senator Bernie Sanders, the Democratic Socialist from Vermont, was again promising HOPE and CHANGE, inspiring millions across the country. Hillary Clinton, until a few months prior to the election, Obama's shoo-in successor, talked about incremental change while Bernie boldly called for a "political revolution."

There are those of us who were looking for a reincarnation of FDR. We held our breath and hoped through Bill Clinton, Al Gore, and Barack Obama. We're still hoping.

Some of us asked, "What is a Democratic Socialist?" Facebook brought us reams of memes to explain. One, courtesy of True Blue Party, stated:

> A **Democratic Socialist** is not a *Marxist Socialist* or a *Communist*. A Democratic Socialist is one who seeks to **restrain the self-destructive excesses of capitalism** and **channel the Government's use of our tax money into creating opportunities for everyone.**
>
> **Democratic Socialists** believe that both the economy and society should be run **democratically** – to meet public needs, not to make profits for a few.
>
> A **Democratic Socialist** does not want to destroy private corporations, but does want to bring them under greater democratic control. The government could use **regulations** and **tax incentives** to encourage companies to act in the public interest and **outlaw destructive activities** such as **exporting jobs** to low-wage countries and **polluting our environment.** Most of all, socialists look to **unions** to make private business more accountable.

Bernie made the campaign once again about issues and pushed Hillary a little to the left. Democratic Socialist also defines and marries both a political and an economic form of governing. "Republican" and

"Democrat," the labels for the two prevailing parties, leaves plenty of wiggle room for economic policy that is implied by the label rather than boldly stated.

Bernie, if he hadn't been saying the same things for over 30 years, could have been a product of the Occupy Movement, with its message of income inequality and a gamed system meant to profit only the rich.

Occupy Wall Street

> ...while the movement may have helped shift the terms of the debate, its lack of organizational unity, ideological coherence, and institutional support clearly are factors in its inability to coalesce into a serious alternative to our current two-party political party system - one that is clearly dominated by the one-percent.
>
> Mark Dudzic & Katherine Isaac

Back in the early 90s, when the Internet was still in its infancy, I had an online conversation in a chat room with labor types around the nation. "Let's picket Wall Street," I suggested. The idea was enthusiastically received, and we talked into the night about what that would look like. Someone from a branch of my own union that represented social workers in New York City brokered a meeting between the two of us and Communications Workers of America President Morton Bahr. To his credit, he listened to us and commiserated, but ultimately the idea went nowhere.

Flash forward 15+ years.

This from the OWS website:

> Occupy Wall Street is a people-powered movement that began on September 17, 2011, in Liberty Square in Manhattan's Financial District, and has spread to over 100 cities in the United States and actions in over 1,500 cities globally. OWS is fighting back against the corrosive power

of major banks and multinational corporations over the democratic process and the role of Wall Street in creating an economic collapse that has caused the greatest recession in generations. The movement is inspired by popular uprisings in Egypt and Tunisia and aims to fight back against the richest 1% of people that are writing the rules of an unfair global economy that is foreclosing on our future.

Their website, occupywallst.org, includes a guide to building an occupy movement.

The protests were against social and economic inequality, high unemployment, and greed, as well as corruption and the undue influence of corporations on government—particularly from the financial sector. If you happened to follow the 2016 presidential campaign of Bernie Sanders, much of this might sound familiar. The protesters' slogan *We are the 99 percent* refers to the growing income and wealth inequality in the U.S. between the wealthiest 1% and the rest of the population. The greatest criticism of the Occupy movement was the lack of a plan of action following the protests. In a leaderless movement meant to appear as a spontaneous grassroots uprising, the lack of a figurehead means there is no charismatic leader, no Mahatma Gandhi or Martin Luther King, Jr., to say, "This way to the promised land!" It also means there is no head of the snake to sever to kill the movement.

Without Occupy there probably wouldn't have been a Bernie campaign. The class struggle, so evident to a new generation of job seekers facing a gig and rigged economy, cried out for solutions. The Occupy movement looked for inspiration and found this man, this US Senator from Vermont who had railed against income equality for most of his life, a rogue who had not sold out to either significant political power.

Bernie showed us that we need to take the initiative, not merely to resist against the forces now in power, but to proactively educate ourselves and the public, to agitate as we did against the Vietnam War, and to organize one-to-one, and in every platform of the media.

Television has reflected on the lessons learned during June 1989, the student uprising in Beijing's Tiananmen Square. We all remember the image of the solitary man standing in the way of advancing tanks. The reasons for the uprising came from frustration. The working class and others, led predominately by college students, felt the system was holding the nation back. The working class saw increasing prosperity around them. 500 million had been lifted out of poverty in a generation according to the World Bank. The burgeoning Middle Class wanted less control over their daily lives and, in exchange for letting the Communist Party keep power, they wanted the trappings of capitalism, the ability to get rich. One CBS report indicated that Chinese society in the 25 years since had gained some ground on their fundamental demands of freedom of assembly and the ability to redress grievances, but little has changed.

In Lenin's *State and Revolution,* published in 1917, he quoted the writings of Marx and Engels to explain how power corrupts political systems:

> In a democratic republic, ... wealth exercises its power indirectly, but all the more surely, first, by means of the "direct corruption of officials" (America); and secondly, utilizing an "alliance of the government and the Stock Exchange" (France and America).

Lenin contended that Marx, Engels, and he were pointing out that the state serves to divide the classes with only one class having any real power.

> Engels elucidates the concept of the "power" which calls itself the state, a power which arose from society but places itself above it and alienates itself more and more from it. What does this power mainly consist of? It consists of special bodies of armed men having prisons, etc. at their command. A standing army and police are the chief instruments of state power.

Indeed. Whether I have picketed AT&T with other union members to provide leverage at the bargaining table or marched with MoveOn to protest predatory practices at Bank of America, the police have been there to protect corporate property and seem willing to admit that.

> Another reason why the omnipotence of "wealth" is more certain in a democratic republic is that it does not depend on defects in the political machinery or on the faulty political shell of capitalism. A democratic republic is the best possible political shell for capitalism and, therefore, once capital has gained possession of this very best shell, …it establishes its power so securely, so firmly, that no change of persons, institutions or parties in the bourgeois-democratic republic can shake it.

Lenin criticized the way things were, but he understood that democracy and capitalism were not the same things. "We are in favor," he wrote, "of the democratic republic as the best form of state for the proletariat (worker aka middle class) under capitalism. But we have no right to forget that wage slavery is a lot of the people even in the most democratic bourgeois republic." His solution: to abolish the state by turning the means of production into state property. That, in turn, would "abolish class distinctions and class antagonisms."

Lenin and his predecessors argued that change was only possible through violent revolution and maybe that will eventually be proved to be the case. But a more reasoned approach might be employee ownership of the company.

Harley Davidson was rocked by stiff competition from Japanese motorcycles in the 1960s. Harley's own image as a "bad boy's bike," fueled by Hells Angels' loyalty and a marketing campaign by Honda, threatened American market share and American jobs.

In 1969 American Machine & Foundry Company (AMF) bought Harley-Davidson and the huge corporation infused the formerly family-owned business with much-needed capital but ignored the burgeoning interest in "hog lite," the smaller, nimbler bikes with smaller engines. In the 70s, H-D's quality started to slide, and Japanese motorcycle manufacturers went toe-to-toe with them on the bigger, though not heavier, bikes.

AMF was looking around for someone to buy the company, but the officers left over from the old days knew that the next owner could ruin them. According to a quote from Forbes magazine, senior manager Vaughn Beats said, "An experienced, closely knit management team would have been replaced by people who didn't know the motorcycle business at all, and the long-term values of the company would have gone down the drain."

In 1981, twelve Harley Davidson executives, with a consortium of banks pitching in the rest of the $80+ million purchase price bought the company. Much of H-D's current popularity has been attributed to Willie O., William G. Davidson, the grandson of co-founder Arthur. He created Harley-Davidson's retro look, which became very popular and, with his long hair, beard and leathers, he looks like a lot of their customers.

Their quality still threatens their success. They, like many innovative companies of the early 80s, examined Japanese production processes. After all, Japan had moved from a post-WW II economy known for its junk to a powerhouse known for its quality and value. They renamed Japan's Just in Time (JIT) approach to warehousing as Materials as Needed (MAN).

They enlisted input from people on the shop floor, a concept referred to in Japan as "employee involvement." With management, they helped redesign everything from the assembly line to quality control because, after all, who knew more about what didn't work and what could?

In 1984, Pacific Bell tried the same concept of employee involvement with less success.

The corporation was one of the spawn of AT&T's court-ordered dissolution in 1983. On December 31, 1983, I worked for AT&T. On January 1, 1984, I was a Pacific Bell employee.

We were welcomed with cake and balloons. Now my coworkers and I were in a new local of the Communications Workers of America and everyone in the office decided I should be the union steward for my workgroup of about fifty. The new incoming Local 9503 leadership agreed. They introduced us to Quality of Work Life, a program based on Japanese work committees called Quality Circles who were getting a say-so and respect in the workplace. QC's were an apparent success at morale building and were credited with skyrocketing productivity by Japanese workers. American corporations rushed to copy the Japanese model.

We suddenly had input in *our* work-related processes and office aesthetics. Ten of us were trained in negotiations and conflict management so our committee would be able to work in harmony and affect change in the office. Or so we thought. Management never solicited our input on work processes, but we used our new relationship to improve our work environment, setting up smoking areas and a corner of the parking lot with tables and shade for lunch. I was elevated by the union to be a trainer of other QWL committees in other workplaces throughout the local's jurisdiction.

There were little successes, but a year later the committees' frustrations were mounting as they tried to improve working conditions while dealing with authoritarian management. Both management and union were beginning to see QWL as a threat to their power and sovereignty and traditional roles. After several months, the union pulled the plug.

According to *Quality Circles: After the Fad* in the January 1985 issue of the Harvard Business Review:

> Although American and Japanese Quality Circle programs are very similar, several significant differences exist. Programs in Japan give greater emphasis to statistical quality control; employees often meet on their own time rather than on company time; and finally, in Japan, all company employees usually receive a financial bonus for the performance of the organization.

The feel-good accomplishments faded with time, but it wasn't the end of experimentation at work, an attempt to prod the most productive workforce in the world.

Corporate Free Speech

"There can be no effective control of corporations while their political activity remains. To put an end to it will be neither a short nor an easy task, but it can be done." President Theodore Roosevelt, 1910

When so many talk about capitalism and democracy as synonyms for each other, it opens our system of government to the possibility of corruption and outlandish court decisions like Citizens United v the Federal Election Commission. The Citizens United case said that corporations were people and money was a form of free speech afforded everyone, just more affordable for some.

In 2008, a conservative lobbying group, Citizens United, wanted to air a film that was very unflattering to Hillary Clinton, a candidate for president. The United States District Court for the District of Columbia labeled the film an "electioneering communication," and decided that even advertising the film would be a violation of the 2002 Bipartisan Campaign Reform Act that ruled such "communications" by either a union or a corporation illegal within 60 days of a general election and within 30 days of a primary.

When the case was appealed and reviewed by the US Supreme Court, they decided in a 5-4 split that the government was abridging the right of a non-profit corporation to make an independent expenditure. After those rights were extended to for-profit corporations and unions, contributions flowed in record numbers virtually unchecked by federal law. US News and World Report:

> A recent analysis of the 2014 Senate races by the Brennan Center for Justice found outside spending more than doubled since 2010, to $486 million. Outside groups provided 47 percent of total spending – more than the candidates' 41 percent – in 10 competitive races in [2014's] midterms.

The concept of Corporate Personhood lies at the crux of the corporate free speech conundrum, and that "right" goes back a long way.

The first corporate victory was in 1886 in *Santa Clara County v Southern Pacific Railroad*. The Supreme Court didn't rule on the concept of corporate personhood, but they determined a corporation was a "natural person." The 14th amendment to the Constitution, granting rights to former slaves, was used to uphold the rights of corporate "citizens." Corporations have used the decision to defeat state laws barring corporate personhood, to dismantle corporate oversight by government and have continuously expanded that definition of personhood to gain more control over the rights of real people and the law.

The Koch brothers have expended many such efforts. Charles and David Koch run Koch Industries, a series of corporations that peddle everything from pipelines to Brawny paper towels and manage philanthropies worth about $52.4 billion according to Forbes. And, like all evil people, they're not all bad. They have given money to the United Negro College Fund, the Lincoln Center and Memorial-Sloan Kettering Cancer Center, and funded at-risk youth groups even as they founded Citizens United and attempted to control elections and legislation through their group, Americans for Prosperity, FreedomWorks, the Tea Party movement and the American Legislative Exchange Council (ALEC). ALEC has upped the ante on corporate control of our government by influencing legislation at all levels of government. They're pro-big business and anti-labor.

The website, OurFuture.org reports:

> [Through ALEC, the Koch brothers are pushing] legislation that allows energy companies to avoid fines for polluting, that pushes privatization of public education, and that prevents states and localities from regulating the rogue behavior of financial institutions.

The business of business is to influence legislation, to roll back laws that might restrict their profits, dismantle government oversight and "intrusion" in the workplace, the environment, and consumer protection. Lawmakers on both sides of the aisle and their corporate benefactors are trying to disenfranchise voters with voter ID laws. We will consider the implications of that practice in another chapter.

There are more millionaires and billionaires and Wall Street tycoons, (but I'm repeating myself), willing to spend lots of money to ensure their continued success. We have Warren Buffett and George Soros and most of Hollywood on our side. We have Move to Amend and American Promise trying to outlaw corporate personhood by changing the US Constitution. Will both major parties continue this mad race for market share in the political arena? Will democracy suffer? Hasn't it already?

Chapter 4

ALEC, the Powell Manifesto and the Heritage Institution

> "The American Legislative Exchange Council is a 501(c)3 organization whose mission is to increase individual liberty, prosperity and the well-being of all Americans by advancing and promoting the principles of limited government, free markets and federalism." ALEC website

As a union leader, there was controversy over any labor involvement in the Chambers of Commerce. Many of our peers cited the Chambers' repeated opposition to pro-labor legislation as "job killers." I felt that it was imperative for labor folks to put a human face on unions, to let management realize that their next-door neighbor was probably a union guy. I also wanted to put a face on layoff statistics and unemployment numbers. I want every layoff and downsizing to be an agonizing decision for management. I also hope to awaken small business owners to the realization that they have more in common with a labor leader than a CEO of a massive corporation.

In 1989, when telecom workers walked out across the nation over the issue of health care benefits, news commentator Bill Press said in an on-air editorial, "They're not just striking for themselves; they're striking for you and me." He understood and tried to draw the connection between the benefits labor bargains for, fights for, and sometimes must strike to achieve, and the benefits that others receive and take for granted as part of their employment benefits package.

We have to do a better job of drawing those connections for those who have never been in a union or known anyone in a union. We can't just count on our friends. We need more institutions like the Economic Policy Institute to do the research and make our case for a voice in our economic future. Corporations have invested heavily in the war to win the hearts and minds of the middle class.

A document referred to alternately as the Powell Memo or Manifesto, was first drafted by Lewis F. Powell, Jr. for his friend and neighbor, Eugene B. Sydnor, Jr., education director of the U.S. Chamber of Commerce. Meant to be a critique of the left's agenda as well as a plan of action for conservative business, the 1971 document inspired and influenced CEOs and Republican presidential candidates alike.

With this lengthy defense of Big Business and his recommended counter-offensive, Powell had proved his staunch loyalty to Big Business. As a corporate lawyer on the board of Philip Morris, he had disputed the connection between smoking and lung cancer and accused the media of fomenting socialism. President Nixon appointed him to the Supreme Court later that year.

The document is now in the public domain so here is the Powell Manifesto in its entirety:

Confidential Memorandum: Attack of American Free Enterprise System

DATE: August 23, 1971
TO: Mr. Eugene B. Sydnor, Jr., Chairman, Education Committee, U.S. Chamber of Commerce
FROM: Lewis F. Powell, Jr.

This memorandum is submitted at your request as a basis for the discussion on August 24 with Mr. Booth (executive vice president) and others at the U.S. Chamber of Commerce. The purpose is to identify the problem and suggest possible avenues of action for further consideration.

Dimensions of the Attack

No thoughtful person can question that the American economic system is under broad attack. This varies in scope, intensity, in the techniques employed, and in the level of visibility.

There always have been some who opposed the American system, and preferred socialism or some form of statism (communism or fascism). Also, there always have been critics of the system, whose criticism has been wholesome and constructive so long as the objective was to improve rather than to subvert or destroy.

But what now concerns us is quite new in the history of America. We are not dealing with sporadic or isolated attacks from a relatively few extremists or even from the minority socialist cadre. Rather, the assault on the enterprise system is broadly based and consistently pursued. It is gaining momentum and converts.

Sources of the Attack

The sources are varied and diffused. They include, not unexpectedly, the Communists, New Leftists and other revolutionaries who would destroy the entire system, both political and economic. These extremists of the left are far more numerous, better financed, and increasingly are more welcomed and encouraged by other elements of society, than ever before in our history. But they remain a small minority and are not yet the principal cause for concern.

The most disquieting voices joining the chorus of criticism come from perfectly respectable elements of society: from the college campus, the pulpit, the media, the intellectual and literary journals, the arts and sciences, and from politicians. In most of these groups, the movement against the system is participated in only by minorities. Yet, these often are the most articulate, the most vocal, the most prolific in their writing and speaking.

Moreover, much of the media, for varying motives and in varying degrees, either voluntarily accords unique publicity to these "attackers," or at least allows them to exploit the media for their purposes. This is especially true of television, which now plays such a predominant role in shaping the thinking, attitudes, and emotions of our people.

One of the bewildering paradoxes of our time is the extent to which the enterprise system tolerates, if not participates in, its own destruction.

The campuses from which much of the criticism emanates are supported by (i) tax funds generated mainly from American business, and (ii) contributions from capital funds controlled or generated by American business. The boards of trustees of our universities overwhelmingly are composed of men and women who are leaders in the system.

Most of the media, including the national TV systems, are owned and theoretically controlled by corporations which depend upon profits, and the enterprise system to survive.

Tone of the Attack

This memorandum is not the place to document in detail the tone, character, or intensity of the attack. The following quotations will suffice to give one a general idea:

William Kunstler warmly welcomed on campuses and listed in a recent student poll as the "American lawyer most admired," incites audiences as follows:

"You must learn to fight in the streets, to revolt, to shoot guns. We will learn to do all of the things that property owners fear." The New Leftists who heed Kunstler's advice increasingly are beginning to act — not just against military recruiting offices and manufacturers of munitions, but against a variety of businesses: "Since February 1970, branches (of Bank of America) have been attacked 39 times, 22 times with explosive devices and 17 times with fire bombs or by arsonists." Although New Leftist representatives are succeeding in radicalizing thousands of the young, the more significant cause for concern is the hostility of respectable liberals and social reformers. It is the sum total of their views and influence which could indeed fatally weaken or destroy the system.

Stewart Alsop wrote a chilling description of what is being taught on many of our campuses:

"Yale, like every other major college, is graduating scores of bright young men who are practitioners of 'the politics of despair.' These young men despise the American political and economic system...(their) minds seem to be wholly closed. They live, not by rational discussion, but by mindless slogans." A recent poll of students on 12 representative campuses reported that: "Almost half the students favored socialization of basic U.S. industries."

A visiting professor from England at Rockford College gave a series of lectures entitled "The Ideological War Against Western Society," in which he documents the extent to which members of the intellectual community are waging ideological warfare against the enterprise system and the values of western society. In a foreword to these lectures, famed Dr. Milton Friedman of Chicago warned: "It (is) crystal clear that the foundations of our free society are under wide-ranging and powerful attack — not by Communist or any other conspiracy but by misguided individuals parroting one another and unwittingly serving ends they would never intentionally promote."

Perhaps the single most effective antagonist of American business is Ralph Nader, who — thanks largely to the media — has become a legend in his own time and an idol of millions of Americans. A recent article in Fortune speaks of Nader as follows:

"The passion that rules in him — and he is a passionate man — is aimed at smashing utterly the target of his hatred, which is corporate power. He thinks, and says quite bluntly, that a great many corporate executives belong in prison — for defrauding the consumer with shoddy merchandise, poisoning the food supply with chemical additives, and willfully manufacturing unsafe products that will maim or kill the buyer. He emphasizes that he is not talking just about 'fly-by-night hucksters' but the top management of blue-chip business."

A frontal assault was made on our government, our system of justice, and the free enterprise system by Yale Professor Charles Reich in his widely publicized book: "The Greening of America," published last winter.

The preceding references illustrate the broad, shotgun attack on the system itself. There are countless examples of rifle shots which undermine confidence and confuse the public. Favorite current targets are proposals for tax incentives through changes in depreciation rates and investment credits. These are usually described in the media as "tax breaks," "loopholes" or "tax benefits" for the benefit of business. As viewed by a columnist in the Post, such tax measures would benefit "only the rich, the owners of big companies."[8]

It is dismaying that many politicians make the same argument that tax measures of this kind benefit only "business," without benefit to "the poor." The fact that this is either political demagoguery or economic illiteracy is of slight comfort. This setting of the "rich" against the "poor," of business against the people, is the cheapest and most dangerous kind of politics.

The Apathy and Default of Business

What has been the response of business to this massive assault upon its fundamental economics, upon its philosophy, upon its right to continue to manage its own affairs, and indeed upon its integrity?

The painfully sad truth is that business, including the boards of directors' and the top executives of corporations great and small and business organizations at all levels, often have responded — if at all — by appeasement, ineptitude and ignoring the problem. There are, of course, many exceptions to this sweeping generalization. But the net effect of such response as has been made is scarcely visible.

In all fairness, it must be recognized that people in business have not been trained or equipped to conduct guerrilla warfare with those who propagandize against the system, seeking insidiously and constantly to sabotage it. The traditional role of business executives has been to manage, to produce, to sell, to create jobs, to make profits, to improve the standard of living, to be community leaders, to serve on charitable and educational boards, and generally to be good citizens. They have performed these tasks very well indeed.

But they have shown little stomach for hard-nosed contest with their critics, and little skill in effective intellectual and philosophical debate.

A column recently carried by the Wall Street Journal was entitled: "Memo to GM: Why Not Fight Back?" Although addressed to GM by name, the article was a warning to all American business. Columnist St. John said:

"General Motors, like American business in general, is 'plainly in trouble' because intellectual bromides have been substituted for a sound intellectual exposition of its point of view." Mr. St. John then commented on the tendency of business leaders to compromise with and appease critics. He cited the concessions which Nader wins from management, and spoke of "the fallacious view many businessmen take toward their critics." He drew a parallel to the mistaken tactics of many college administrators: "College administrators learned too late that such appeasement serves to destroy free speech, academic freedom, and genuine scholarship. One campus radical demand was conceded by university heads only to be followed by a fresh crop which soon escalated to what amounted to a demand for outright surrender."

One need not agree with Mr. St. John's analysis. But most observers of the American scene will recognize that the essence of his message is sound. American business "plainly in trouble"; the response to the full range of critics has been ineffective, and has included appeasement; the time has come — indeed, it is long overdue — for the wisdom, ingenuity, and resources of American business to be marshaled against those who would destroy it.

Responsibility of Business Executives

What specifically should be done? The first essential — a prerequisite to any effective action — is for people in business to confront this problem as a primary responsibility of corporate management.

The overriding first need is for people in business to recognize that the ultimate issue may be survival — survival of what we call the free enterprise system, and all that this means for the strength and prosperity of America and the freedom of our people.

The day is long past when the chief executive officer of a major corporation discharges his responsibility by maintaining a satisfactory growth of profits, with due regard to the corporation's public and social obligations. If our system is to survive, top management must be equally concerned with protecting and preserving the system itself. This involves far more than an increased emphasis on "public relations" or "governmental affairs" — two areas in which corporations long have invested substantial sums.

A significant first step by individual corporations could well be the designation of an executive vice president (ranking with other executive VP's) whose responsibility is to counter-on the broadest front-the attack on the enterprise system. The public relations department could be one of the foundations assigned to this executive, but his responsibilities should encompass some of the types of activities referred to subsequently in this memorandum. His budget and staff should be adequate to the task.

Possible Role of the Chamber of Commerce

But independent and uncoordinated activity by individual corporations, as important as this is, will not be sufficient. Strength lies in organization, in careful long-range planning and implementation, in consistency of action over an indefinite period of years, in the scale of financing available only through joint effort, and in the political power available only through united action and national organizations.

Moreover, there is the quite understandable reluctance on the part of any one corporation to get too far out in front and to make itself also visible a target.

The role of the National Chamber of Commerce is therefore vital. Other national organizations (especially those of various industrial and commercial groups) should join in the effort, but no other organizations appear to be as well situated as the Chamber. It enjoys a strategic position, with an excellent reputation and a broad base of support. Also — and this is of immeasurable merit — there are hundreds of local Chambers of Commerce which can play a vital supportive role.

It hardly need be said that before embarking upon any program, the Chamber should study and analyze possible courses of action and activities, weighing risks against the probable effectiveness and feasibility of each. Considerations of cost, the assurance of financial and other support from members, adequacy of staffing and similar problems will all require the most thoughtful review.

The Campus

The assault on the enterprise system was not mounted in a few months. It has gradually evolved over the past two decades, barely perceptible in its origins and benefiting (sic) from a gradualism that provoked little awareness much less any real reaction.

Although origins, sources, and causes are complex and interrelated, and difficult to identify without careful qualification, there is a reason to believe that the campus is the single most dynamic source. The social science faculties usually include members who are unsympathetic to the enterprise system. They may range from a Herbert Marcuse, Marxist faculty member at the University of California at San Diego, and convinced socialists, to the ambivalent liberal critic who finds more to condemn than to commend. Such faculty members need not be in the majority. They are often personally attractive and magnetic; they are stimulating teachers, and their controversy attracts student following; they are prolific writers and lecturers; they author many of the textbooks, and they exert enormous influence — far out of proportion to their numbers — on their colleagues and in the academic world.

Social science faculties (the political scientist, economist, sociologist and many of the historians) tend to be liberally oriented, even when leftists are not present. This is not a criticism per se, as the need for liberal thought is essential to a balanced viewpoint. The difficulty is that "balance" is conspicuous by its absence on many campuses, with relatively few members being of conservative or moderate persuasion and even the relatively few often being less articulate and aggressive than their crusading colleagues.

This situation extending back many years and with the imbalance gradually worsening, has had an enormous impact on millions of young American students. In an article in Barron's Weekly, seeking an answer to why so many young people are disaffected even to the point of being revolutionaries, it was said: "Because they were taught that way."10 Or, as noted by columnist Stewart Alsop, writing about his alma mater: "Yale, like every other major college, is graduating scores' of bright young men ... who despise the American political and economic system."

As these "bright young men," from campuses across the country, seek opportunities to change a system which they have been taught to distrust — if not, indeed "despise" — they seek employment in the centers of the real power and influence in our country, namely: (i) with the news media, especially television; (ii) in government, as "staffers" and consultants at various levels; (iii) in elective politics; (iv) as lecturers and writers, and (v) on the faculties at multiple levels of education.

Many do enter the enterprise system — in business and the professions — and for the most part, they quickly discover the fallacies of what they have been taught. But those who eschew the mainstream of the system often remain in key positions of influence where they mold public opinion and often shape governmental action. In many instances, these "intellectuals" end up in regulatory agencies or governmental departments with significant authority over the business system they do not believe in.

If the foregoing analysis is approximately sound, a priority task of business — and organizations such as the Chamber — is to address the campus origin of this hostility. Few things are more sanctified in American life than academic freedom. It would be fatal to attack this as a principle. But if academic freedom is to retain the qualities of "openness," "fairness" and "balance" — which are essential to its intellectual significance — there is an excellent opportunity for constructive action. The thrust of such action must be to restore the qualities just mentioned to the academic communities.

What Can Be Done About the Campus?

The ultimate responsibility for intellectual integrity on the campus must remain on the administrations and faculties of our colleges and universities. But organizations such as the Chamber can assist and activate constructive change in many ways, including the following:

Staff of Scholars

The Chamber should consider establishing a staff of highly qualified scholars in the social sciences who do believe in the system. It should include several of national reputation whose authorship would be widely respected — even when disagreed with.

Staff of Speakers

There also should be a staff of speakers of the highest competency. These might include the scholars, and yes, those who speak for the Chamber would have to articulate the product of the scholars.

Speaker's Bureau

In addition to full-time staff personnel, the Chamber should have a Speaker's Bureau which should include the ablest and most effective advocates from the top echelons of American business.

Evaluation of Textbooks

The staff of scholars (or preferably a panel of independent scholars) should evaluate social science textbooks, especially in economics, political science, and sociology. This should be a continuing program.

The objective of such evaluation should be oriented toward restoring the balance essential to genuine academic freedom. This would include assurance of fair and factual treatment of our system of government and our enterprise system, its accomplishments, its fundamental relationship to individual rights and freedoms, and comparisons with the operations of socialism, fascism, and communism. Most of the existing textbooks have some sort of comparisons, but many are superficial, biased and unfair.

We have seen the civil rights movement insist on re-writing many of the textbooks in our universities and schools. The labor unions likewise insist that textbooks be fair to the viewpoints of organized labor. Other interested citizens groups have not hesitated to review, analyze and criticize textbooks and teaching materials. In a democratic society, this can be a constructive process and should be regarded as an aid to genuine academic freedom and not as an intrusion upon it.

If the authors, publishers, and users of textbooks know that they will be subjected — honestly, fairly and thoroughly — to review and critique by eminent scholars who believe in the American system, a return to a more rational balance can be expected.

Equal Time on the Campus

The Chamber should insist upon equal time on the college speaking circuit. The FBI publishes each year a list of speeches made on college campuses by avowed Communists. The number in 1970 exceeded 100. There were, of course, many hundreds of appearances by leftists and ultra liberals who urge the types of viewpoints indicated earlier in this memorandum. There was no corresponding representation of American business, or indeed by individuals or organizations who appeared in support of the American system of government and industry.

Every campus has its formal and informal groups which invite speakers. Each law school does the same thing. Many universities and colleges officially sponsor lecture and speaking programs. We all know the inadequacy of the representation of business in the programs.

It will be said that few invitations would be extended to Chamber speakers.11 This undoubtedly would be true unless the Chamber aggressively insisted upon the right to be heard — in effect, insisted upon "equal time." University administrators and the vast majority of student groups and committees would not welcome being put in the position publicly of refusing a forum to diverse views; indeed, this is the classic excuse for allowing Communists to speak.

The two essential ingredients are (i) to have attractive, articulate and well-informed speakers; and (ii) to exert whatever degree of pressure — publicly and privately — may be necessary to assure opportunities to speak. The objective always must be to inform and enlighten, and not merely to propagandize.

Balancing of Faculties

Perhaps the most fundamental problem is the imbalance of many faculties. Correcting this is indeed a long-range and challenging project. Yet, it should be undertaken as a part of an overall program. This would mean the urging of the need for faculty balance upon university administrators and boards of trustees.

The methods to be employed require careful thought, and the apparent pitfalls must be avoided. Improper pressure would be counterproductive. But the basic concepts of balance, fairness, and truth are difficult to resist if adequately presented to boards of trustees, by writing and speaking, and by appeals to alumni associations and groups.

This is a long road and not one for the fainthearted. But if pursued with integrity and conviction it could lead to a strengthening of both academic freedom on the campus and of the values which have made America the most productive of all societies.

Graduate Schools of Business

The Chamber should enjoy a particular rapport with the increasingly influential graduate schools of business. Much that has been suggested above applies to such schools.

Should not the Chamber also request specific courses in such schools dealing with the entire scope of the problem addressed by this memorandum? This is now essential training for the executives of the future.

Secondary Education

While the priority should be at the college level, the trends mentioned above are increasingly evidenced in the high schools. Action programs, tailored to the high schools and similar to those mentioned, should be considered. The implementation thereof could become a significant program for local chambers of commerce, although the control and direction — especially the quality control — should be retained by the National Chamber.

What Can Be Done About the Public?

Reaching the campus and the secondary schools are vital for the long-term. Reaching the public generally may be more important for the shorter term. The first essential is to establish the staffs of eminent scholars, writers, and speakers, who will do the thinking, the analysis, the writing, and the speaking. It will also be essential to have staff personnel who are thoroughly familiar with the media, and how most effectively to communicate with the public. Among the more obvious means are the following:

Television

The national television networks should be monitored in the same way that textbooks should be kept under constant surveillance. This applies not merely to so-called educational programs (such as "Selling of the

Pentagon"), but to the daily "news analysis" which so often includes the most insidious type of criticism of the enterprise system. Whether this criticism results from hostility or economic ignorance, the result is the gradual erosion of confidence in "business" and free enterprise.

This monitoring, to be effective, would require constant examination of the texts of adequate samples of programs. Complaints — to the media and the Federal Communications Commission — should be made promptly and strongly when programs are unfair or inaccurate.

Equal time should be demanded when appropriate. Effort should be made to see that the forum-type programs (the Today Show, Meet the Press, etc.) afford at least as much opportunity for supporters of the American system to participate as these programs do for those who attack it.

Other Media

Radio and the press are also relevant, and every available means should be employed to challenge and refute unfair attacks, as well as to present the affirmative case through these media.

The Scholarly Journals

It is especially important for the Chamber's "faculty of scholars" to publish. One of the keys to the success of the liberal and leftist faculty members has been their passion for "publication" and "lecturing." A similar passion must exist among the Chamber's scholars.

Incentives might be devised to induce more "publishing" by independent scholars who do believe in the system.

There should be a reasonably steady flow of scholarly articles presented to a broad spectrum of magazines and periodicals — ranging from the popular magazines (Life, Look, Reader's Digest, etc.) to the more intellectual ones (Atlantic, Harper's, Saturday Review, New York, etc.) and to the various professional journals.

Books, Paperbacks, and Pamphlets

The newsstands — at airports, drugstores, and elsewhere — are filled with paperbacks and pamphlets advocating everything from revolution to erotic free love. One finds almost no attractive, well-written paperbacks or pamphlets on "our side." It will be difficult to compete with an Eldridge Cleaver or even a Charles Reich for reader attention, but unless the effort is made — on a large enough scale and with appropriate imagination to assure some success — this opportunity for educating the public will be irretrievably lost.

Paid Advertisements

Business pays hundreds of millions of dollars to the media for advertisements. Most of this supports specific products; much of it promotes institutional image making, and some fraction of it does support the system. But the latter has been more or less tangential, and rarely part of a sustained, significant effort to inform and enlighten the American people.

If American business devoted only 10 percent of its total annual advertising budget to this overall purpose, it would be a statesman-like expenditure.

The Neglected Political Arena

In the final analysis, the payoff — short-of revolution — is what government does. Business has been the favorite whipping-boy of many politicians for many years. But the measure of how far this has gone is perhaps best found in the anti-business views now being expressed by several leading candidates for President of the United States.

It is still Marxist doctrine that the "capitalist" countries are controlled by big business. This doctrine, consistently a part of leftist propaganda all over the world, has an extensive public following among Americans.

Yet, as every business executive knows, few elements of American society today have as little influence in government as the American businessman, the corporation, or even the millions of corporate stockholders. If one doubts this, let him undertake the role of "lobbyist" for the business point of view before Congressional committees. The same situation obtains in the legislative halls of most states and major cities. One does not exaggerate to say that, regarding political influence for the course of legislation and government action, the American business executive is truly the "forgotten man."

Current examples of the impotence of business, and of the near-contempt with which businessmen's views are held, are the stampedes by politicians to support almost any legislation related to "consumerism" or to the "environment."

Politicians reflect what they believe to be majority views of their constituents. It is thus evident that most politicians are making the judgment that the public has little sympathy for the businessman or his viewpoint.

The educational programs suggested above would be designed to enlighten public thinking — not so much about the businessman and his role as about the system which he administers, and which provides the goods, services, and jobs on which our country depends.

But one should not postpone more direct political action while awaiting the gradual change in public opinion to be effected through education and information. Business must learn the lesson, long ago learned by labor and other self-interest groups. This is the lesson that political power is necessary; that such power must be assiduously cultivated; and that when necessary, it must be used aggressively and with determination — without embarrassment and without the reluctance which has been so characteristic of American business.

As unwelcome as it may be to the Chamber, it should consider assuming a broader and more vigorous role in the political arena.

Neglected Opportunity in the Courts

American business and the enterprise system have been affected as much by the courts as by the executive and legislative branches of government.

Under our constitutional system, especially with an activist-minded Supreme Court, the judiciary may be the most important instrument for social, economic and political change.

Other organizations and groups, recognizing this, have been far more astute in exploiting judicial action than American business. Perhaps the most active exploiters of the judicial system have been groups ranging in political orientation from "liberal" to the far left.

The American Civil Liberties Union is one example. It initiates or intervenes in scores of cases each year, and it files briefs amicus curiae in the Supreme Court in some cases during each term of that court. Labor unions, civil rights groups, and now the public interest law firms are extremely active in the judicial arena. Their success, often at business' expense, has not been inconsequential.

This is a vast area of opportunity for the Chamber, if it is willing to undertake the role of spokesman for American business and if, in turn, business is willing to provide the funds.

As for scholars and speakers, the Chamber would need a highly competent staff of lawyers. In special situations it should be authorized to engage, to appear as counsel amicus in the Supreme Court, lawyers of national standing and reputation. The greatest care should be exercised in selecting the cases in which to participate, or the suits to institute. But the opportunity merits the necessary effort.

Neglected Stockholder Power

The average member of the public thinks of "business" as an impersonal corporate entity, owned by the very rich and managed by over-paid executives. There is an almost total failure to appreciate that "business" actually embraces — in one way or another — most Americans. Those for whom business provides jobs, constitute a fairly obvious class. But the 20 million stockholders — most of whom are of modest means — are the real owners, the real entrepreneurs, the real capitalists under our system. They provide the capital which fuels the economic system which has produced the highest standard of living in all history.

Yet, stockholders have been as ineffectual as business executives in promoting a genuine understanding of our system or in exercising political influence.

The question which merits the most thorough examination is how can the weight and influence of stockholders — 20 million voters — be mobilized to support (i) an educational program and (ii) a political action program.

Individual corporations are now required to make numerous reports to shareholders. Many corporations also have expensive "news" magazines which go to employees and stockholders. These opportunities to communicate can be used far more effectively as educational media.

The corporation itself must exercise restraint in undertaking political action and must, of course, comply with applicable laws. But is it not feasible — through an affiliate of the Chamber or otherwise — to establish a national organization of American stockholders and give it enough muscle to be influential?

A More Aggressive Attitude

Business interests — especially big business and their national trade organizations — have tried to maintain low profiles, especially for political action.

As suggested in the Wall Street Journal article, it has been fairly characteristic of the average business executive to be tolerant — at least in public — of those who attack his corporation and the system. Very few businessmen or business organizations respond in kind. There has been a disposition to appease; to regard the opposition as willing to compromise, or as likely to fade away in due time.

Business has shunted confrontation politics. Business, quite understandably, has been repelled by the multiplicity of non-negotiable "demands" made constantly by self-interest groups of all kinds.

While neither responsible business interests nor the United States Chamber of Commerce, would engage in the irresponsible tactics of some pressure groups, it is essential that spokesmen for the enterprise system — at all levels and every opportunity — be far more aggressive than in the past.

There should be no hesitation to attack the Naders, the Marcuses and others who openly seek destruction of the system. There should not be the slightest hesitation to press vigorously in all political arenas for support of the enterprise system. Nor should there be a reluctance to penalize politically those who oppose it.

Lessons can be learned from organized labor in this respect. The head of the AFL-CIO may not appeal to businessmen as the most endearing or public-minded of citizens. Yet, over many years the heads of national labor organizations have done what they were paid to do very effectively. They may not have been beloved, but they have been respected — where it counts the most — by politicians, on the campus, and among the media.

It is time for American business — which has demonstrated the highest capacity in all history to produce and to influence consumer decisions — to apply their great talents vigorously to the preservation of the system itself.

The Cost

The type of program described above (which includes a broadly based combination of education and political action), if undertaken long-term and adequately staffed, would require far more generous financial support from American corporations than the Chamber has ever received in the past. High-level management participation in Chamber affairs also would be required.

The staff of the Chamber would have to be significantly increased, with the highest quality established and maintained. Salaries would have to be at levels fully comparable to those paid key business executives and the most prestigious faculty members. Professionals of the great skill in advertising and in working with the media, speakers, lawyers and other specialists would have to be recruited.

It is possible that the organization of the Chamber itself would benefit from restructuring. For example, as suggested by union experience, the office of President of the Chamber might well be a full-time career position. To assure maximum effectiveness and continuity, the chief executive officer of the Chamber should not be changed each year. The functions now primarily performed by the President could be transferred to a Chairman of the Board, annually elected by the membership. The Board, of course, would continue to exercise policy control.

Quality Control is Essential

Essential ingredients of the entire program must be responsibility and "quality control." The publications, the articles, the speeches, the media programs, the advertising, the briefs filed in courts, and the appearances before legislative committees — all must meet the most exacting standards of accuracy and professional excellence. They must merit respect for their level of public responsibility and scholarship, whether one agrees with the viewpoints expressed or not.

Relationship to Freedom

The threat to the enterprise system is not merely a matter of economics. It also is a threat to individual freedom.

It is this great truth — now so submerged by the rhetoric of the New Left and of many liberals — that must be re-affirmed if this program is to be meaningful.

There seems to be little awareness that the only alternatives to free enterprise are varying degrees of bureaucratic regulation of individual freedom — ranging from that under moderate socialism to the iron heel of the leftist or rightist dictatorship.

We in America already have moved very far indeed toward some aspects of state socialism, as the needs and complexities of a vast urban society require types of regulation and control that were quite unnecessary in earlier times. In some areas, such regulation and control already have severely impaired the freedom of both business and labor, and indeed of the public generally. But most of the essential freedoms remain private ownership, private profit, labor unions, collective bargaining, consumer choice, and a market economy in which competition largely determines price, quality, and variety of the goods and services provided the consumer.

In addition to the ideological attack on the system itself (discussed in this memorandum), its essentials also are threatened by inequitable taxation, and — more recently — by inflation which has seemed uncontrollable. But whatever the causes of diminishing economic freedom may be, the truth is that freedom as a concept is indivisible. As the experience of the socialist and totalitarian states demonstrates, the contraction and denial of economic freedom are followed inevitably by governmental restrictions on other cherished rights. It is this message, above all others, that must be carried home to the American people.

Conclusion

It hardly need be said that the views expressed above are tentative and suggestive. The first step should be a thorough study. But this would be an exercise in futility unless the Board of Directors of the Chamber accepts the fundamental premise of this paper, namely, that business and the enterprise system are in deep trouble, and the hour is late.

The Business Agenda

The reader may find himself gasping at the implications and enormity of this document. *The blueprint for corporate control of America is all here.* The memo brought about the creation of the American Legislative Exchange Council (ALEC), the Heritage Foundation, the Manhattan Institute, the Cato Institute, Citizens for a Sound Economy, Accuracy in Academe, and other powerful conservative organizations. President Reagan was a convert. Under his administration, business could do no wrong; he went to war against so-called leftist organizations, including unions. More on Reagan's involvement will be explored in a later chapter.

Powell's tenure on the Supreme Court helped shore up Big Business' claim that they had a right to contribute campaign funds as a form of free speech and gave us a glimpse into a philosophy now termed neo-liberalism that finds a way to justify a "centrist" viewpoint that sells out New Deal democracy to cozy up to corporations. Powell's decision to join with other justices to legalize abortion gave him a chance to show he was still a good Democrat at heart.

History has certainly frowned upon other decisions during his time on the bench. The Supreme Court ruled in 1978 for the first time that corporations had a First Amendment right to free speech in First National Bank of Boston v. Bellotti. At a time when voters were trying to limit corporate influence at the ballot box, SCOTUS ruled for the first time that contributions to ballot initiative campaigns were a permissible way for corporations to exercise their right to free speech. The US Chamber of Commerce weighed in against a lower court's decision and were rewarded with a 5-4 decision and a majority opinion delivered by their old friend, Justice Powell.

Conservative business interest in the Powell Manifesto grew, his seat on the bench underlined his credibility. Big Business invested heavily in think tanks to spread their gospel. The American Legislative Exchange Council was founded in 1973, as was the Heritage Foundation with the Libertarian think tank, the Cato Institute and the Manhattan Institute for Policy Research following in 1977.

Joseph Coors contributed $200,000 to the fledgling Heritage Foundation whose stated mission was, and still is to "formulate and promote conservative public policies based on the principles of free enterprise, limited government, individual freedom, traditional American values, and a strong national defense." What about, "the common good?"

The Heritage Foundation came into its own with the newly-elected Ronald Reagan. They produced a 20 volume conservative wish list called *Mandate for Leadership* that included income tax cuts and a presidential line-item veto. Reagan was so impressed, he handed out copies to his cabinet and implemented 60 percent of the suggested programs within his first year of office.

Heritage's latest target has been the repeal and replacement of the Affordable Care Act aka Obamacare. Despite their efforts using the carrot approach and the stick (running ads to call out Republicans who weren't marching to the "Kill Obamacare" drum), after several failed attempts in Congress, the winds of change are now focused on screwing the middle class with tax cuts for the rich.

In 1984, there was *Mandate II, Mandate III* in '88. They published updates in 1996 and 2000 without numbering them, probably sensing overkill on sequels and comparisons to *Rocky* movies, and issued *Mandate VI* in 2005, when sequels became cool "franchises" like *Fast and Furious* and Star Wars films.

The Heritage Foundation maintains its clout despite several recent PR disasters, including an immigration report written by Jason Richwine, who was found to have a Harvard dissertation in his past that argued that immigrants have lower IQs than white Americans and that immigration policy should be based on the disparity. Other conservative think tanks panned the report for its shoddy research.

The Foundation budget is $80 million strong. The organization's Center for Data Analysis crunches numbers to go toe-to-toe with the Congressional Budget Office reports and has a longtime partnership with the Republican Study Committee, a conservative caucus in the House with a majority of House Republicans in its ranks.

Then there's the annual three-day retreat for GOP lawmakers somewhere in the environs of the capital and the Wednesday Chick-fil-A luncheon where Republicans, *Atlantic* magazine says, "talk policy, plot legislative strategy, and seek out cosponsors for legislation."

The Center for Media and Democracy calls out the actions of another monster hatched in 1973: the American Legislative Exchange Council (ALEC). ALEC"s influence is all-pervasive. Their members write the bills to benefit their members then shepherd them through Congress or state legislatures. These are just a few such measures:

- Altria/Philip Morris USA benefits from ALEC's newest tobacco legislation -- an extremely narrow tax break for moist tobacco that would make fruit flavored tobacco products cheaper and more attractive to youngsters.
- Health insurance companies such as Humana and Golden Rule Insurance (United Healthcare), benefit directly from ALEC model bills, such as the Health Savings Account bill that just passed in Wisconsin.
- Tobacco firms such as Reynolds and pharmaceutical firms such as Bayer benefit directly from ALEC tort reform measures that make it harder for Americans to sue when injured by dangerous products.
- Corrections Corporation of America (CCA) benefits directly from the anti-immigrant legislation introduced in Arizona and other states that requires expanded incarceration and housing of immigrants, along with other bills from ALEC's crime task force. (While CCA has stated that it left ALEC in late 2010 after years of membership on the Criminal Justice Task Force and even co-chairing it, its prison privatization bills remain ALEC "models.")
- Connections Academy, a large online education corporation and co-chair of the Education Task Force, benefits from ALEC measures to privatize public education and promote private online schools.

Our duty as Progressives is to learn from corporations' successes and build our own foundations and think tanks. In the marketplace of ideas, we can offer an alternative that will stand on its own merits. Our current institutions focus on damage control and short-term goals rather than playing the long game required to swing the pendulum of political influence in the other direction. We need to win hearts and minds, not just repeat the mantra of NO that was the GOP's blueprint for change during the eight years of an Obama administration. We need bold, innovative systemic change to reverse growing corporate dominance. How do we accomplish such a lofty goal?

ALEC's influence is noted throughout this book. For all our railing against government R or D, the true danger to democracy is the invidious presence of pro-business policies that undermine the Peoples' will and allow unsafe conditions back into the work environment and community. Often called a plutocracy, ALEC primes the pump with key campaign contributions, concocts and then presents legislative templates to state and federal legislators they have helped elect. The next step: they lobby all other legislators of that house to support their colleague's bill. Then it's on to the next legislature to repeat the process. This is the way we will continue to lose on comprehensive legislation against questionable business practices and products from corn additives in our fuel to minimally-tested genetically modified foods.

The Powell Memo continues to be the bible for business. The Trump administration adheres to it.

Chapter 5

What's wrong with a two party system?

> "The two-party system is the greatest political evil under our Constitution. There is nothing which I dread so much as a division of the republic into two great parties, each arranged under its leader, and concerting measures in opposition to each other." John Adams

The functions of political parties are to marshal voters around principles that are central to that organization's core standards known as a platform. The Green Party in this country and throughout the world first raised the issue of protecting the environment, making it the central part of the Green Party platform. As these organizations attempt to expand and attract new members, they discuss in caucuses other issues that are near and dear to their members. These additional "planks" become part of the Party platform. The party looks for candidates that seem to personify that platform best to champion those causes once they are elected to public office.

Traditionally, labor unions have been closely allied with the Democratic Party. As a member of the Communications Workers of America, I found that candidates and elected officials courted the labor movement. They talked about worker protections, the threat that others would take away our hard-earned victories like the 40-hour work week, paid overtime, and something my friends in the Building Trades called "prevailing wage." A prevailing wage in government contracts includes the hourly wage and usual benefits and overtime paid to workers, laborers, and mechanics in a certain municipality or region where the work is being performed.

Over the years, just as I walked many a picket line in support of my brothers and sisters on strike, I also walked precincts and called voters in support of candidates. I joined my local's legislative political committee and lobbied on workers' bills in Sacramento and Washington, D.C. because some corporations were trying to take away overtime pay in specific industries and, in the Building Trades, prevailing wage benefited all workers because, whether union or not, workers would still be paid the same salary. Union construction workers knew that their advanced skills, when pay wasn't the issue, would be the deciding factor in landing lucrative building contracts. A prevailing wage in government contracts includes the hourly wage and usual benefits and overtime paid to workers, laborers, and mechanics in a certain municipality or region where the work is being performed.

Meanwhile, I advanced within my union, serving as an Executive Board member as well as continuing my work on legislation. I was elected Chair of the Legislative Political Committee of all the CWA locals in Southern California. Now I met with legislators to talk about bills we wanted to be considered in the state Capitol. I handed out checks to candidates from our voluntary Committee on Political Education (COPE) fund. And I trained the next generation of labor grassroots lobbyists.

Did we always get what we wanted from Democratic lawmakers? No. And more than once I heard a labor leader say, "We're not going to be an ATM for the Party anymore!"

So, would we have had greater response from another Party?

Let's look at various parties and see which hold the promise of "lifting all boats."

Does the Libertarian Party look out for the middle class? In a Pew Research Study, about eleven percent of Americans asked to define libertarianism said a libertarian was "someone whose political views emphasize individual freedom by limiting the role of government."

More than twice as many self-identified Libs are college graduates than those with no more than a high school education. About 14 percent of independents and 12 percent of Republicans said they are libertarian, compared with 6 percent of Democrats. More figures from the study:

> Libertarians are somewhat more likely than the public overall to say government regulation of business does more harm than good (56 percent vs. 47 percent). However, about four-in-ten libertarians say that government regulation of business is necessary to protect the public interest (41 percent).
>
> The attitudes of libertarians similarly differ from the public on government aid to the poor; they are more likely than the people to say "government aid to the poor does more harm than good by making people too dependent on government assistance" (57 percent vs. 48 percent), yet about four-in-ten (38 percent) say it "does more good than harm because people can't get out of poverty until their basic needs are met."

Members of the Libertarian Party seem a little vague on the definition of a Libertarian, but the Libertarian Party's stance on economics includes the following statement pulled from their national website:

> On unions: *Employment and compensation agreements between private employers and employees are outside the scope of government, and government-mandated benefits or social engineering should not hinder these contracts. We support the right of private employers and employees to choose whether or not to bargain with each other through a labor union. Bargaining should be free of government interference, such as compulsory arbitration or imposing an obligation to bargain.*

That platform, if enacted as law, would rule out any attempt to raise the minimum wage at any level of government. And frankly, without compulsory arbitration or an obligation to bargain, companies would be reluctant to negotiate a contract or settle an impasse. Even without a Libertarian government, workers often find it hard to get respect. The threat of "government interference" sometimes makes an equitable settlement possible.

> *Retirement planning is the responsibility of the individual, not the government. Libertarians would phase out the current government-sponsored Social Security system and transition to a private voluntary system. The proper and most effective source of help for the poor is the voluntary efforts of private groups and individuals. We believe members of society will become more charitable and civil society will be strengthened as government reduces its activity in this realm.*

Those in power would like us to forget the way things were before we had programs in place to catch those who were falling through the social net: the disabled, the homeless, the elderly. Left to their own devices, corporations will lie, cheat and steal from their employees, the consumer, and each other in a vicious grab for market share and profits.

We as a nation had over 100 years where the working class was on their own in their golden years. Under FDR, we took a more enlightened approach and created Social Security. This program allowed dignity in old age and opened up the job market for younger workers.

Libertarians also believe the free market system should govern health care and education. Until recently, healthcare operated on the free market and meant higher premiums for those of us enrolled in the system who subsidized emergency care for the uninsured, and it meant the possibility of infection from those who weren't. Would an emergency room be forced to turn away the uninsured under a Libertarian majority? How would homeschooling fit into a Libertarian paradigm? Speaking personally with parents with a ninth grade education my education would have suffered. Some say schools would have to up their game to stay viable in a free market educational system; others say that only the wealthy would receive a quality education. Public education is guaranteed in our Constitution and should be a right, not a privilege.

The Libertarian Party is often considered the closest aligned in ideology with the Republican Party.

The Grand Old Party, the Party of Lincoln and Ronald Reagan, is proud of their alliance with the powerhouse of Big Business. As with all other parties I looked into, I went to their public face, the official Republican Party website and pulled up their platform from 2012. Within a document entitled, "Restoring the American Dream: Rebuilding the Economy and Creating Jobs," I found the following:

> *Republicans support employee ownership. We believe employee stock ownership plans create capitalists and expand the ownership of private property and are therefore the essence of a high-performing free enterprise economy...*

They, of course, admonished the Obama Administration:

> *[They're] clinging to antiquated notions of confrontation and concentrating power in the Washington offices of union elites. [The current administration] has strongly supported the anti-business card check legislation to deny workers a secret ballot in union organizing campaigns and, through the use of Project Labor Agreements, barred 80 percent of the construction workforce from competing for jobs in many stimulus projects.*

Project Labor Agreements, otherwise known as Community Workforce Agreements or PLAs, are a tried and true way of building the basics of America from the Hoover Dam to the Washington Nationals baseball stadium. These agreements benefit working men and women, contractors, communities and taxpayers by ensuring projects are completed on time and on budget, requiring employee training, and encouraging that public investment benefits local communities. Card check legislation was promoted as a way to avoid what was happening all too often – employer coercion. Companies, especially in the anything-against-labor-goes Reagan 80s, leaned on employees through threats of a plant shutdown, one-on-one talks with the boss, and mandatory meetings where actors pretended to be victims of the unsuccessful union drive one town over. Companies have also tried promotions and temporary raises, usually lasting until the union either lost the election or went away due to lack of employee interest. The Republican Party, not surprisingly, takes a strong anti-labor stance:

> *We will restore the rule of law to labor law by blocking "card check," enacting the Secret Ballot Protection Act, enhancing the Hobbs Act against labor violence, and passing the Raise Act to allow all workers to receive well-earned raises without the approval of their union representative.*

I had never heard of the Hobbs Act, so I looked it up and found this on Wikipedia: The Hobbs Act, enacted in 1946, stipulates, "Whoever in any way or degree obstructs, delays, or affects commerce or the movement of any article or commodity in commerce, by robbery or extortion or attempts or conspires so to do, or commits or threatens physical violence to any person or property in furtherance of a plan or purpose to do anything in violation of this section shall be fined under this title or imprisoned not more than twenty years, or both." Labor violence, or even the threat, would fall under a broad interpretation of the Act. Business owners could probably find a judge who would declare the act of picketing to fall under the reach of the Hobbes Act. Very often, when scabs cross the picket line intimidation dissuades many others from following. In over 30 years experience in the labor movement, most of the violence has been at the hands of those crossing the line.

According to congress.gov, the Rewarding Achievement and Incentivizing Successful Employees Act or RAISE Act:

> Amends the National Labor Relations Act to declare that neither its prohibition against interference by an employer with employees' right to bargain collectively, nor the terms of a collective bargaining agreement entered into between employees and an employer after enactment of this Act shall prohibit an employer from paying an employee higher wages, pay, or other compensation than the agreement provides for.

I have never, ever met a union rep who stood in the way of a member's raise! The union receives a tiny percentage of that raise as the negotiating party. The National Labor Relations Act (NLRA) states and a contractual agreement between a company and a union declares the union to be the sole negotiator regarding wages, hours and working conditions. The Republicans would have you believe that labor is against Senator Rubio's bill because only the "union bosses" should get you that raise. BS! Labor is against arbitrary raises. Boss' pet? A raise for you! Marge took Care of Newborn Child time to care for her newborn son? So sorry! Pretty soon, you have worker pitted against worker, stabbing each other to make themselves look good.

Back to the Republican platform for workers:

> *We salute the Republican Governors and State legislators who have saved their States from fiscal disaster by reforming their laws governing public employee unions. We urge elected officials across the country to follow their lead to avoid State and local defaults on their obligations and the collapse of services to the public.*

They quickly forget that these pensions and benefits to public employees were negotiated in good faith by both parties and, like their "obligations" to the public, these contracts deserve to be honored or reconsidered by both parties.

> *We support the right of States to enact Right-to-Work laws and encourage them to do so to promote greater economic liberty. Ultimately, we support the enactment of a National Right-to-Work law to promote worker freedom and to promote greater economic liberty.*

Right-to-work weakens the power of labor unions by saying workers cannot be forced to join labor unions or pay union dues to keep their jobs. No dues: no funds to provide services to members like grievances, arbitration and training, and lost leverage at the bargaining table. Right-to-work is currently the law of the land in half the nation after Wisconsin Governor Scott Walker persuaded a majority of his state legislature to pass it, and it's being wielded as a weapon to bludgeon the labor movement, and workers, to death – or at least into submission. Many in the middle class, those at the upper end fretting about unfettered capitalism, will be gripped with fear when they see how precarious their own perch in the social order actually is!

RIGHT TO WORK STATES: Alabama, Arizona, Arkansas, Florida, Georgia, Idaho, Indiana, Iowa, Kansas, Louisiana, Michigan, Mississippi, Nebraska, Nevada, North Carolina, North Dakota, Oklahoma, South Carolina, South Dakota, Tennessee, Texas, Utah, Virginia, Wisconsin, and Wyoming.

In summation: the Republican Party wants to do away with labor unions. Why? Because Big Business hates that layer between management and worker. Why should the loss of labor unions concern the rest of us? Union workers set the standard in wages and benefits and safety. Unions, through various battles over the years, brought about the 8-hour day, the 40-hour work week, paid vacation, health care, and health and safety laws. Some or all of this could be dismantled overnight. Union leaders have always understood the ambivalence of laws and the impressionable support of non-union family members, neighbors, and friends. "That's why we have contracts," explained former Communications Workers of America President Morton Bahr.

So where are the Democrats on these crucial issues? I failed to find a national website like the Republicans have so I went to my state's platform site. California Dems tend to lean further left than the Party elsewhere due to California's solidly blue status. Every elected statewide official is a Democrat and both houses of the state legislature are controlled by a Democratic Party majority. If Dems are going to push the envelope anywhere in the country, it will happen here.

On the economy, the Trans-Pacific Partnership with Fast Track authority did not sit well with the majority of Dems in the state. I checked out cadem.org, the official site for the California State Democratic Party, and found the 2014 platform. I found a lot to like. The Party supports many of the issues I care about including worker rights:

> *Support the rights of all employees to organize, select a bargaining representative of their choice through card check recognition,*

> work in a safe environment and be free from intimidation and retaliation tactics.
>
> Oppose privatization of essential government services and outsourcing of public sector jobs, promote the development and purchase of goods that are made in America, and support the modification of the US tax code so that corporations are incented to hire workers in the U.S. instead of abroad.
>
> Oppose new and unfair trade agreements and renegotiate existing agreements.

Those above "planks" of the Democratic Party platform convinced me – and apparently most members of organized labor – that the Party has our back. Sometimes it may not seem so: Democrats received more corporate contributions than their Republican counterparts in the last election cycle according to Sunlight Academy, a nonpartisan group that advocates for transparency in government; they report that labor unions spent their time and money almost exclusively with the Democrats. No surprise there.

The Green Party is probably closest in appearance to the Democratic Party. The federal Party is an outgrowth of state efforts from 1996 to 2001 and is considered a federation of state Green Parties. "Our goal," states the 2014 Platform, "was to help existing state parties grow and to promote the formation of parties in all 51 states (?) and colonies (??)." They have won a few elections here and there and in 2000, upset more than a few Democrats who felt the Green candidate, Ralph Nader, pulled enough support from Al Gore for the Republicans to take the White House. Of course, there was the matter of Florida and hanging chads, and a Supreme Court decision that awarded the election to George W. Bush.

"Whether the issue is universal health care, corporate globalization, alternative energy, election reform or decent, living wages for workers, Greens have the courage and independence necessary to take on the powerful corporate interests."

Let's take a look at their platform:

> *There's only one plausible excuse left for ... voters to remain loyal to the Dems in the realm of electoral politics: to prevent the GOP from winning. Some progressives insist that we need to continue supporting Democrats because of Supreme Court appointments (although Dems in Congress have approved some of the most ideologically rigid Republican appointees) and to save reproductive rights (already watered down, with Democratic help),*

> *The Green Party opposes the privatization of Social Security. It is critical that the public protections of Social Security are not privatized and subjected to increased risk. The bottom 20 percent of American senior citizens get roughly 80 percent of their income from Social Security, and without Social Security, nearly 70 percent of black elderly and 60 percent of Latino elderly households would be in poverty.*

In 2010, Hugh Giordano, at the time a 26-year-old from a suburb of Philadelphia, a union organizer for United Food and Commercial Workers Local 152 and a candidate for office, had enough of partisan politics and issued the following letter on official Green Party stationery:

Open Letter to Union Leaders

It's Time to Put An End to The Two-Party System
What We, As Labor Leaders, Must Do!

Dear Union Brothers and Sisters,

This letter is more of a "cry for action" rather just an informational or ideological statement or platform. It is meant to be severe and intense, and I hope you take this letter in that form! This letter is being sent to as many union brothers and sisters as possible.

I have been involved in the labor movement now for about ten years, from non-union worker/union activist to member, and officially becoming a union representative for UFCW Local 152. I have been a part of every aspect of the union movement, and now I must take the next step – Labor leader.

What do I mean by a leader? Being a leader does not mean having the title of Business Manager or President of a local. It means standing up and saying what needs to be said against the status quo. There were numerous forms of this leadership before me, and there will be numerous ones after me – but I am worried about what is happening in today's present labor environment.

Many of you might have heard about my run for State Representative as an Independent with the Green Party and I am proud of that decision. I ended up getting the highest vote of any third party [candidate] in Philadelphia and I am pretty sure I received the highest in a three-way race. This is what needs to be done! I did this using basic union organizing skills and having a handful of unions behind me. Imagine what would have happened if I had all of the Philadelphia unions behind me?

Why do we support Democrats and Republicans when all they do is take our money, use our manpower, and then leave us out to dry? Why do we support CEOs, corporate consultants, and corporate attorneys, when 365 days of the year when they are not running for office, they are fighting unions, breaking labor laws, and spreading their greed? But all of a sudden when they run for office as a 'Democrat", they have changed their ways? This just proves that the Democrats are as corporate as the Republicans.

Labor has the power to change this and we must! Many labor unions still believe the Democrats are "labor's friend." Really? How can this be when they failed to pass EFCA [the Employee Free Choice Act which would have given employees the ability to vote in a union simply by a majority interest]? They bail out the super rich, failed to pass Single-Payer healthcare, pass horrible trade laws (NAFTA), attack pensions, and most of all – are in the pockets of the same people we fight every day, the corporations? I am not writing this letter so I can fill it with boring facts, but the Democrats took 53% of the total "corporate" contributions – 53 percent!

Why are we, the strong men and women of the labor movement, bowing down to the corporate bosses and politicians, when we could run for office, win, and do what we need to do – enact laws that benefit working people and poor people.

We have the manpower, money, and knowledge to run OUR UNION REPRESENTATIVES and win!

But here is the catch: we CANNOT run as a Democrat or Republican; those two parties are too corrupt and entrenched. We must strengthen and build a THIRD PARTY! Yes, we must do what our past labor leaders tried to do, and that is building a party that is about us. Some of you might say, "That will never work, and it can't happen." Well, I would say you are dead wrong! The corporate Democrats ONLY win because we fuel them, but then they turn their backs on us. If we run with a clean and fresh party such as the Green Party, we can call the shots and be as progressive as we choose.

It amazes me how some local leadership bows down to the Democrats and "fears" them. Union brothers and sisters, when any one of us becomes "fearful" or "controlled" by a political party – it's time to step down and pass the torch on. WE are the voice of working people, and WE should be telling these politicians what to do, not the other way around.

We owe the Democrats and Republicans NOTHING because they have done NOTHING for our members, for our contracts, and for the movement. How much longer are we going to support a bunch of failures? WE don't have to because WE can blackball them just like they blackballed our members and the movement. We gave them plenty of time and opportunities and each time, they spat in our face!

Here is what needs to happen:

We have to come together and make a collective of progressive, fearless, and strong locals that will run with the Green Party.

We have to talk about the issues we want to be passed in City Council and the State Legislature.

We then must pick union representatives to run for these seats in City Council and the State Legislature.

We must stick together and focus on winning for once!

WE CAN DO IT AND WE WILL DO IT!

The Green Party is the party of labor. They have a platform that is 100% pro-labor (repeal Taft-Hartley, NAFTA, and prosecute CEOs who break the law). Other labor unions around the country are supporting Green Party candidates in local races; I say we RUN AS GREEN PARTY CANDIDATES.

It's time we make history and do the right thing. We have an obligation to our members, to our future, and we have an obligation to the men and women who died to form and join unions. If we keep on doing what we are doing, then we have slapped everyone in the face that fought for us.

Sincerely,
Hugh Giordano, Union Organizer

Other members and friends of organized labor are aligning with the Green Party. Tom Clements a "Greenie" running for the state Senate in South Carolina, picked up the endorsement of the Greater Columbia Central Labor Council of the South Carolina AFL-CIO. Ben Manski, Wisconsin State Assembly candidate, won the endorsement of Madison Teachers Inc. Mark Swaney, who ran for a state representative seat in Arkansas, had the support of the state AFL-CIO. Howie Hawkins, a Teamster, ran as a Green Party candidate for governor of New York.

I, too, wrote a heartfelt letter when I ran for California State Assembly. I urged my brothers and sisters to look around and see how working people were being attacked in Wisconsin and Michigan. I said it was time to circle the wagons and protect what we had. I had three times the amount of experience in the labor movement as Brother Giordano. I had risen in the leadership of both the Communications Workers of America and the United Auto Workers, and I lived in a solidly blue state. But both races, in 2008 and 2013, included a staff member from a popular, pro-labor Congressman's office. I had some support from labor; I'm forever indebted to the Steamfitters and others, but I was flabbergasted when I encountered outright hostility from some of my brothers and sisters in 2008. In 2013, I was treated better, but the endorsement of union pragmatists for the "establishment" candidate prevailed in both races. They knew that with a Congressman's endorsement the staffer would likely win and labor wanted to be there when they were showered in gratitude. Without the support of my base, the campaign was doomed. How do you not become jaded and cynical in the face of overwhelming ambivalence?

Giordano's letter raises some questions that strike at the heart of a two-party system: In a political landscape where both major parties are beholden to monied, corporate interests, how do we hear and respond to the voice of working people and the middle class? Is the answer to run mean, lean and Green? There are at least 39 other declared political parties recognized at the federal level. There are nine listed parties with the word "Socialist" or "Socialism" in their title. Interestingly, all of them predate the rise of Bernie Sanders as a Democratic Socialist running under the banner of the Democratic Party.

To date, coalitions among parties, as in Europe, have not been necessary to move legislation. No minor or third party has created an atmosphere of influence in the political realm that would lead to such an arrangement in this country.

Some ask why there's no labor party in the United States. After all, wouldn't the voice of the working class carry significant weight in a national conversation about issues like income inequality, jobs, and infrastructure?

Chapter 6 Why Don't We Have a Labor Party?

Chapter 6

What About a Labor Party?

> "If a labor party had been established, it is highly likely that business interests would have had less influence over public policy, that income and wealth would have been more equally distributed, that trade unions would have been stronger and that a more comprehensive welfare state would have developed." Robin Archer, *Why Is There No Labor Party in the United States?*

Why is there no Labor Party?

Robin Archer asked that question in his book of the same name. His answer differed from the usual observation that its part of our maverick American makeup. Academics had always compared the history of Europe's labor movement with ours, but Archer believed our labor movement was more akin to Australia's at a crucial time in history for both countries, the late 1800's.

> In the early 1890s, both countries suffered from the worst depression of the nineteenth century, and a series of major industrial confrontations took place in which governments sided with employers and left the unions completely defeated.

This is where the two countries diverged. Some machinations behind the scene of the 1894 American Federation of Labor convention by A F of L President Samuel Gompers sidelined the issue of a U.S. Labor Party, but the Australian Labour Party became an official political party in 1901, predating even the Labour Party in England. The ALP was also the first political party established in Australia.

The idea of an American Labor Party has emerged at various times in our country's history and first formed formally in the aftermath of World War I, but its roots and the belief that workers should map their own destinies were planted in Europe and Australia in the late 1800s. In America, the Workingmen's Party was established in 1876 with the goal of transforming society through the combined political and industrial action of the working class organized in industrial unions. All workers in a particular industry were to be organized into one union to gain leverage at the bargaining table. The following year they changed their name to the Socialist Labor Party of America.

During the first World War, the prices of virtually every US-made product rose while workers' wages stayed flat, yet crop prices were bringing farmers less and less. The Wilson Administration frowned on labor's attempts in bargaining that brought on any form of labor dispute. They made it clear that they regarded any affront to business as usual as disloyal and un-American.

Farmers and industrial workers found themselves on the same side in the ensuing recession and depression. They resented the sacrifices they had made for the war effort and blamed these hard economic times on business' failure to share in the sacrifices. Arthur C. Townley, a former organizer for the Socialist Party of America, formed the Non-Partisan League in North Dakota in 1915 who, on behalf of small farmers and merchants, advocated state control of mills, grain elevators, banks and other farm-related industries in order to reduce the power of corporate political interests from Minneapolis and Chicago. The Union Labor Party was formed in Duluth, Minnesota in 1917 and a year later the Minnesota arm of the Farmer's Non-Partisan League merged with the Union Labor Party and the Worker's Non-Partisan League to form the Farmer-Labor Party of Minnesota. The organization promoted a platform of farmer and labor union protection, government ownership of certain industries, and social security laws and reached its apex in the 1920s and 1930s. Future Democratic Presidential candidate Hubert H. Humphrey and former Minnesota governor Elmer Benson were instrumental in having the organization absorbed into the Democratic Party in 1944.

By August 1919, labor parties existed in seven states. A convention to establish a national Labor Party was planned for November and organizing efforts by unions in the other 41 states ensured that there would be labor parties in all 48 by the time the convention was convened.

The convention adopted a challenging declaration of principles and a party constitution. Wikipedia reports:

> The list of principles included
>
> - complete repeal of the Espionage Act of 1917, which had included in the original bill presidential authority to censor the press
> - complete equality for all sexes and races
> - an end to labor injunctions
> - cost of living reductions
> - nationalization of public utilities and natural resources
> - enactment of the Plumb Plan to nationalize the railroads
> - free public education "from kindergarten to university" and democratic education
> - introduction of the powers of popular initiative, referendum and recall at the federal level
> - dissolving the United States Senate
> - a maximum term of four years for federal judges
> - introduction of a nationwide age of consent of 18 years
> - the end of employment of all minors under the age of 16 years
> - institution of minimum wages and minimum prices for agricultural goods
> - an end to the use of convict labor and foreign labor to undercut American workers' wages

- a maximum workday of 8 hours and a maximum workweek of 44 hours
- full employment.

In the 1920s, former members of the Socialist Labor Party of America founded the Industrial Union League. One of the founding members of the League, Joseph Brandon, was convinced that before workers could form their own party, a socialist industrial union had to be established. The Industrial Union Alliance was founded in April 1932 and attempted to bring all the factions back together under one banner. The Alliance became the Industrial Union Party a year later. Later that same year, 1933, the unified IUP splintered again, tossing out Brandon and his followers and morphed into the American Labor Party. The ALP published a manifesto entitled Labor and State Capitalism in four chapters in 1934. They declared themselves Marxist and predicted the destruction of the "capitalist state by the capitalist class through world war" as Marx and Engels prophesied in their writings. The working class would be around to pick up the pieces. "...The Labor Party will not concern itself about the industrial and political action and struggle of the working class. It will be the function of the Labor Party to teach the working class to be prepared to take over the power of government..." The ALP published another pamphlet Socialism – the Basis for Happiness that substituted Socialism for Marxism and made some familiar-sounding comments:

> According to statistics supplied by the U.S. Government, 1 percent of the population of America owns 60 percent of the wealth.

The last gasp of the American Labor Party came in June of 1935. Labor Party 1.0 was over.

Labor Party 1.5

New York, that bastion of workers' sound and fury, has given birth to quite a few attempts at balancing management/worker power. In 1936, it was in the form of a redux struggle from 1932: the formation of an American Labor Party.

The Old Guard was dominated by middle-aged Socialist Party veterans and stood for everything the Militants and Progressives hated: an entrenched bureaucracy with little or no fire left in them. The Progressives saw democracy as merely a tool of those in power.

Historian Irving Howe, a young Militant in the SP in the early 1930s, later recalled his own perception of the "Old Guard":

> On the right stood the Old Guard, hard and unyielding. As a youthful newcomer to the socialist movement, I was, of course, contemptuous of the Old Guard, and so was almost every other new member... In the American left of those days, anything not 'revolutionary' was dismissed as beneath discussion; but that didn't bother the Old Guard, which gloried in its distance from the vulgar ferment of popular radicalism. Perhaps the Old Guard carried within itself too large a weight of historical pain — its admirers would say, historical knowledge. It had won the struggle against the communists in the garment unions during the 1920s, but that had drained much of its socialist spirit.

Differences came to a head, and the Old Guard was forced out of leadership at the 1934 Convention of the Socialist Party. A year and a half later the Old Guard took on the militant wing for control of the Socialist Party. By then they were on the outside looking in and after their charter was revoked, left to form the Social Democratic Federation of America (SDF).

In New York's municipal elections of 1935, Socialists turned out 200,000 voters. Suddenly the Socialist Party seemed a real threat to the re-election of FDR. The SDF shored up its connections to the labor movement, in those days a political juggernaut who turned out their members to vote and canvass for candidates. Labor leaders from both the American Federation of Labor and the blue-collar Congress of Industrial Organizations formed the Labor Non-Partisan League. They filed papers in New York to create a new political party, the American Labor Party, that would also declare FDR as their candidate of choice, putting his name on the ballot twice and pulling votes from any Socialist candidates.

The ALP's early successes drew union members affiliated with the Communist Party. That taint was used against them in future elections and meant the ALP's demise during the McCarthy era. Dwindling turnout doomed the Party; its charter was pulled in 1956.

Labor Party 2.0

In the early 1970s, the name of Lyndon LaRouche first gained national recognition. Formerly known as Lyn Marcus, LaRouche headed a movement that had originated in radical leftist student politics of the 1960s. His group's physical altercations with other left-wing organizations, including the Students for a Democratic Society and the American Communist Party, alienated him from possible political allies.

In the 1970s and 1980s hundreds of candidates, some with only limited knowledge or connection to LaRouche or the movement, ran as Democrats in the United States on the LaRouche platform but had little success.

In 1988, LaRouche and 25 associates were convicted on fraud charges related to fund-raising. Of course, the movement cried foul, calling the prosecutions politically motivated.

Labor Party 3.0

Let's connect the dots to this latest effort:

In 1988, a progressive caucus led by Bob Wages and Tony Mazzocchi won election to national office in the Oil, Chemical and Atomic Workers union.

The Labor Party website states:

> Mazzocchi was widely regarded as a visionary at the forefront of the labor movement's involvement in the major struggles

for social justice in the postwar period - from the civil rights movement, nuclear proliferation, and the Vietnam War to environmental justice and the movement for occupational health and safety, in which he and the OCAW played a crucial role. He conceptualized health and safety issues as a fight against corporate power and for worker empowerment. Wages and Mazzocchi campaigned on the promise of breaking away from labor's lockstep allegiances to the Democratic Party.

This Labor Party moment reflected the merging of a number of significant developments in the 1990s:

1. A realization by the rest of the labor movement that the events surrounding the PATCO strike and the mass firing of so many air traffic controllers revealed how business was going to treat the working class in the future.
2. Union members were connecting the dots and the feeling was the Democratic Party had sold us out in their support of NAFTA. Globalization was a threat to workers everywhere.
3. We remembered our roots. After our misplaced support of the Vietnam War, we were again proud to declare ourselves labor/left, proud of our tradition of bottom-up activism, a sense of solidarity, and boots-on-the-ground political action. Many of us found a new militancy that inspired the troops.

By the end of 1992, three major labor unions had endorsed the idea of organizing a Labor Party; the California State Federation became the first state AFL-CIO body to endorse. Momentum grew with the passage of the North American Free Trade Agreement in December 1993, that made the newly-elected Clinton Administration's neoliberal loyalties painfully clear. The effort picked up steam as more labor unions signed on.

In 1995, newly-elected AFL-CIO President John Sweeney, while skeptical about the Labor Party's chances for success, commented: "I would be the last person to discourage the dedicated brothers and sisters who are organizing the Labor Party movement from taking their best shot and I hope the progress they are making sends a clear signal to a Democratic Party that has moved away from working families just as surely as it has moved away from the old, the young, the disabled, and the poor."

But in a duh! moment, the AFL-CIO proudly "defied convention" and made an early endorsement (March 1996) for the re-election of President Clinton and Vice President Gore. Forget the hue and cry about NAFTA from rank and file members and local leaders. The fix was in. Unions assessed themselves $25 million for a union education effort, voter registration, and boots on the ground.

"First, none of the $25 million—or an additional $10 million coming out of our regular operating funds—will go to the DNC," swore Sweeney. "In fact, we've given less than $10,000 to the DNC this year because of our concern with their policies and practices. Second, the endorsement of Clinton and Gore should not be read as an endorsement of the DNC or of Democratic Party candidates in general. We endorsed the President and the Vice President because their performance on behalf of working Americans over the past four years merits it (70 percent of our 13.1 million members agree)." Traditionally top-down, the organization ignored the angry members who already had or would soon be losing their jobs as the work headed south of the border.

In June 1996, this Labor Party was founded as a new political party when 1400 delegates at the founding convention, including representatives from hundreds of local and international unions as well as individual activists, came together on issues most agreed were the most important to working people - trade, health care, and the rights to organize, bargain, and strike – and recognized that both the Democrats and Republicans have failed working people.

From 1996 through 2007, the idea of a Party "for the rest of us" took hold. Six national unions and thousands of individual members joined the Labor Party. Labor Party organizers launched national issues campaigns: the right to a job, health care, tuition-free higher education, and the right of all workers to organize and bargain. The movement put out a monthly newspaper, ran worker education programs, held forums and events in major cities across the country and promoted working-class culture. The support the Labor Party threw behind the launch of a state Labor Party in South Carolina was the beginning of the end for the national Labor Party.

Nineteen local unions, the state AFL-CIO and the Charleston and Columbia central labor councils endorsed the founding meeting. Activists and union delegates adopted an organizing strategy for the 2007 and 2008 elections. In the end, they collected 16,000 signatures, enough to appear on the South Carolina ballot.

But the drive for a national Labor Party was losing momentum. Many unions were losing members and scaling back their ambitions due to the effects of globalization and technology that moved jobs at the flip of a switch. The union that had been a driving force, the Oil, Chemical and Atomic Workers (OCAW), went through two mergers, eventually becoming part of the United Steel Workers of America. In the meantime, the support for a Labor Party dwindled. After G.W. Bush stole the 2000 Presidential election, Green Party candidate Ralph Nader took the heat for the outcome, which seemed to suggest that an independent party wasn't such a good idea. Labor went into defense mode with the Bush Administration's attacks on unions. Unions hunkered down to weather the storm of the G.W. Bush years and abandoned any political aspirations. By the end of 2007, Labor Party 3.0 organizing efforts were over.

They left us with this parting challenge:

> ... the ongoing economic crisis and the failures of the Obama administration seem to provide an opening to begin to challenge labor to move some of its resources towards long-term projects that would advance a broad working-class program that goes beyond the next election and is geared toward building independent political power for working people. We could launch such a project if labor contributed just 10 percent of the resources and finances that it spent in the 2012 election cycle.
>
> What could we do with those resources and commitments? We could connect with the 10 million Americans who are

underwater on their mortgages. We could reach out to the 42 million Americans forced to rely on food stamps to feed their families, and the 50 million without healthcare, the 15 million unemployed, the 15 million underemployed, the 20 million immigrants with no rights to a secure life, the millions of college graduates condemned to a lifetime of debt peonage, the tens of millions of workers trapped in a series of Wal-mart-style jobs and facing the prospect of the loss of even the minimal social insurance benefits that used to be the birthright of everyone in the United States. In short, we could begin to mobilize and speak on behalf of a working class that has become fragmented and disenfranchised because of a political system that inexorably distributes wealth and power upward to the "one percent."

Why is there no American Labor Party? Ask the Marxists:

> In primary elections, candidates must first win the nomination of the party and then proceed to the general election. In practice, it takes lots of money and media coverage to win the primary campaign and then even more money to win the general election. This is perfect for the capitalist class. They have the money, and they own the newspapers, magazines, book publishers, and radio and television stations. Even many billboards on highways are owned by the same companies that own the television networks and cable channels. This is one example of how they control the candidates of both major parties long before they are even elected.

Did we mention the consultants? According to The Young Turks Network, one political consulting firm, GMMB, earned $236.3 million from Hillary For America and $5.3 million from the Democratic National Committee in 2016. Joel Benenson, a pollster and strategist who frequents cable news, collected $4.1 million from HFA while simultaneously earning $3.3 million from the DNC. Perkins Coie law firm collected $3.8 million from the DNC, $481,979 from the Convention fund and $1.8 million from HFA in 2016.

Working Families

According to Wikipedia, the Working Families Party of New York was first organized in 1998 by a coalition of labor unions, community organizations, members of the now-inactive national New Party, and a variety of advocacy groups such as Citizen Action of New York and the Association of Community Organizations for Reform Now (ACORN). The party's main concerns are jobs, healthcare, raising the minimum wage, universal paid sick days, the student debt crisis, higher taxes on the rich, public education, and energy and environmental reform. It has usually cross-endorsed progressive Democratic or Republican candidates through fusion voting, a process legal in only nine states that allows minor parties to endorse major party candidates with an additional line on the ballot, but Working Families will occasionally run its own candidates. In the 2016 elections in California, the American Independent Party endorsed Donald Trump, giving him two positions on the ballot. This was the first time in 80 years, electoral fusion had occurred on the California ballot.

Chapter 7

We the People: Abdicating Oversight of our Political Systems and our Politicians

"If there is one eternal truth of politics, it is that there are always a dozen good reasons for doing nothing." John le Carre

"All politics are based on the indifference of the majority." James Barrett Scotty Reston

"We must never allow ourselves to lapse into thinking, 'That's just the way things are now.'" Senator Jeff Flake, AZ (R)

"It is not only what we do, but also what we do not do, for which we are accountable." Molière

I grew up poor and one thing we were taught early on was, we don't matter. The implicit message: don't get involved, don't think you're as good as everybody else. Politics were a lofty goal for those with money and nobody else.

It wasn't until I was brought into the labor movement that I found the little people apparently *did* matter and candidates listened to us with respect. We had monetary contributions raised voluntarily from our members to spread around and, often, more importantly, we had "boots on the ground." Our activists would gather together to make phone calls on behalf of a candidate and/or walk door-to-door with literature to get out the vote.

We found some interesting data on the stump. Internally, our own members would vote against their own self-interest, backing another candidate who demonstrated strong support for one of their hot-button issues, what we called the three Gs: God (for), gays (against), or guns (enthusiastically for). Many of our members fell under the sway of the National Rifle Association's Chicken Little approach that warned them the government, specifically Democrats, were coming for their guns. Under President Obama that irrational fear grew. Homophobia is still alive and well; it has just gone underground and is closely associated with the views of those in the Bible Belt who still consider homosexuality to be an abomination. And though there are lots of God-fearing, church-going Democrats, Republicans have been more successful in wearing the mantle of righteous indignation.

Externally, we found that our members mirrored the views of the general population. Some understood that you sometimes had to set aside the three G's and take the long view: without a job, without decent pay, you couldn't afford more guns and couldn't tithe as well on Sunday. But many times we came up against a potential voter who didn't plan to leave the house on Election Day.

Many working class folks, shockingly, don't want to be bothered with politics.

"I come home from work and just want to plop down in front of the TV."

"Why should I bother getting involved? It doesn't make a difference anyway."

We're all very close to the political process, but if you're not involved, you have no way to know that. I was fortunate in that leaders in the labor movement dragged me along for precinct walks and phone banking. It's tough when the door is slammed in your face, or they slam down the phone, but when someone actually *thanks you* for knocking on their door, that almost makes up for other responses.

Walking precincts is one of the best ways to take the pulse of the community. When an educated voter is engaged, actual information may be exchanged.

What happens when two candidates, Republican against Democrat, run for office and you don't like either one? Or you really want to elect a woman, and the one who's running is not acceptable? Or it's a Primary, and you don't like any of the choices for your Party?

To tell the truth, none of these is a thorny issue for the typical American because the average American is not even voting!

Voter turnout is abysmal – usually somewhere between 12 percent and 15 percent. Why? Folks state a variety of reasons: My vote doesn't matter. I live in a district where the other Party will always be in power. I'm sick of the whole system. Things never change. There's an election?

In a New York Times article titled, "Who Turned My Blue State Red? Why poor areas vote for politicians who want to slash the safety net" by Alec MacGillis, the author observes:

> The people who most rely on the safety-net programs secured by Democrats are, by and large, not voting against their own interests by electing Republicans. Instead, they are not voting, period. They have, as voting data, surveys and my reporting suggest, become profoundly disconnected from the political process.

I'm assuming, because the question is left unanswered that, much like my own childhood, the beneficiaries of such programs as welfare and Medicaid feel they haven't earned a voice in the political process, they feel that due to the stigma attached to public assistance their contributions are inconsequential. And the people just above them who, because of more fortunate circumstances have never been in a similar predicament, turned their situation around by finding a job or don't see their Medicare or Social Security payments as entitlements, look down at "those people" as undeserving leeches on their tax dollars.

MacGillis continues:

> The people in these communities who are voting Republican in larger proportions are those who are a notch or two up the economic ladder — the sheriff's deputy, the teacher, the highway worker, the motel clerk, the gas station owner, and the coal miner. And their growing allegiance to the Republicans is, in part, a reaction against what they perceive, among those below them on the economic ladder, as an increasing dependency on the safety net, the most visible manifestation of downward mobility in their declining towns.

Those who do become engaged with politics usually turn into junkies and armchair pundits. How deeply folks become involved depends on their desires to influence policy and become educated on the minutia that goes into lawmaking and political campaigns.

In the dustup between Hillary Clinton and Bernie Sanders, there was an apparent abdication of a different kind: labor's bow to the wife of the man who brought us NAFTA. Two former staff members of Service Employees International Union (SEIU), a union that endorsed Clinton, had this to say:

Leighton Woodhouse: "…one of the biggest disappointments of this primary for me was, for the hundredth time, from the labor movement. Despite all of its endless rhetoric about the 99 percent and building a mass movement against corporate power, not only did the majority of labor fail to align itself with the biggest electoral uprising against monopoly capitalism in decades, it actively fought to suppress it."

Henry: "I lost faith in the labor movement years ago. It will always align itself with institutional power above principle because it simply does not believe it will ever have real power."

Woodhouse again: "Still some good unions left, and some good people in not-so-good unions. Not enough of them in leadership positions."

I admit I'm confused, too. Why wouldn't labor support the candidate who was and is talking with passion about our issues: campaign finance reform, income inequality, minimum wage, and healthcare for all? Was it as American Postal Workers President Mark Dimondstein suggests, a belief that labor "can't win?"

The truth as I see it: many labor leaders have climbed the ladder of stature and responsibility within the Democratic Party and now more closely identify with the Party than with their members. And some of these unions, while professing to be member-driven, are top-down organizations. Frankly, I was surprised when my first union, Communications Workers of America, polled their members and announced that Senator Bernie Sanders was members' favored Democratic candidate for President in 2016 and the union was endorsing him. But even that poll doesn't prove that CWA is more democratic – small d – than SEIU, UAW or others, because shortly after the poll results were published the international president of CWA, Larry Cohen, stepped down to run Bernie's campaign. At first blush, it appeared that the tail was wagging the dog, that the members were calling the shots, but after Cohen's quick exit, it looked like leadership may have offered up the membership in exchange for a plum position on the Sanders campaign, but it turns out Brother Cohen took a non-paying position. Here in California, a union activist who holds a high position within the Democratic Party chose to disregard her union's endorsement of Sanders and threw her support to Clinton. Senator Sanders, in my opinion, was the superior candidate.

During the primary season, like many, I wanted to express my opinions. I was in full Bernie defense mode when I argued with a Hillary supporter.

DAN: *[Hillary Clinton] won't fight for a public option/Medicare for All because it's just too hard. You also left out [when you praised her] that she was a Wal-mart board member while they fought off labor organizing.*

SCOTT: Dan, if you're a member of a board, you're not always aware of the day-to-day... but she did resign from the board (or did you not know that).

DAN: *I met her in May, '92 and was impressed, but she has been too corporate for me. Bernie, I believe, is the new FDR and his concerns are my concerns and should be everybody's: income inequality, campaign finance reform including Citizens United, tuition-free college, $15 an hour not $12, bold ideas that we Dems used to embrace. We've sold out to corporate donors and I want my country and my party back!*

SCOTT: I find it fascinating that you talk of Hillary's coronation bandwagon... I did not leap on as quickly as you might surmise. I have supported Bernie's platforms for as long as I've been listening to him, which frankly is a lot longer than a great many "come-latelys". He and Thom Hartmann would have an hour-long one-on-one every Friday, and I would tune in to listen to his positions which have not changed over the years.

Bernie is an articulate and passionate statesman and I agree with much of what he says. I was not here in California when Reagan changed the education landscape, but there was a time when college was affordable for all. During the anti-war movement era, Ronald Reagan recognized the "question authority" attitude could become problematic, so he altered the landscape making it financially difficult to gain an education beyond high school. This helped to crush activism contrary to conservative thought.

Back to Bernie. I did change my position although I do have issues with Hillary (perhaps her corporate approach... as you put it). But I do see the larger picture. I believe that there can be a shift in the country, but it takes an engaged electorate and frankly from the "feel the bern" supporters, I have little faith that they'll come to realize there is a place under the big tent. If there is no engagement, there will never be change.

And to your point about FDR and Sanders: If you know anything about FDR, he was a flawed politician. If not for Eleanor, he would not be standing on the progressive pedestal that he occupies today as it was Eleanor who pushed him in that direction.

This running the country will take someone with a vast knowledge of the political environment and the tenacity to make it happen. And it takes a whole lot more, so instead of tossing in the towel, I truly hope people will acknowledge Clinton's strengths at the same time they point out her failings because during her time on the planet she has accomplished more than most.

DAN: I agree that FDR was a flawed individual, and neither is perfect, but both are men recognizing a time in history that calls for bold action, not incremental baby steps. Sanders was known as the amendment king because his issues were often tagged onto legislation as amendments and thus flew under Republican radar and passed. I know Elizabeth Warren is being floated as a possible running mate [for Hillary] to pull in the angry independents, but A.I.'s don't have a history with Hillary and see her as a warmonger, a manipulative insider whose stances on issues depend on her audience and a felon one step from an FBI indictment and see Warren's endorsement of Hillary as a sell-out and a refutation of the ideals that she purported to share with Bernie. The endorsement set off a flurry of unfriending on Warren's Facebook page, so the ploy of enticing Bernie supporters to the fold has failed. How do you propose we engage these angry independents? Even on the issue of TPP where the UAW was able to push Hillary to the left, I believe the union, despite their endorsement, knows realistically that she will probably drift back to her assessment of TPP as the "Gold Standard" of "fair" trade agreements. BTW, Hillary stepped down from the Wal-Mart board when Bill was running for president, NOT in protest of anti-union activity!

Donald J. Trump, a man who voters either hated or loved, was mocked by the mainstream media because he spoke in grandiose fashion. He made sweeping generalizations and was caught fudging on the facts on a regular basis. Politico reported that Trump's statements were lies 70 percent of the time compared to Hillary Clinton's 25 percent. In his own autobiography, ghostwritten, of course, his ghostwriter called it "truthful hyperbole." He showed tremendous disrespect for the disabled, women, Latinos, and Muslims. Whatever, the public bought it. Trump was elected by more than the necessary 270 electoral votes. "We had a massive landslide victory, as you know, in the Electoral College." Clinton, after all votes were counted, won the popular election by over 3 million votes. Trump promptly blamed California.

How did he do pull off the win? Many blame the structure of the Electoral College, which tries to balance the densely populated urban areas with rural, less densely populated areas. The rural regions went heavily for Mr. Trump. It didn't help that Clinton had referred to half of them as a basket of deplorables. She also stated at a private fundraiser during primary season that Sanders' followers were over-idealistic political newbies who "live in their parents' basement."

Wikileaks proved what Bernie supporters had suspected all along: the fix was in. Amid cries of foul, we discovered that the Democratic Party machine – and, without a doubt, the Clinton Presidential machine – threw obstacle after obstacle in Sanders' way: arcane rules, the purging of voter rolls, and last minute changes and eliminations in polling locations. There were accusations that CNN's Donna Brazile shared questions with the Clinton campaign. Bill Clinton popped into primary polling locations, throwing voting into disarray with his entourage and attending media. Party loyalists seethed about Bernie, "He's not even a real Democrat!" through clenched teeth and had choice criticisms of his young followers, many of whom had never voted before because they were too young or simply not engaged. For the most part, the media that had fawned over Barack Obama seven years before ignored the huge rallies and the meteoric rise of Bernie Sanders' popularity. When nasty emails were brought to light that exposed the Party's opposition to Bernie and favoritism to Clinton, the Party's national chair, Congresswoman Debbie Wasserman Schultz, was forced to resign. The Clinton campaign immediately hired her. After all, as a good soldier who fell on her sword to protect her candidate, a reward was due!

And then the rapprochement, the "better together" moment of unity at the Democratic National Convention – that wasn't. Bernie had a look on his face of a bitter pill swallowed, as promised, as he urged his supporters to elect Hillary as President. Hillary supporters continued to thwart efforts by Bernie supporters to oppose the Trans-Pacific Partnership and endless, senseless war with signs, banners, and shouts at the Convention. Their signs and banners were bigger, their shouts louder and in a cadence meant to drown out the earnest cries of Sanders supporters. At that moment of resignation and tears, some of us vowed to stay true to Bernie to the point of writing in his name on the ballot in November. Some of us decided to abandon the Democratic Party for "Greener" pastures and Jill Stein, and some of us decided to work to transform the Democratic Party from within, a sacrifice of our principles to deny the Presidency to Donald Trump.

Why do voters abandon their Party? Why is "independent" or "decline to state" or "no Party preference" the fastest-growing segment of the voting public?

In California, where the no party preference designation is labeled decline to state, the San Diego Union-Tribune reported in 2015 that registered voters without a Party preference had jumped about three percent over two years to 23.6 percent and, according to the Secretary of State, climbed to 24.5 percent in 2017, reflecting a national trend. Looking at real numbers: 8.7 million Californians are registered Democrats while just under 4.8 million have registered with no party preference. The Democrats, who control all statewide offices and both legislatures, increased their majority from 2015 to 2017 from 43.2 percent to 44.8 percent while Republican registration dropped from 28 percent to under 25.9 percent.

Why does Party affiliation continue to drop? The 2016 presidential race disenfranchised a lot of voters, especially those in the Middle Class. Two populist candidates talked about income inequality, about the decline of infrastructure and wages and the need for bold action: Bernie Sanders and Donald Trump.

Those Democrats who pinned their hopes on Sanders saw them dashed by machinations of the Old Guard. There was an exodus from a Party they felt owed their allegiance to corporations and no longer represented their interests. Republicans who were turned off by Trump's crass behavior and hype abandoned the GOP. Others felt neither Party represented them anymore.

There was a rush to separate from Party affiliation by those who were considering voting across the aisle for a change. Voters in the Rust Belt who had voted for Obama liked Trump's brazen approach to politics-not-as-usual and bought into the "Crooked Hillary" rhetoric. On the morning after election day, though Clinton had clinched the popular vote, the Electoral College, with its skewed representation of small towns and farms, gave the presidency to Trump.

As of this writing, the new Democratic Party Chair, Tom Perez, has just purged many Progressives from leadership positions at a time when we should be uniting to take back the House of Representatives. The question is, do Progressives leave or stay and fight?

Clean Money

One success in California has been the new DISCLOSE Act signed into law by Governor Jerry Brown on October 7, 2017. The new law requires ballot measure ads and independent expenditure ads for or against candidates to clearly and prominently disclose the identity of their top three funding sources, casting light on campaigns that affect all Californians. Some compromises were made to ensure passage, but for those who have been trying to get this bill passed, or others like it for the past seven years, AB 249 is considered a success.

"No more fine print," said the bill's author, Speaker Pro Tem Kevin Mullin. "California voters will now be able to make informed decisions, based on honest information about who the true funders are of campaign ads."

Clean money is campaign finance reform. From the disclosure of where a candidate's contributions are coming from to the powers behind a particular ballot initiative, campaign finance reform is the effort to change the involvement of money in politics, at both the state level and nationally.

SCOTUS' decision in *Citizens United* loosened restrictions on political expenditures and goosed campaign financing to new heights. Campaign consultants organized Super PACs, and the country's wealthiest of the wealthy contribute enormous amounts of cash into both parties to determine who gets into office to ultimately influence policy. As I mentioned in previous chapters, there is actual collusion between the rich and powerful and those who purport to represent their constituents. The one percent are writing laws, and their puppets at state and federal levels are rubber stamping bills that will, at the very least, disregard our wishes and, at the worst, will reverse all the successes we have achieved in protecting the working class, the poor and disabled.

The ultimate goal of campaign finance reform, then, is publicly financed campaigns. The constant pursuit of contributions subverts the will of constituents and the law-making process and corrupts legislators. Once elected, checks roll in with some frequency to elected officials, and it gets easier and easier to ignore the origin of the funds. During the design phase of the Affordable Care Act, some pundits thought that President Obama capitulated too quickly on the question of a public option and the Plan's ability to negotiate drug prices. "He's beholden to Big Pharma and the insurance agency," they said. Others close to the Obama Administration counseled compromise to ensure the bill's passage sidelined those issues for another day.

When I ran for the California State Assembly, I was met with derision from many prospective voters. They knew what I had long refused to acknowledge: the fix was in a long time ago and our democracy stands between a plutocracy, government by the wealthy and fascism, rule by a dictator. Donald Trump has indicated through his executive orders and his priorities his faith in business as the solution to all of our country's problems. A safety regulation stands in the way of progress? Gone. Oil in the pristine Alaskan wilderness? Go get it!

Even as the president's numbers continue to hover in the low 40s, his supporters remain loyal and resolute. Yet, despite control of the presidency and, until recently, both houses of Congress, Gallup Daily tracking throughout May 2017, indicates that 45 percent of U.S. adults self-identify as Democrats or say they are independents who lean Democratic, while 38 percent identify as Republicans or lean Republican. Gallup doesn't credit the Democratic Party for the uptick of seven points. "The growing Democratic advantage in recent months is mostly attributable to a decline in Republican affiliation rather than an increase in Democratic affiliation."

During the 2016 elections, the difference was only three percent, but President Trump appears to be unpopular with many within his party, reflected by a four percent drop in the Republican Party's membership. The Democratic Party's numbers have increased only one percent. According to Gallup, Republicans haven't defected to the Democratic Party; they've gone rogue. They're no longer associated with a party.

The Public Policy Institute of California analyzed the trend in September 2016.

> Most independent likely voters have unfavorable views of both the Democratic Party (55 percent) and the Republican Party (69 percent). When independents are asked why they are registered as "no party preference" nearly half say they are not satisfied with the parties or that parties don't reflect their views (48 percent); one in five say they vote for candidates, not a party (21 percent). When asked if the major parties do an adequate job representing the American people, or if they do such a poor job that a third major party is needed, independent likely voters (69 percent) are much more likely than partisans (57 percent Republicans, 52 percent Democrats) to say a third party is needed.

The rapid growth of the no party preference electorate indicates the continued desire to vote, which is good, but also suggests that voters are turned off by partisan Party propaganda. Much of that dissatisfaction is due to the way parties vilify the opponent. Democrats painted John McCain as unbalanced. The Swift Boat Veterans for Truth portrayed John Kerry as a fake Vietnam War hero. A third party, some believe, wouldn't resort to such divisive tactics, but others, party insiders, resent the idea that a third party is needed. Democrats are afraid a left-leaning candidate, a Green, might pull votes away from their candidate. Some within the Democratic Party still blame Gore's loss to GW Bush on Ralph Nader's Green campaign. Republicans voice the same concerns about a strong Libertarian candidate. In 1912, after Teddy Roosevelt lost the Republican Party's endorsement, his Bull Moose Party, aka the Progressive Party, took 25 percent of the Republican vote from William Howard Taft, giving us Democrat Woodrow Wilson. A third party candidate could change the outcome of a presidential election, but it's not very likely. Of course, most political pundits wouldn't have considered a Trump presidency likely. Now they see it as inevitable.

HERE IS THE UNVARNISHED TRUTH: It is our duty as participants in this society, as parents, as friends, to do our homework. We need to know who's running to represent us at all levels of government and where they stand on multiple issues we deem important. We can examine their records, check our favorite website, check out what other groups are saying, talk to our friends and neighbors - all of that, skimping on nothing - to arrive at a balanced view of the candidate. Issues also arise, some on the ballot, some not, that deserve our attention and informed consent to become law. In Northridge, California, we successfully fought off an attempt to put a Wal-Mart in our community with picket signs and petitions and with no politician in sight. Don't be lazy. Don't just rely on your favorite source to get it right every time. According to Wikipedia, some eleven democracies, including Australia and Belgium, have made compulsory voting the law of the land. Should we force every citizen to vote? If we do, can we insist on mandatory education, too?

If we continue to cling to our representative system of democracy, aren't we abdicating some of our rights to self-government? Don't the rich and powerful use their money to game the system to their own advantage? American society is rigged, and in our gut, we know it.

In March 2003, during my tenure as president of Local 9503 of the Communications Workers of America, I was invited to a back room meeting at the Democratic state convention in Sacramento. Democratic Party Chair Howard Dean asked labor leaders, "What should our message be to voters this time around?" and then had one-on-one conversations to hear our responses.

Considering the race between George W. Bush and Senator John Kerry, I poured my heart into my answer. "We should let voters know this election is nothing less than an attack on working people." I ranted away for another five minutes and left feeling someone was listening. Most of the slogans that campaign season were developed with a glance back three years to 9-11 and used the word "strong" in many of the messages, but there was nothing in those messages that spoke to me, that addressed my inability to get ahead of my bills or guaranteed job security.

The importance of great slogans can't be understated. Most of the memorable ones tend to be from advertising because they're the most pervasive, but there are those political turns of phrase that still speaks to our hearts: "I have a dream." "Ask not what your country can do for you…" We need to craft a message that reaches everyone. We need to find a way to honor working people, invoke a spirit of community that inspires. The slogan I found on a button on the AFL-CIO website reflected the sentiment of my state Assembly campaign in 2008, and I wore "Kickin' Ass for the Working Class" to every event and debate. I won a union election invoking the "power of one."

In summary, be involved as much or as little as you can be. If you're not registered to vote, why aren't you? People say if you don't vote, you can't complain about the outcome. I don't agree. This is a democracy. Of course, you can complain, but not voting does undermine your credibility.

Learn who's running and figure out who best represents your views and vote for that candidate. If your state has the initiative process, proposals must first collect signatures to qualify for the ballot. Stop and meet a signature gatherer and test their knowledge on the ballot measures. Sign them if you agree with them.

We can't allow the foxes to watch the hen house. We never could, but in these days of Scorched Earth policies and handouts to big business, it has become more imperative to watch them daily. Watch Democrats, Republicans, Independents. Watch them all.

I would recommend running for office, but do your homework before sending out your press release. As they say, if you're out marching and there's no one behind you, you're just out for a walk.

There are clubs and caucuses, Facebook groups, chapters of national organizations. If nothing else, follow them online. Post opinions, ask questions. It is called social media, after all.

County and State party representatives get some say-so regarding policy. Run for party delegate. Inject new voices into the debate over party priorities.

Attend town halls. Some of our members of Congress still have them. You can also reach them by email, phone and by appointment in either the home office or in Washington, D.C. State reps are also supposed to listen to you. Find your state capitol and visit sometime.

We need an informed electorate who vote regularly and know who and what we're voting for. This is OUR country, damn it, and we need to get some respect around here!

Chapter 8 The Vanishing Middle Class

Chapter 8

The Vanishing Middle Class

"Here in Missouri we hear about those jobs being created, but they are newer jobs that replace the quality jobs being lost. What a different world it is for the generation behind us. They don't ever expect to be as affluent as we are, even though we are middle class." Missouri State Senator Joan Bray

"We don't use the term "working class" here because it's a taboo term. You're supposed to say "middle class," because it helps diminish the understanding that there's a class war going on." Noam Chomsky

"Admittedly, we have a long way to go before we succeed in transforming the AFL-CIO from 'a Washington-based institution concerned primarily with refining policy positions' into a 'worker-based movement against greed, multi-national corporations, race-baiting, and labor-baiting politicians…" AFL-CIO President John Sweeney

Uh, thank you?

LinkedIn reported in 2016 that CEO Jeff Weiner would pass along his stock options worth $14 million to employees after a weak earnings report caused the company's stock to drop 43 percent in one day. The action wasn't unprecedented. Twitter CEO in Jack Dorsey had passed along $200 million in stock to employees in October 2015. Both tech companies had shown some recent earnings disappointments and both CEOs wanted to show confidence in their futures. Word on the street revealed there was a tech bubble that looked a lot like the dot-com disaster of 2000.

I don't pretend that the telecommunications industry was the first in recent years to slash their workforce. A region of our country is called the rustbelt because of what happened to the steel industry in the 1970s. Our workers and our mills were undercut in price by cheap steel from China.

In the aftermath of NAFTA, homegrown manufacturing was the victim. The search for ever-cheaper manufacturing bases has been termed a "race to the bottom." As a country begins to grow a middle class because of financial gains, corporations move somewhere they can make the product for less: Mexico to India to the Philippines to Qatar, Bangladesh…

The effects of NAFTA and the loss of manufacturing jobs have taken their toll on good paying jobs and the impacts on local community continue to be felt. We covered those job losses in a previous chapter, but it's important to note that President Trump has vowed to rewrite that trade agreement. Unfortunately, if we examine the ways he has "fixed" other areas of concern, dismantling social safety nets, allowing unfettered access to pristine wilderness to drill for oil, excuse our reluctance.

Newly-elected as the head of the AFL-CIO on a status quo challenge ticket, John Sweeney wrote for Cornell University, "… shame on us if we don't take advantage of a rare opportunity created by the over-reaching of profit-hungry corporations and opportunistic conservatives in the United States Congress."

There was the printing industry. Suddenly everyone could play with fonts, print business cards and letterhead from home.

"Nobody is reading newspapers anymore," said newspaper publishers, who quickly consolidated our news sources. Massive layoffs ensued. There used to be a law against owning a certain percentage of a broadcasting market in any particular geographical area. People stopped sending letters. The post office's monopoly on package delivery was usurped by FedEx, established in Little Rock, Arkansas in 1971. Others including DHL and UPS followed.

Technology marches on... Taxis were shoved aside by the seemingly hip Uber car service which was followed by Lyft, which gave birth to associated food delivery services Uber Eats, Courier, and Postmates. As truck drivers fight at the piers to be recognized as employees rather than free agents, there is talk of driverless trucks carrying our produce throughout the country.

Automation has replaced many of the good-paying jobs of the past. The robots that used to do menial, repetitive tasks have been programmed to turn every job into a series of menial, repetitive tasks and so threaten us all.

Proponents of automation sing the praises of our brave new world. One is Steve Westly, a former California State Controller and gubernatorial candidate. Westly is currently serving on the board of advertising technology company, Radium. He has also been a board member of eBay and Tesla, and the self-proclaimed "pragmatic progressive" seems blinded by science.

"Who would've thought an online flea market would be worth $70 billion today?" Westly gushed when talking about eBay.

Meanwhile, at the phone company, healthcare was one of the major sticking points at the bargaining table. The company was insisting that we pick up part of the cost of our policies for the first time since we had first won health benefits in 1968. In a heartfelt message on the local news, TV reporter Bill Press reported that our fight to keep our healthcare was a noble pursuit. We kept our paid healthcare for the next couple contracts, but with management paying for theirs, a change was inevitable.

The Affordable Care Act (ACA) aka Obamacare and, in the future, Single Payer, may undermine consistent, affordable health care for working families. Single Payer has been touted as a way to remove the middlemen – insurance companies – and take healthcare off the table as a negotiable item in labor contracts. Other items like higher wages could, instead, take their proper place. Healthcare will come up again in a later chapter in a more comprehensive way, but it was mentioned here because forces in the corporate world are working to make healthcare seem an entitlement rather than a right for all workers. That misinformation campaign is how we lose those rights that we have won over the decades in our tug-a-war with management.

Education costs continue to skyrocket and there was fear the new tax plan would end write-offs on student debt. Thousands of graduate students walked out in protest across the nation. Congress got the message. According to the *Washington Post*, the tax plan will not tax tuition waivers; students can still deduct loan interest payments. We're still far from tuition-free college that would allow more students to break the cycle of poverty and enter the middle class.

We lost 5 million manufacturing jobs since 2000 and lost an opportunity for others to earn enough to realize the American dream. Since 1960, according to CNN, the number of American workers in manufacturing dropped from one in four to one in ten. The fastest growing jobs are now nurses, personal caretakers, cooks, waiters, and retail sales. Other than nursing, none of those jobs holds the earning potential in manufacturing.

Then there's the Wal-mart effect.

In the book of the same name by Charles Fishman, he lays out the statistics:

> Every seven days more than one hundred million Americans shop at Wal-mart – one-third of the country. Each year 93 percent of American households shop at least once at Wal-mart.

I'm not one of them. Charles Kernaghan, a union brother with UNITE HERE, (a union merger of UNITE *Union of Needle trades, Industrial, and Textile Employees,* formerly known as the International Lady Garment Workers Union, and HERE, the union of Hotel Employees, Restaurant Employees), called the shopping empire on their claim that everything in the store was American-made. (It isn't.) Despite the best organizing efforts of the United Food and Commercial Workers Union, (UFCW) very few stores have gone union. Employees of a store in Canada voted in the union to see the corporation close the doors permanently, claiming there was no connection.

When Wal-mart enters a local market, the first to suffer are the mom and pop stores. Local customers are a finicky lot who head to Wal-mart when local shops aren't able to match Wal-mart's prices. First, it's the hardware store, then locally-owned department stores, supermarkets, and others in a massive ripple effect. Soon, the only jobs to be had are at Wal-mart. The newly-unemployed spend their dwindling cash reserves on the cheaper prices at Wal-mart, but the bean counters at Wal-mart's corporate headquarters in Bentonville, Arkansas realize the money isn't rolling in anymore and they pull the plug on the store, throwing a downward spiraling local economy into a death plunge.

Wal-mart teaches their employees how to navigate government assistance to get welfare and food stamps rather than pay their workers a working wage. In the nineties, we in California lobbied successfully to keep Wal-mart and other corporations from purchasing life insurance policies on employees with the company listed as the beneficiary, which they used to pay management bonuses.

The corporate office indicated they were closing 63 Sam's Club stores in 24 states and Puerto Rico, affecting some 11,000 workers after announcing they were raising the minimum wage from $10 to $11 an hour. Again, they claimed there was no connection. In January 2016, the corporation announced it would be closing 269 stores worldwide affecting, according to Wal-mart about 16,000 workers. The company hopes laid-off employees will get jobs at stores nearby.

According to CNS News, a conservative news site, the US has lost about 191,000 mining jobs since 2014, down from an industry high of 1.1 million in 1981 to a current level of 661,600. Three-fourths of those jobs were in "support activities," peripheral businesses that provide everything from the tools of the trade to transportation services to move their product. The job losses of major industries create a ripple effect in a community that hits everyone in the wallet.

That miner doesn't take the family out for Sunday dinner anymore. He's got nothing for the collection plate at church. The pastor's hurting, the restaurant has to cut back on staff, and that waitress that used to serve you just got laid off. The taxes these folks used to pay – sales tax in the restaurant, federal and state taxes for government programs that help the old, disabled and indigent – those funds have dried up and can't handle the increased demand from the miner, the pastor, the restaurant and the waitress. The system begins to fail us all.

The loss of good-paying union jobs with the creation of McJobs to replace them has lowered the expectations of those just entering the workforce. We have seen the results in other countries. A 2016 study by the European Commission and the International Labor Organization (ILO) indicate almost every EU country is witnessing a shrinking middle class.

The World Bank reports middle-class growth has stagnated throughout Latin America after rising out of poverty into the "vulnerable" tier, not quite middle class, just above "poor," but in a position that leaves them in a precarious position, living paycheck to paycheck.

China has seen the most successful rise out of poverty, but workers are only inching toward middle-class existence. The World Bank reports 18 percent of China's population qualifies as middle class, a much better lifting of all boats than experienced by India with only three percent. Pew research found 12 percent of Chinese are considered poor while 20 percent of Indians would fall into that category. The World Economic Forum points to a thriving middle class as a sign of economic activity and prosperity. The European Commission and the ILO that measures are necessary to protect the middle class around the world with sustainable wages, quality education, and an adequate social safety net.

Back in the US, a May 2016 CNBC report attributed this "hollowing out" of the middle class to households who have failed to bounce back from the 2008 Recession. Rakesh Kochhar, Associate Director of research at the Pew Research Center points to rising income inequality as a contributing factor to the shrinking middle class and recommends learning a skill. "Being skilled is useful. High tech will always rule the income ladder. And global changes matter."

Jobs in the service-based sector constitute the largest rise in employment numbers. Many of them pay substantially less than jobs in the manufacturing or goods-based sector that have disappeared overseas. Some service sector jobs show a promising future: healthcare, legal. Others – call center jobs, for instance, are designed to be flexible in terms of longevity and focus. (Many sell a variety of products under a variety of contracts). These centers can be moved or shut down at a moment's notice and the flick of a switch. During strikes at AT&T, the call center work was funneled to locations where management and scab employees could work unopposed unrecognized. After the strike, work would resume at their previous locations, but one can imagine that without a labor contract and leverage at the bargaining table, that work could continue in the new site or in another country. Other ways that jobs can be moved, eliminated or outsourced will be explored in another chapter.

Let's examine what happens down in the trenches when an imbalance of power is felt on the shop floor or in the boardroom or…

Chapter 9 Workplace Balance of Power

Chapter 9

The Workplace Balance of Power

"If people feel like the boss doesn't respect them, they don't stretch for the boss." John Dickerson

"Clients do not come first; employees come first. If you take care of the employees, they will take care of your clients." Richard Branson

When I started at the phone company in 1973, I was greeted with an authoritarian style of management. It was do it or else, my way or the highway. After many of us barely survived a massive layoff in my first six months, employees in the department slowly grew to trust each other more, and the boss loosened the reins a little bit.

Then management decided to install a brand new computer system next door, one of the first of its kind. They dropped the office temperature on our floor by 20 degrees to accommodate the computers' susceptibility to heat. Suddenly we were wearing sweaters in July.

When we complained, they said "tough." We decided our only option was to walk out one morning and picket the building. The office union steward appeared and advised us we were participating in a wildcat strike, illegal and unsanctioned by the union. By noon, we were home watching ourselves on TV. We were back to work two days later, eventually recovered our lost wages and a cold room was created for the computer, maybe for the first time.

There is a delicate balance among the four parties of interest in the commercial realm, four market forces: the consumer, the employer, the stockholder, and the employee. If employees aren't treated with dignity, if the stockholder is taken for granted, if management fails to lead and inspire, if the "brand" fails to engage the customer, the whole arrangement lacks balance and leads to instability at all levels.

Companies brag about customer focus but have been driven to bankruptcy in the sometimes futile attempt to deal with a fickle public or economic trends that drive the business in other directions. The current auto market has designed Sports Utility Vehicles to meet the demand for safe, roomy vehicles with most of the comforts of home. Meanwhile, rising fuel costs have created a demand for hybrids and other fuel-efficient cars and trucks. Companies that are ruled by a marketing department that sell myriad variations of the same product have to pay close attention to what's selling. There is such a thing as too many choices. Ask anyone from the former Soviet bloc overwhelmed by options just in the cereal aisle.

Stockholders' Role

If the employer is beholden to only the stockholders, employees will be treated with disdain or indifference. This will be demonstrated by new, stringent rules in the workplace, intensified monitoring and/or draconian discipline for minor infractions. If there's an abrupt change in the way the company treats its employees, a "crack of the whip," there will be an attendant drop in morale, growing distrust between management and workers, and ultimately, a company torn with internal strife, constant conflict, and employee turnover. The focus is on the bottom line and labor, at about 80 percent, is a company's greatest cost. But any effort to jettison employees in the interest of lowering company overhead makes the company more attractive to Wall Street, raises stock prices and leads to bonuses for upper management.

For the customer, this could result in degradation in service or a rise in prices or both. If the customer has to deal with the company over the phone or have an employee dispatched for a problem, the employee may display an attitude of defensiveness, ambivalence, or frustration. If the company has adjusted its pricing structure (almost always upward), the employee may exhibit any or all of the above behaviors because they bear the brunt of customer dissatisfaction. In turn, if the customer encounters a price increase or a sullen employee, the customer may move their service to another provider. The company, its stockholders and employees, will suffer as a consequence.

After the breakup of the Bell System in 1984, stockholders were given an equal number of shares in each of the seven "Baby Bells." Our holdings as employees were relatively small, but we tried to pool our shares through the union to have more of a voice and possibly a position on one or more Boards of Directors. Union leaders thought a Board seat would be the ultimate level of corporate involvement, though others were more realistic in their expectations. Only a majority of positions on a Board would have impacted corporate decisions.

The smoke cleared and SBC seemed poised to gobble up its siblings. The corporation bought Pacific Telesis for $16.5 billion in 1997, Southern New England Telecommunications for a little over $5 million the next year, Ameritech for $61 billion the year after. SBC consumed its "mother" in 2005, changed its name to the better-known AT&T moniker and bought BellSouth for $85.8 billion in 2007.

With the changes at the highest levels of the corporation came a callous and indifferent culture. The original AT&T and its parts had felt like family. When someone took a vacation, an employee didn't have to worry if the work was getting done in their absence. As the workforce shrank and fewer were forced to do more, the company seemed sincerely puzzled by dwindling loyalty from their employees. "Change," said management, "is the only constant."

Locals of the Communications Workers of America (CWA) continued to use stockholder proxies as leverage with the new AT&T. Other stockholders groups have been more successful in creating change.

Artur Raviv, a professor of finance at the Kellogg School of Management, states:

In theory, a corporation's board of directors represents the interests of the shareholders. However, it is commonly believed that board members do not exercise sufficient control over self-interested managers because directors are typically handpicked by management insiders who control the proxy process. Eventually, a conflict develops between the shareholders, who are the owners of the corporation, and the management, which is supposed to represent them, and the board, which is supposed to be supervising management. The conflict has given rise to the "shareholder democracy movement," in which many stock owners seek a greater voice in corporate decision-making.

The article points out the efforts of such heavyweight stockholders as Carl Icahn and Kirk Kerkorian to control corporations from outside the boardroom – with mixed success. There have been attempts to push companies to adopt green policies. As higher wages were replaced by stock options and 401(k)s, employees have become more interested in market share, company growth, and rising stock prices. As shareholders, then, employees experience mixed emotions when massive layoffs raise the value of their stock at the expense of their coworkers.

Employee Engagement

If employees, due to ineffective management, a murky or nonexistent corporate vision, or because they lack input into work processes, may pay less attention to customer satisfaction. Managers may play favorites with employees, surrounding themselves with sycophants. That, in turn, creates resentment in the ranks and may hurt customer service.

Then there are the companies who have structured policies that aren't flexible. Rigid policies act as a barrier to criticism and are a symptom of a layered system of management meant to protect positions in the hierarchy. Workers in the public sector (your local Department of Motor Vehicles) and other, formerly semi-oligarchic empires like the old Bell System are examples of these groups. Communication needs to be an essential part of business to get everyone rowing in the same direction. Goals and roles play a vital part of a business/labor partnership.

A study by Temkin Research Group in 2016 showed that companies that excelled at customer service had 1.5 times as much engaged staff than companies with poor customer experience. They recommended improving employee engagement by mastering the five I's: inform, inspire, instruct, involve and incent.

Their follow-up study in 2017 found "...engaged employees are almost five times more likely than [forgotten] disengaged employees to recommend the company's products and services, over four times more likely to something that is good, yet unexpected, for the company, are three times more likely to stay late if needed, and are five times more likely to recommend an improvement at the company."

David Macleod, on the Engage for Success website, explains:

> Employee engagement is about understanding one's role in an organization and being energized by where they fit in the organization's purpose and objectives.
>
> Employee engagement is about having a clear understanding of how an organization is fulfilling its purpose and objectives, how it is changing to fulfill those better, and being given a voice to offer ideas and express views that are considered as decisions are made.
>
> Employee engagement is about being included fully as a member of the team, focused on clear goals, trusted and empowered, receiving regular and constructive feedback, supported in developing new skills, thanked and recognized for achievement.
>
> Engaged organizations have strong and authentic values, with clear evidence of trust and fairness based on mutual respect, where two-way promises and commitments – between employers and employees – are understood and fulfilled.

To its credit, AT&T has a history of trying different forms of employee engagement. Between 1924 and 1932, at a Western Electric factory outside Chicago called the Hawthorne Works, management played with the lights. They wanted to see if making the lights burn brighter or less intense would affect productivity. It did. Until the study was over. It seemed that workers responded to the increased attention from the company rather than any change in lighting. They slacked off when all the behavioral scientists left.

As mentioned before, there was the Quality of Worklife program, modeled on Japanese work circles, at Pacific Bell following divestiture that created worksite committees to address issues in the workplace. The union trained committees on negotiating changes in the office, prioritizing and dealing with conflict, but management shied away from employee suggestions on work processes and union officers felt their role in negotiating working conditions was being superseded. Both management and union pulled the plug. The committees were dissolved though some perks lived on in the form of outside eating areas and other cosmetic improvements.

AT&T's problem child had reduced its workforce from 118,000 in 1981 to 81,500 just before the court-ordered breakup of the Bell System in 1984. Divestiture brought its own list of problems, chief among them a growing realization that this former monopoly and all its former parts would be competing in the open market. Acting entrepreneurial would require an entirely new skill set for all employees.

Pac Bell CEO Donald Guinn wanted to convince employees that they had a personal stake in the success of the company. Middle management, in an effort to adapt to this new competitive culture, pushed employees to generate revenue by tripling sales quotas in 18 months. The California Public Utilities Commission found the company guilty of heavy-handed sales tactics and issued a cease and desist decree and levied a hefty fine.

Pacific Bell adopted business/labor partnership in the late 80's. Suddenly we in the labor movement were asked our opinions on the direction of the business.

Business/Labor Partnership, as we called it, was a product of the company's Leadership Development program. LD attempted to improve thinking by making people conscious of their thought processes. It also tried to foster teamwork by giving all employees involved in the management process a common language and framework for solving business problems.

Leadership Development was an attempt to develop managers who could thrive in the new competitive environment post-Bell System without coercing employees into aggressive sales practices and alienating customers. Union leaders were brought in to get buy-in and help sell the new program to non-management. At first, we were all excited, because the company seemed to care about what we thought. When the company tried to push LD into the rest of the organization, union employees balked. "Thinking about thinking," employees called the program derisively, but accurately. We were taught there are two types of thinking: systems thinking or associative (rational) thinking and LD concentrated on making us think in holistic "systems" thinking. If you could put a concept into the strict wording that LD called for, it could very well be adopted at the office level. Whatever. The real perk of the program? Union stewards were suddenly being treated as equals by management. Rank-and-file employees hated the rigidity of the program's structure, the attempt by the company to cram round heads into square holes. Or maybe they hated the tumultuous, seemingly never-ending changes that divestiture had brought to our lives.

The California Public Utilities Commission stepped in again and surveyed employees about the program. They determined LD was too expensive and ordered the company to charge stockholders, not customers, with $25 million of the program's $40 million price tag. The company, in the meantime, had already abandoned Leadership Development in favor of more traditional training and pending contract negotiations.

The union and the company have maintained a love/hate relationship since SBC's takeover in 1995. Their managers, coming from a right-to-work state, chaffed at the rules and regulations they had to adhere to in California, their new cash cow. Employees and the union were lulled into complacency when SBC purchased Pacific Bell and all the draconian changes we had anticipated failed to materialize. Five years later, it became clear that they had spent those years combing over the contract, studying our practices and were ready to institute change.

Those changes included massive layoffs by creating an airtight paper trail that led to disciplinary measures and individual attrition by firing. Actions that had earned a slap on the wrist were now grounds for dismissal. The company put GPS in technicians' trucks to keep track of them in real time. Though now called AT&T, it's telling that they run their national operations from Texas.

When AT&T absorbed the wireless side of the business, they signed a neutrality agreement with the union that kept management coercion at bay and almost guaranteed wireless employees would become members of the Communications Workers of America (CWA). The last two strikes in the western region were weekend affairs and indicated the union's willingness to cooperate and avoid any militancy that might provoke the company into moving jobs elsewhere, but it may have suggested we knew we didn't have any leverage.

When workers band together in a union, there are certain protections guaranteed under the National Labor Relations Act, a federal agency created in the years of the FDR administration and embattled since its inception. Non-union employees may not realize they have some of the same rights. Workers in the railroad and airline industries are protected under the National Railway Act, established in 1926. The Railway Act seeks to avoid strikes except in circumstances where negotiation and arbitration have failed to succeed.

As union density has shrunk, so has the leverage in the workplace, though union wages are still used as a benchmark for non-union employees within a particular industry. In fact, many companies use wage equivalence to demonstrate to employees that they don't need a "third-party" coming between them to negotiate wages, hours or working conditions. Unions have often pointed to the contract between the company and the union as protection against capricious action by an employer.

Circuit City alarmed employees of other companies in their industry by suddenly declaring that 3,400 of their employees were now making too much money (somewhere in the $11 an hour range) and they were subsequently laid off. They were told they could reapply and be rehired at the minimum corporate rate. This practice, if unchecked and unchallenged, could have meant a devastating reworking of wages up and down the spectrum, stopping just short of upper-level management, one would assume. Other corporations, marveling at Circuit City's chutzpah and "innovation," would be encouraged to boldly follow suit. The current disparity in wages between the upper echelons of management and those at the bottom would be turned from a chasm into a canyon.

Fortunately for the majority of us, though not, lamentably, for the workers at Circuit City, management's egregious actions failed to save the company from the effects of Chapter 11 and was only one of several well-established corporations that went under that year. No other company has attempted similar stunts to stay in business.

Management's Role

"When I started back in 1961, it was an honor to work for a supervisor that had come up through the ranks. This person was able to help you if you had a problem. This person had the experience to manage a team. This person made you PROUD to be a telephone [company] employee," Cyrus Douglas, Pacific Bell retiree

Douglas, a second level manager by the time he retired from Pacific Bell, looks back with mixed emotions. With the name change to Pacific Telesis following the court-ordered breakup of the Bell System, Douglas states:

> Things started to change. [Recent college graduates] were being hired to be managers with a possible promotion to higher management. They had NO knowledge of the job they were hired to manage. Costs became a problem; time management was impossible due to stretching goals/targets. Lying, cheating, backstabbing became the norm. Pride in your job was not respected. Due to lack of personnel, forced overtime was mandatory by management. Maintaining

family values went out the window. Soon you found that some of your teammates were divorcees, alcoholics, and drug users just so they could weather the tough and stringent requirements of the job. Once we were a BELL family with pride in our employment.

But the situation deteriorated further. There was a change of culture that demanded results with no investment or development for employees. It was all about the numbers, Douglas says:

> The second [level managers] were, at times, clueless. They demanded faster repair, more extended hours, fewer people, no training from plant schools. Never mind the weather, get out there and work. The bottom line became the object under the microscope. I may sound bitter. I am. I loved my job until the end. The end came sooner than I had planned.

Government's Role

Government through oversight by such agencies as the Department of Labor, the Federal Trade Commission and a host of other bodies, has the responsibility to become involved and restore economic balance. Though Corporate America decries this "intrusion" into laissez-faire, government has brought reason and compromise (and more oversight) in the aftermath of such bloodbaths as the Depression and, more recently, the Great Recession of 2009.

State and federal levels of government have intervened in labor disputes in the form of mediation to force both parties back to the bargaining table and injunctions to shut down strikes. The Department of Labor and the National Labor Relations Board have jumped in on multiple occasions to investigate malfeasance. We as a government and as citizens have been fighting the collusion among government, the banks, and the stock market.

The Consumer Financial Protection Bureau was established by the Dodd-Frank Wall Street Reform and Consumer Protection Act of 2010 following the meltdown of 2008 and serves as a firewall between consumers and the sometimes rapacious practices of financial institutions.

The CFPB is charged with overseeing the Federal financial laws that protect consumers—people who keep their money in banks and credit unions, pay for goods and services with their credit cards, and rely on loans to buy homes or pay for college, among other services. It's their job to make sure people understand the fine print in financial transactions with banks, credit union, and other institutions.

By 2014, the CFPB, established by Senator Elizabeth Warren, had instituted an impressive list of consumer protections. Those will be addressed in another chapter.

Meanwhile, the sometimes mind-numbing details of the 2008 Meltdown proved to be too nuanced and complicated for the little people and those who bring us the news.

Government is full of checks and balances and overlapping duties and agencies. That overlap is what Congress calls "waste," "fraud," and inefficiency. If that overlap had existed in the days leading up to 9/11, with the FBI and other national security agencies communicating across lines of responsibility, those deaths might have been prevented.

That overlap has also provided our country with a diverse overview of policy and a solid grounding in mutually agreed-upon fact. Let's examine our media as they existed a few short years ago and how they look today.

Chapter 10 Who's Telling out Story?

Chapter 10

Who's Telling Our Story? Media Consolidation

"Our founding fathers could not have foreseen that freedom of the press might eventually be threatened just as much by media consolidation as by government." -- Marshall Herkovitz

"The dumbing down of America is most evident in the slow decay of substantive content in the enormously influential media, the 30 second sound bites (now down to 10 seconds or less), lowest common denominator programming, credulous presentations on pseudoscience and superstition, but especially a kind of celebration of ignorance." — Carl Sagan, *The Demon-Haunted World: Science as a Candle in the Dark*

"There are 1500 newspapers, 1100 magazines, 9000 radio stations, 1500 TV stations, 2400 publishers owned by only six corporations and 272 executives that control 90 percent of what 27 million Americans see, hear and read." – Liberal And Proud of It

When the Communications Workers of America went on strike against AT&T for three weeks in 1989, I was tapped to be Local 9503's PR guy. I didn't have my journalism degree yet, but I had a reputation as a writer/editor. The media was looking for a local spin on a national strike so a typical day would find me writing and faxing press releases, inviting speakers to our weekly rallies, putting out a mini-newsletter for the picket lines, and getting interviewed on TV, radio and the papers. It was hectic and fun. Now there are fewer workers, on strike or not, and fewer reporters covering strikes or workers' issues, all due to a shrinking workforce.

The consolidation of media has meant less local coverage and fewer eyes on the newsmakers, with six corporations owning 90 percent of the media in the nation. That consolidation has meant fewer voices, fewer viewpoints, less analysis, more fluff, and more fake news, with those in power controlling information.

An article in the *Columbia Journalism Review* spells out the implications:

> This means that national and even local news coverage priorities are dictated from afar — and by business leaders, not by journalists on the ground. It means that as print and broadcast journalism struggles to remain profitable in the face of free, online alternatives, hard financial decisions that affect reporters and the stories they tell will be made in corporate boardrooms. And it assures that some issues — issues in which corporate America is uninterested — go uncovered, while some voices — particularly female, minority and immigrant voices — rarely make it into print or onto the airwaves.

How did this happen?

An act of Congress formed the Federal Communications Commission in 1934. The new agency was given oversight of the fledgling television business as well as an ongoing commitment to radio. The FCC's jurisdiction also extended to telecommunications.

From the beginning, it seemed broadcast media existed to push soap to soup, but of course, newspapers had started as shipping notices with a short jump to advertising. Yellow journalism appeared on the scene in the late 1880's and was not too concerned with facts and was willing to peddle sensationalism.

Joseph Patrick McKerns, in his 1976 *History of American Journalism*, described yellow journalism at its most sensationalistic:

> The yellow journalism of the 1890's and tabloid journalism of the 1920's and the 1930's stigmatized the press as a profit-motivated purveyor of cheap thrills and vicarious experiences. To its many critics, it seemed as though the press was using the freedom from regulation it enjoyed under the First Amendment to make money instead of using it to fulfill its vital role as an independent source of information in a democracy.

As newspapers undermined their own credibility, readers began to question what they read. W.E. Miller of the St. Mary, Kansas *Star* developed the first Code of Ethics for Newspapers, adopted by the Kansas State Editorial Association at the 1910 State Convention, but yellow journalism continued unabated into the 1930's.

Victor Pickard, a professor at the Annenberg School for Communication at the University of Pennsylvania, blamed the media and explained the efforts they made to change:

> The 1940s saw widespread public discontent with commercial media institutions, stemming from a perceived lack of local accountability, the rise of media monopolies, and increasingly obtrusive advertising. ...The FCC forced NBC to divest itself of its Blue Network, which became ABC; the Supreme Court's 1945 antitrust ruling against the Associated Press called for government to encourage "diverse and antagonistic voices" in media; the 1946 FCC Blue Book, which outlined broadcasters' public service responsibilities, advocated for more local news, public affairs, and experimental noncommercial programming; the 1947 Hutchins Commission on Freedom of the Press established

journalistic ethics; and the 1949 Fairness Doctrine mandated public interest parameters for broadcasters.

World War Two and the years following brought the era of responsibility, credibility, and ethics to journalism that had eluded many for decades thanks to war correspondents like Edward R. Murrow and Walter Cronkite. The transition of these respected journalists to television brought integrity to the relatively new industry.

Commercialization of our news has always influenced what we receive as pertinent to our lives, and the media has determined everything from the top story of the evening to the depth of the reportage. Even as a child, I wondered why they cut away from the news for commercials. Wasn't what was happening in the world more important than selling a Timex? With news limited to a half-hour or even more, we have been subjected to sound bites, car chases, and TV show previews. All of this "news," of course, sandwiched between commercials. Local news, even in major metropolitan areas like Los Angeles, does little to inform citizenry on candidates, ballot issues, or agenda items being considered by the city council or in Sacramento. Of course, now we have streaming news video on the internet, Arab Spring on Facebook and proliferation of "fake news" that has not been adequately vetted or corroborated. The eighties brought us CNN with 24/7 news and ads for pharmaceuticals.

The Fairness Doctrine

The eighties also saw the end of the 1949 Fairness Doctrine. The FCC required stations to air controversial issues of public interest and to present more than one perspective on those issues in a fair and balanced manner. The FCC under the Reagan administration dumped the requirement in 1987.

Two more 24-hour news networks went on the air in 1996: MSNBC, which was a ticker tape for stocks in the beginning, and the uber-conservative Fox News Network. Fox called itself "Fair and Balanced," either ironically or to convince the simple-minded that if Fox was telling it straight, why watch anything else?

The Telecommunications Act of 1996, another item on the GOP wish list for deregulation, was passed at the insistence of Democrat Bill Clinton. A frenzy of mega-mergers brought Hearst, Knight-Ridder and Gannett ownership of most of the nation's newspapers. Clear Channel Communications owns many radio stations. Disney owns ABC and ESPN and the Disney Channel, Viacom owns CBS and MTV. Media Corporation, Rupert Murdoch's empire, own all Fox channels, several radio networks, satellite television providers, and newspapers in many countries. Time-Warner owns dozens of magazines, including Time, Life, and Sports Illustrated, as well as CNN and Turner television networks. The mainstream media had very little to say about the implications of the new Act.

The FCC voted to eliminate a rule first adopted in 1975, which prevented entities from owning a radio or TV station and a newspaper in the same market. The agency has also loosened restrictions even more in the Trump administration to make it easier for a company to own multiple TV stations in one market.

Ajit Pai, the Trump-appointed chairman of the FCC, framed the move as an attempt to "strengthen local voices" and update regulations for the internet era.

When Rupert Murdoch created the Fox network and named Roger Ailes, the former Republican image-maker, to run its news division, Bill Moyers, a former spokesman in the LBJ administration, saw what was coming.

He predicted that the demise of the Fairness Doctrine and the rise of skewed reporting by "Fox and Friends" would spell the downfall of Hillary Clinton and the rise of Trump's agenda in a symbiotic relationship with the network that started with Trump's very public support for the birther movement claiming Barack Obama was not a US citizen. That relationship continues as the network and "friends" continue to vilify Trump's critics, fawn over his every move and feed the 24/7 Trump Twitter account.

As Moyers further elaborated:

> The United States is the only advanced country in which the denial of climate science is taken seriously in governing circles. ExxonMobil and the other fossil-fuel companies that spent decades and hundreds of millions of dollars promoting this denial are the number-one culprits, but Fox and Friends rank a close second: It was their ceaseless repetition of such corporate disinformation that embedded climate denial in right-wing ideology and made it a litmus test for Republican politicians.

The conservative movement and the Republican Party have produced a coalition of cable-TV outlets, talk-radio stations, websites, newspapers, magazines, and publishing houses that have exerted enormous influence on America's public and political discourse for nearly 30 years, ever since Rush Limbaugh's radio show went national in 1988. The right-wing drowns out what the left is saying because we lack the resources and the brash on-message cacophony of half-truths, misdirection, and bullshit that makes up most conservative rhetoric. Is anyone surprised, then, that right-wing views enjoy so much more visibility and influence in today's United States?

Nineteen percent of all voters named Fox as their primary source of campaign news, according to a Pew Research Survey—ahead of CNN, the other TV networks, and even social media platforms like Facebook. After a dustup with Megyn Kelly, CNN, and the president have not only remained at odds, CNN is openly critical of Trump's administration while Trump constantly calls their credibility into question.

Moyers has warned a small group of very wealthy progressive philanthropists that, with Murdoch's fortune behind it, Fox could transform the US media and political landscape by distributing well-produced if journalistically fraudulent "news" to vast numbers of Americans. Though Ailes has died, the mission and its relentless onslaught on real news progresses.

If progressives want to be part of the national conversation, the other side needs to enter the fray in a serious way. If we allow Fox and Friends to shape the news and push their political agenda, Moyers argued, they need to build an equivalent empire to Fox. According to Moyers, "…a journalism more in the mold of the BBC at its best—unafraid of power and not complicit with it, reporting what conventional journalism overlooked or wouldn't touch, getting its viewers as close as possible to the verifiable truth…with a strong and independent muckraking mission."

The mainstream or commercial media usually doesn't deliver fair and balanced news because they're reacting to a deliberate campaign to tarnish them as the "liberal media." Addressing those accusations in a futile attempt to counter them has pushed mainstream media's coverage further to the right. Claims of media bias in the United States include claims of liberal bias, conservative bias, mainstream bias, and corporate bias.

In his book, *What Liberal Media? The Truth About Bias and the News*, author Eric Alterman calls the so-called liberal bias a "lie" pushed by conservatives and the Republican Party.

The coverage of Bernie Sanders' presidential campaign is a case in point. He was ignored even as crowds grew to fill stadiums. After all, people wouldn't really vote for a democratic socialist, would they? Pundits saw the election of Hillary Clinton by pundits as a *fait accompli,* Sanders won primaries and polls showed he had a better chance of defeating Donald Trump, but his ideas of income inequality, a $15 minimum wage, and tuition-free college weren't part of the nightly news. Newspapers, when they discussed his campaign at all, called his ideas "pie in the sky." Add to that an orchestrated campaign waged by both the Clinton campaign and the Democratic National Committee to hand Hillary the election, and it's bye-bye, Bernie.

A study for The Center for Media and Public Affairs found that the average length of a presidential candidate's soundbite on the evening news dropped from 42 seconds in 1968 to less than 10 seconds in 1992.

This shove further to the right begun under Reagan, with the Powell memo as their bible, has worked well in dividing the general public almost to the point of Civil War. In fact, many of those icons of the South have been resurrected to divide the country further. Somehow the twisted logic used to defend the Confederate flag AND the American flag and anthem justifies the rise of white supremacy and the chest-thumping of the "True Patriot."

The shift began with innuendoes of wrong-doing to absurd allegations that started in right-wing media and ended up on the evening news, most of the time never questioned or subjected to the traditional rules of corroboration and fact-checking. There were hints of multiple mob-like "hits" of people close to Hillary and Bill Clinton, the birther accusations that Barack Obama wasn't born in the United States and thus wasn't a legitimate president, and whispered allegations of Hillary's human trafficking of girls out of a DC pizza restaurant. Donald Trump followed along on Fox and waded in on Twitter at 3 A.M. rants. The mainstream dutifully reported it all.

Jeremy Dear, Deputy General Secretary of the International Federation of Journalists, expressed concern about the state of US journalism. He looks on so-called fake news and President Trump's statements accusing mainstream media as the source as dangerous. "He is undermining the credibility of genuine news," he says. "And the world still looks on the US as the standard-bearers of an open, transparent press."

What happened to the Tea Party?

For a while, the Tea Party was making the news every night. Republican politicians heeded their every statement and courted their endorsement. MoveOn.org, some say the equivalent organization representing the left, plays more by the rules and gets mostly ignored.

The Tea Party movement, according to Fox pundit Juan Williams, formed from disenfranchised followers of Ron Paul after he lost the 2008 Republican presidential primary. Their public coming-out occurred when member angrily protested the bailout of mortgage companies when homeowners went bankrupt. For those of us at home, their attention-getting antics made them appear more comical than serious.

They organized a Taxpayer March on Washington in 2009 with the so-called liberal media hanging on their every word. Individual members were Republican Party activists and brought in others who dogged Democrats in their home districts, protesting everything from the deficit to the health insurance mandate of Obamacare. Though many times they looked like they had just left the set of The Price is Right, serious money from David H. Koch of the infamous Koch Brothers bought them media coverage and a level of credibility.

MoveOn.org was also making waves having appeared in the wake of Bill Clinton's impeachment in 1998. Formed by members of the House of Representative with a decidedly Progressive outlook, they were virtually ignored by mainstream media. Full disclosure: I was an organizer for MoveOn.org, putting together street corner protests and pickets at banks. My Congressman showed up, but the media who had followed the Tea Party with such fervor was nowhere to be seen.

A 2016 Pew Research Center study found that 57 percent of Americans get their news from television, 25 percent from radio and 20 percent from newspapers. Online media was responsible for 38 percent, with millennials skewing higher at 50 percent. Most online news outlets are owned or funded by the same large corporations. Those that aren't part of some conglomerate have no stake or interest in presenting local news. Those who get their news on mobile devices jumped from 54 percent in 2013 to 72 percent in 2016.

A recent film on Facebook revealed the effects of lazy local station managers, the pervasive influence of public relations when they showed about a dozen news desks reporting the same news story, the exact same news story with identical verbiage, making it evident that when *Mother Jones magazine* reported in 2014 that only 25 percent of local TV stations actually produce their own content, that number may have been high.

Trump's FCC Chairman Ajit Pai continues efforts to dismantle media ownership laws further. Sinclair Broadcasting, a company that already owns/operates 193 local news stations around the country, is planning to buy Tribune media, giving the company control of 233 stations, over 100 markets in 40 percent of households including Los Angeles, New York, and Chicago. Sinclair also owns four radio stations, four digital networks, and the Tennis Channel. Julian Sinclair is well known in conservative circles. He hired Boris Ephshteyn, a former senior advisor on the Trump presidential campaign, as chief political analyst. Sinclair has a list of "must-runs," editorials and reports, right-wing commentaries, that politicize local news, undermining the objective nature of other station programming and the stations' credibility as reliable sources of news. There are rumors that Trump TV may be in the preliminary stages of moving from Facebook and establishing its own news network. Already there's a Trump News Network on YouTube. Add to this the constant threats to shut down networks that criticize or question Trump's actions.

Academics were concerned with the changing landscape of news before Trump took the oath of office. The *Columbia Journalism Review* printed "An Open Letter to Trump from the US Press Corp on the eve of the inauguration:

> Reports over the last few days that your press secretary is considering pulling news media offices out of the White House are the latest in a pattern of behavior that has persisted throughout the campaign: You've banned news organizations from covering you. You've taken to Twitter to taunt and threaten individual reporters and encouraged your supporters to do the same. You've advocated for looser libel laws and threatened numerous lawsuits of your own, none of which has materialized. You've avoided the press when you could and flouted the norms of pool reporting and regular press conferences. You've ridiculed a reporter who wrote something you didn't like because he has a disability.

CJR announced that the press would determine the narrative and that Truth would prevail. Editor in Chief Kyle Pope stated a year later in a podcast, "We've shirked our duty. The real news is getting drowned out by all the other nonsense."

For over 30 years Fairness and Accuracy in Reporting (FAIR), a national media watch group has fought media bias and censorship and reminds us of the stories that mainstream media fails to cover.

Their website, fair.org, exposes some of the misdirection TV news uses to obscure the very issues they should be analyzing more in-depth. "Perseverance porn" are heartwarming personal stories that FAIR says are "shared to shame the poor under the guise of inspirational life advice." Examples include a low-wage worker who buys shoes for a child because his mother can't afford them and a teen who returns to work after a serious car accident.

FAIR's Adam Johnson explained the media's role in reporting these stories:

> One particularly vulgar example was CBS News referring to an "inspiring" African-American kid who had to work at his fast-food job with an arm sling and a neck brace after a car accident. To compound the perseverance porn, he was, at least in part, doing so to help donate to a local homeless charity. Here we have a story highlighting how society has colossally failed its most vulnerable populations—the poor, ethnic minorities, children and the homeless—and the take-home point is, "Ah gee, look at that scrappy kid." A healthy press would take these anecdotes of "can do" spirit and ask more significant questions, like *why* are these people forced into such absurd hardship?

FAIR blames the media for going for the easy story and uses traffic on the website GoFundMe to show how the facts are right in front of journalists. As always, FAIR presents the facts: "About one-half the money raised from the website has been used to pay healthcare expenses." Single payer is the obvious answer to many of us, but revealing statistics like these are rarely used to draw a connection to a systemic problem.

Thomas Frank, a Progressive author of such works as *Listen, Liberal* and *What's the Matter with Kansas?* blames an insular press corp.

> The *Washington Post*, with its constant calls for civility, with its seemingly genetic predisposition for bipartisanship and consensus, is more than the paper of record for the capital—it is the house organ of a meritocratic elite, which views the federal city as the arena of its professional practice. They are professionals in the full sense of the word, well-educated and well-connected, often flaunting insider credentials of one sort or another. ... And when they look around at the comfortable, well-educated folks who work in government, academia, Wall Street, medicine, and Silicon Valley, they see their peers.

Freedom of Information Act

It seems as though the media is keeping information from the general public rather than performing its role of informing the public. Reporters have used the Freedom of Information Act, a 1966 federal freedom of information law that allows for the full or partial disclosure of previously unreleased information and documents controlled by the United States government, to uphold the public's right to know. As Muckrock, "a non-profit, collaborative news site," reports, "When Donald J. Trump took office, our data found that the average federal FOIA request that took 162 days to complete from the time it was filed. Now, that average has crept up to 169 days." The allowed response time under FOIA is supposed to be 20 days.

The Environmental Protection Agency is using FOIA, too. Both *Mother Jones* and *The New York Times* have reported how a consulting firm called Definers Corp., an opposition research firm frequently used by Republicans to get dirt on their opponents, was hired with a no-bid contract by the EPA to work on media affairs. Definers VP, Allan Blutstein, has filed at least 40 FOIA requests, reports the *New York Times*, aiming for "resistance" figures in the federal government. In an interview, he said he hoped to discover whether they had done anything that might embarrass them or hurt their cause. The witch hunt has had a number of employees and former employees looking over their shoulder.

MuckRock reports:

> The State Department beefed up its FOIA resources, but here, too, was a political angle: Much of that work was focused on releasing emails related to Hillary Clinton's time as Secretary of State... A scrubbing of the EPA's climate change resources was widely noted with teams preparing to archive information. Similar information released by the National Park Service disappeared, although the agency later promised it would return.

No surprise: Freedom of Information Act (FOIA) lawsuits have skyrocketed. In the year since Trump took office, FOIA lawsuits have jumped 26 percent compared to the year before, according to The FOIA Project, up 70 percent in the last five years with over 900 cases on backlog.

What the heck is Net Neutrality and why does it matter?

Net Neutrality mandates all Internet Service Providers (e.g., AT&T, Verizon) to treat all data on the internet equally. An ISP is not allowed to block, charge extra for, or deliberately slow down (throttle) an internet related service or websites such as Google or Facebook. They can't discriminate against certain services, users, content, applications, or methods of communication.

FCC chairman Ajit Pai called California's new net neutrality bill "egregious," "radical, anti-consumer," and "illegal." The bill was passed last month but has not yet been signed by the governor. When signed into law, it will create tougher net neutrality rules than those the FCC recently overturned. The FCC recently ruled against state's individual efforts to overturn what many see as a giveaway to big business.

Pai says that internet traffic is an interstate service, so "it follows that only the federal government can set regulatory policy in this area."

His spin reflects the administration's belief that business should be unencumbered in its pursuit of market share and that "nanny-state California legislators" want to take choice away from consumers.

Net neutrality matters because, without it, our voices are further diminished and the free flow of communications is dictated by the level of service you've paid for. We need a level playing field for the exchange of ideas and information and access to educate ourselves on the issues of the day in a democracy governed by angry tweets.

Communication Rights

Jean D'Arcy was a French pioneer in the early days of TV in Europe, and as the 1969 Director of Radio and Visual Services Division of the UN realized that the right to freely communicate was a universal human right. The United Nations Educational, Scientific and Cultural Organization's (UNESCO) International Commission for the Study of Communication Problems, Many Voices, One World, also known as the MacBride Report, further defined these rights in a 1980 document entitled, "Communication rights involve freedom of opinion and expression, democratic media governance, media ownership, and media control, participation in one's own culture, linguistic rights, rights to education, privacy, assemble, and self-determination."

We are fortunate enough in this country to have many watchdog organizations and individuals reporting on these assaults on our press and the information we receive, but it is imperative that we keep government accountable.

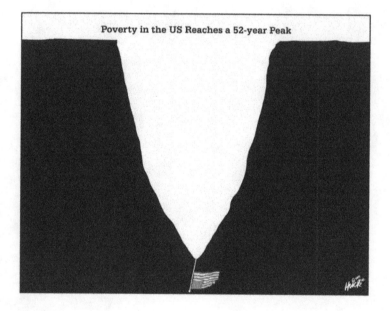

Chapter 11

The American Caste System

"The forces in a capitalist society, if left unchecked, tend to make the rich richer and the poor poorer." Jawaharlal Nehru

"The U.S. has a class problem. It has a race problem. And it may just have a caste problem, too." Subramanian Shankar

When I was growing up in a small Texas town, I was reminded almost daily that there were different classes of people. Many of my classmates lived on the other side of the railroad tracks. I lived on the wrong side in "N" town. My stepdad cut, or rather shaved, my hair whenever he thought I needed it. I wasn't allowed to see a dentist because it was "too expensive." My clothes were ragged. I was the eldest, so they weren't hand-me-downs, but they were cheap. My dad warned me, "We're poor and we'll always be poor. You might as well get used to working with your hands." Apparently, he had either never heard of American exceptionalism like the Horatio Alger story (very likely), or didn't buy it.

Controversial books published over the last 150 years in America and within the neo-Nazi movement have promoted the antiquated and long-disproved notion of Social Darwinism. The theory of eugenics furthered this belief that the rich and powerful were in positions of power due to their superior breeding. According to white supremacists, the "inferiority of African-Americans and poor people" have undermined the evolution of the human race because those with lower IQs have been allowed to breed and proliferate. These beliefs go beyond class distinction or racism because in a caste system one is locked in by a matter of birth.

Those of us near the bottom of the ladder look up and see that we're trapped. The system is rigged by those in power, a system that buoys their prosperity while applying downward pressure on the middle and working classes. We see that very few of us can move upward, that we're playing a rigged game. Even those who win millions in the lottery are revealed to be unworthy of the climb upward. In a Business Insider magazine article in 2016, writer Pamela Engel reported on 21 lottery winners who "blew it all." My response to her?

> I just stumbled upon your article from January 2016, entitled, "21 Lottery Winners Who Blew it All." Your article perpetuates the belief that the poor and middle class are that way because they don't know how to manage money. How about an article about those who won the lottery and successfully made the transition into the upper class? I don't think I've found one!

Many of the insights into the caste system come from articles written by those most familiar with its history: Indians. They have become alarmed at the obvious parallels in America that the native-born seem not to have noticed. Those who have written on the subject attribute an American caste system for the exclusion of people of color, women, and occupation.

The difference between class and caste, as explained in an article by Subramanian Shankar, is the permanency of the situation. Shankar was born in India, and he points out some apparent parallels that resonated with his American students of color and working class:

> First, caste cannot be transcended. Unlike class, people of the "low" Mahar caste cannot educate or earn their way out of being Mahar. No matter how elite their college or how lucrative their careers, those born into a low caste remain stigmatized for life.

> Caste is also always hierarchical: As long as it exists, so does the division of people into "high" and "low." That distinguishes it from race, in that people in a caste system cannot dream of equality. Caste, in other words, is societal difference made timeless, inevitable, and cureless. Caste says to its subjects, "You all are different and unequal, and fated to remain so."

Shankar was not the first to recognize alarming comparisons between American society Indian castes. Gerald Berreman compared north Indian villages with the Jim Crow South in his 1960 essay, *Caste in India and the United States*. "A caste system may be defined as a hierarchy of endogamous (self-contained) divisions in which membership is hereditary and permanent." Here, said Berreman, "hierarchy includes inequality both in status and in access to good and services."

Berreman's wrote in 1960 that the position of African Americans in our society is littered with obstacles has been corroborated by the findings of the Brookings Institutio nalmost 60 years later: "Accessibility to a prestigious university and the possibility of forming relationships that can lead to better employment opportunities is an uphill battle for those who are the first generation in their families to attend college, black and Hispanic students."

First-generation, black, and Hispanic students are getting a lower-quality education than their more socially advantaged peers. Gaps in college quality reflect disparities in education in the preceding years, of course. But right now, if anything, the college years see those gaps widen even further—which puts the ideal of equal opportunity even further out of reach.

The dynamic of race since *Caste and Class in a Southern Town* by John Dollard was published in 1937 is not so in-your-face, though we're seeing a resurgence of police shooting of young black men that gave rise to the Black Lives Matter movement. The racism in 1937 was a way of life:

> A Negro boy's automobile was sideswiped by another car, and the impact threw it against a white worker on the road.

> The worker was slightly injured. The boy was brought to jail, tried and given thirty days at the county farm. An informant intervened on behalf of his protégé and talked to an officer of the law who thought that the boy had come off lucky not to be killed for hitting a white man; the fact that the other driver caused the accident did not appear to matter. It seemed to be taken for granted that a Negro would hit a white man if he could get away with it under cover of an "accident."

In her book, *The New Jim Crow: Mass Incarceration in the Age of Colorblindness,* writer Michelle Alexander calls the mass incarceration of young black men a new caste system.

> It may be helpful, in attempting to understand the fundamental nature of the new caste system, to think of the criminal justice system—the entire collection of institutions and practices that comprise it—not as an independent system but rather as a gateway into a much larger network of racial stigmatization and permanent marginalization. The term mass incarceration refers not only to the criminal justice system but also to the larger web of laws, rules, policies, and customs that control those labeled criminals both in and out of prison. Once released, former prisoners enter a hidden underworld of legalized discrimination and permanent social exclusion.

Writer Rajesh Sampath also refers to America's caste system in terms of race:

> Let's look at how both caste and racial discrimination perpetuate hierarchy, privilege, discrimination, marginalization, and exclusion. It is after the successes of the African American Civil Rights movement that we have witnessed the birth of the school-to-prison pipeline, state violence against a disproportionate number of African American men in police killings, and the turning back of affirmative action at public universities in some states' constitutional amendments, such as Michigan.

"The US has a class problem. It has a race problem. And it may just have a caste problem, too," states Professor Shankar.

In America, terms such as "inner city African Americans," "urban Hispanics," "suburban whites," "second generation Asian," etc., are demographic segments in consumer marketing, but they're comparable to the very rigid levels of a caste system where no one rises above his station.

Rajiv Raholtra has stated and recognized that types of work sometimes define one's place in society.

> Caste systems in India evolved, just as they have done in the US, as a labor group by the kind of work. This is why each of India's castes corresponds to a category of labor, much like the modern guild of American workers of a given profession, with its own procedures for membership and strategies to compete with outsiders. In India, this segmentation got perpetuated because training was done through work apprenticeship under one's parents, thereby turning family lineages into specialized labor.

Writer Kate Wells pondered the question of an American caste in December 1881, issue of *The Atlantic*."…we become conscious that caste rules in American life with an iron rod, tempered only by the fiery furnace of much wealth or rare intellectual ability: the lower we descend, in what is called social life, the more perceptible become its demarkations (sic)."

The writer used caste to define levels of work in society: workingmen against working women, tailoresses against sewing-girls with each group guarding their status jealously. Wells quotes an anonymous woman identified only as "one who is doing all she can to elevate the character of her fellow-workers":

> Caste is a nuisance to those who want to get into what you call society, and it is our curse. There is among us (1) the sensuous class, those who dance; (2) the domestic class, who

stay by themselves and get their own meals, or live with their parents in rooms, who work all day and sew all night, and go to church on Sunday, or remain at home without gadding about; (3) then the God-forsaken class, who stay honestly in their attics and die by inches, who are not skilled workwoman by birth, and who never can be, any more than all can be artists, but they can do slop-work and starve to death (why don't the skilled pity the unskilled, and look only to the slow process of better-born generations to do away with the amount of unskilled labor?); and (4) there are the servants."

So now we have a caste defined in terms of race and type of work. In an American caste system which we all don't agree even exists, the opportunity, no matter how small, allows a minute number to rise above their station. To deny the existence of a rigged system leaves us susceptible to the whims of the powerful and makes us powerless to challenge and change the status quo.

Sam Amer sees the issue as the rich and powerful keeping the poor in check. "If you were born poor, you and your progeny are likely to remain that way as well. In America the newly developing caste system appears to encompass more than just income inequality. It encompasses inequality in opportunity, in health, in life expectancy, in happiness and in all other aspects of life itself."

The rich don't cross paths with the "little people" very much. They travel in very different circles, attending their own schools, traveling separately even on the same transport, party at their private exclusive social functions, and don't shop at the same stores. They are our government officials, our judges, our corporate CEOs, only occasionally, often accidentally, glimpsing a part of our lives. They write the laws and establish the rules for the rest of us as the wealth gap in the United States continues to grow; only Russia, Ukraine, and Lebanon are worse.

The rich in America have no interest in expanding Social Security, don't want to deal with single payer or Medicare. They don't want to increase the minimum wage or raise Social Security. Home base may or may not be in the States, but they show no real allegiance to any particular country. They're not concerned about the workers – in any country.

A caste system widens income equality, creates a gulf between those at the top and those at the bottom and is not sustainable in the long run. Those who used to be consumers, who purchased the products they made, can no longer afford them. Diminished demand spurs layoffs. Cities and states watch infrastructure crumble that would have been maintained by taxes that dried up. Workers move to the end of the unemployment line seeking assistance in feeding their families and keeping the lights on. The rest could be the plot of a dystopian novel. We need to find a solution or solutions.

Growing up poor is traumatizing, a sense of not belonging keeps one at arms' length. During my lifetime, I managed to move up the ladder one rung because of family and stay there because of a good-paying union job. Getting a college education didn't improve my lot by raising my income or promotion. Many of those who toil away inside the "phone company's" windowless nondescript beige buildings are content. Many come from a long line of family members past and present who spent a lifetime there. Many of us find a spouse at the water cooler or in the union hall. The positive side, then, is a sense of community. The negative that it has all been preordained and permanent.

Several recent studies indicate that Americans still believe that anyone, with enough hard work, can become anything they want, but the reality is we here in the United States are less mobile than comparable nations. Markus Jantti, an economist at a Swedish university, found that 42 percent of American men raised in the bottom fifth of incomes stay there as adults.

In 2013, the US government forecast that inequality would rise in the next 20 years by just as much as it did in the past 25 years. If corporations and the wealthy receive as much of a relative tax break under President-elect Donald Trump as researchers say they will, the income gap between US earners may grow even larger. Experts have predicted a ballooning deficit.

Caste, by defining all of the issues that certain segments of society feel forever subordinate them to others, explains Americans' sense of persistent marginalization. We talk about class warfare, of exclusion because of gender, color, shade of color, sexual orientation, occupation, country of origin, family income and any combination, that captures us with a sense of permanency in our lack of future upward mobility. Whose American Dream is this?

Chapter 12

Government As Protector

> If the people cannot trust their government to do the job for which it exists - to protect them and to promote their common welfare - all else is lost. Barack Obama

> Many people want the government to protect the consumer. A much more urgent problem is to protect the consumer from the government. Milton Friedman

I first became aware that the police exist to protect property over people during the 1989 nationwide strike of the Communications Workers of America against AT&T. Manhole covers were welded shut and security patrolled the perimeter of offices surrounded by picketers ostensibly to prevent vandalism. I was told the company's policy wasn't new and soon discovered why telecom buildings have few or no windows.

After the Watts riots of 1965, the company decided telecommunications were too vulnerable to angry mobs. Employees were informed that in an insurrection or a revolution, agitators would seize the means of communications, so windows were painted or plastered over, locks and fences installed, and identification cards issued.

I encountered this policy of property over people again in 2008 when activists protested against the banks whose toxic assets had caused a financial meltdown. When we attempted to deliver a list of demands to the Bank of America, police blocked both entrances and threatened us with arrest if we tried to enter the bank. Waving my B of A ATM card, announcing, "See! I'm a customer!" had no effect on my perceived status as a troublemaker.

Ask the Standing Rock Sioux and other area tribes if they felt police at the scene of Dakota Access Pipeline construction since September 2017, were there to protect them or the construction equipment. The pipeline, started in June 2016, was designed to transport oil underground for 1172 miles. Local tribes were worried about leaks and effects on local water quality, and disturbing sacred burial grounds in Iowa and the Dakotas.

Over 400 protestors have been arrested on charges such as criminal trespassing and engaging in a riot in the last year since the protests began. On just one day, 141 protesters were jailed when authorities bulldozed a camp that had blocked the pipeline path on land owned by the pipeline developer. Even Amy Goodman of *Democracy Now* and former presidential candidate Jill Stein were detained for possible vandalism.

Protestors accuse local law enforcement of excessive force. There are reports that pepper spray, tear gas, and bean bag rounds have been unleashed on peaceful demonstrations, pipe ceremonies and prayer circles in a show of militarized force. The people lost when the pipeline delivered its first product in May 2017. The pipeline is expected to pump 470,000 gallons of oil a day. A leak of 210,000 gallons in South Dakota was reported in November 2017. Apparently, concerns were warranted.

Consumer Protection

The CFPB website's Original Mission Statement: "The Consumer Financial Protection Bureau (CFPB) is a 21st-century agency that helps consumer finance markets work by making rules more effective, by consistently and fairly enforcing those rules, and by empowering consumers to take more control over their economic lives." (consumerfinance.gov)

The Consumer Financial Protection Bureau, (CFPB) created just seven years ago, was, until recently, headed by interim Director Mick

Mulvaney who, as a Congressman, vowed to get rid of the agency he called a "sick, sad joke." Seen as an impediment to business, Mulvaney was appointed by President Trump to gut the agency. His influence was felt immediately with his decision to reverse complaints and fines against payday lending companies. Kathy Kraninger was appointed Director in December 2018, and confirmed by one vote in the Senate. She is apparently looking to distance herself from her predecessor.

From out of the collapse of the housing bubble and a meltdown of Wall Street, came the creation of the CFPB in 2011. A provision of the Dodd-Frank Act and conceived by Harvard law professor Elizabeth Warren, the agency was created to protect consumers in the financial arena. From unscrupulous payday lenders to overzealous collection agencies, the agency has developed new avenues to raise concerns about financial institutions and products, to educate the public about their rights, and has established new rules and regulations that have brought restitution of $12 billion to 30 million consumers. Of course, Mulvaney believes the way to give consumers "more control over their economic lives" is to rid the nation of "unnecessary" rules and regulations.

Richard Cordray as the first Consumer Czar, was an effective ombudsman, drawing fire from those who opposed the agency in the first place. CFPB's role of watchdog has put important data online that allows consumers and the media access to trends in the financial sector and continues, (at least for now), to reveal the actions of the financial services sector. There are at least 30 million consumers who appreciate the work of the CFPB under the direction of Cordray. Many times it is said that government action or inaction is invisible to the public, but in this case, this particular agency has been transparent in its dealings on our behalf. The agency should be allowed to continue advocating robustly in the financial sector, posting its findings on the website where all can access the data, and keeping rapacious practices from overwhelming students, the middle class and seniors.

Mulvaney's influence has already been felt; complaints and fines against payday lending companies have been reversed.

Social Security

There's a common belief that Reagan "borrowed" $2.7 trillion from Social Security, GW Bush took $1.37 trillion (more like $708 billion) to pay for the Iraq War, and Bill Clinton hijacked $3 trillion for a variety of programs. The "lockbox" that GW Bush and Al Gore discussed leading up to the 2000 election indicated that Social Security was a sacred cow. Historian Sean Wilentz referred to it as the "third rail" of national politics – touch it and get burned. Are Social Security funds protected as promised?

Some sources equivocate, pointing out that Social Security surplus funds aren't technically "borrowed," unless and until the US Treasury fails to redeem interest-incurring bonds due to mature in 2020. Besides, they say, even though the Social Security trust funds received $1.5 trillion in bonds during the W Bush years, the Treasury only had access to revenue collected every year, and couldn't touch the interest on the entire surplus.

The Social Security program, officially called "Old-age, Survivors, and Disability Insurance" (OASDI), in reference to its three components, was created as a part of FDR's New Deal in 1935 and, until 1982, employees' contributions to Social Security ensured the program paid for the benefits of current recipients. A joint commission was formed in 1983 to deal with the predicted impending shortfalls as Baby Boomers started to retire.

The ideas presented by the commission included a law that raised the payroll tax, which hit working folks harder than the wealthy. The retirement age was increased from 65 to 67 over time and government employees now had to pay into the system. These changes promised to extend Social Security's solvency until at least 2037, kicking the can down the road a couple of generations.

Matthew Dallek cited Congress' 1983 bipartisan deal on April 2, 2009, US News and World Report article as proof that "good politics can happen in the most unforgiving environments."

> Reagan's Social Security Reform Act not only reversed his own ideological opposition to Social Security but also identified

the nation's leading conservative as a defender of liberalism's most cherished achievement: "This bill demonstrates for all time our nation's ironclad commitment to Social Security," Reagan announced when he signed the bill.

President GW Bush addressed the issue in his 2004 State of the Union address: "Younger workers should have the opportunity to build a nest egg by saving part of their Social Security taxes in a personal retirement account. We should make the Social Security system a source of ownership for the American people."

The following year Republican members of Congress and the GW Bush administration tried unsuccessfully to privatize Social Security. The plan included partial privatization of the program, personal Social Security accounts, and options that would allow Americans to divert a portion of their FICA tax into secured investments. Employees could invest up to a third of the 12.4 percent payroll tax that they and their employers pay on their wages. (Workers pay 6.2 percent and their employers pay the other 6.2 percent.)

"We will make sure there are good options to protect your investments from sudden market swings on the eve of your retirement," the President promised.

Annual contributions would be capped at $1,000 in 2009 and rise slightly more than $100 per year. Workers would have a choice of five broadly diversified index funds and a "lifecycle fund," a portfolio that, starting from age 47, would grow increasingly more conservative as retirement approached. Of course, a worker could throw caution to the wind and opt out.

Other options the younger Bush's administration considered "on the table":

- limiting benefits for wealthy retirees aka means testing;
- indexing benefits to prices rather than wages;
- increasing the retirement age; and
- discouraging taking Social Security benefits early.

Fortunately for working people, Bush's obsession never caught on. Every time the president brought it up, his approval ratings took a hit. When unions lobbied against the idea on the hill on behalf of our members, it seemed everyone prowling the halls of Congress was there to protest any changes to Social Security.

The arguments we used in 2005 and every time Republican members of Congress have proposed privatizing Social Security are compelling:

- Privatization does not address Social Security's long-term funding challenges. The program is "pay as you go," meaning current payroll taxes pay for current retirees. Diverting payroll taxes (or other sources of government funds) to fund private accounts would drive enormous deficits and borrowing ("transition costs").
- Privatization converts the program from a "defined benefits" plan to a "defined contribution" plan, subjecting the ultimate payouts to stock or bond market fluctuations;
- Social Security payouts are indexed to wages, which historically have exceeded inflation. As such, Social Security payments are protected from inflation, while private accounts might not be;
- Privatization would represent a windfall for Wall Street financial institutions, who would obtain significant fees for managing private accounts.
- Privatization in 2008, in the midst of the most significant economic downturn since the Great Depression, would have caused households to have lost even more of their assets, had their investments been invested in the U.S. stock market.

The Center for Economic and Policy Research found in a 2013 study income equality affected Social Security. The Center estimated that upward redistribution of income is responsible for about 43% of the projected program's shortfall over the next 75 years. "This is because income over the payroll tax cap ($127,200 in 2017) is not taxed; if individuals generate higher income above the taxable income limit, that lack of additional taxation results in lower funding than possible if there were no income limit." It's time to raise the cap once again.

The 2017 Annual Report Of The Board Of Trustees Of The Federal Old-Age And Survivors Insurance And Federal Disability Insurance Trust Funds seemed optimistic that funds would last longer than the 2037 projected depletion date. They realize how many retirees, their survivors, and disabled workers and their families depend on Social Security payments to make ends meet.

At the end of Fiscal Year 2016, the OASDI program (aka Social Security) was providing benefit payments to about 61 million people: 44 million retired workers and dependents of retired workers, 6 million survivors of deceased workers, and 11 million disabled workers and dependents of disabled workers.

"[Social Security] accounts for more than half of the income for 60 percent of senior households and more than 90 percent for almost one third," reports Dean Baker of The Center for Economic and Policy Research.

In 2017 the Center on Budget and Policy Priorities suggested changes to fix the program that included raising the ceiling on taxable wages in baby steps and taxing any salary reduction plans, including cafeteria plans and health care Flexible Spending Accounts on behalf of Social Security.

A point made in the Center's 2010 report is even more relatable nine years later: "Members of Congress cannot simultaneously claim that the tax cuts for people at the top are affordable while the Social Security shortfall constitutes a dire fiscal threat."

But the hero of the working class has a solution:

"Anyone who tells you Social Security is going broke is lying," Vermont's Senator Sanders said. "We can increase Social Security benefits for millions of Americans and extend the life of Social Security if we have the political will to tell the wealthiest Americans to pay the same rate as everyone else.

Right now, an American who makes $106,800 a year pays the same amount of money into the Social Security system as a millionaire or a billionaire. That is because today, all income above $106,800 is exempt from the Social Security payroll tax. As a result, 94 percent of Americans pay Social Security tax on all of their income, but the wealthiest 6 percent do not."

The Hill website reported Sanders' legislation would increase Social Security benefits by about $1,300 annually for seniors who make less than $16,000, while wealthy earners would pay payroll taxes on income above $250,000.

Pete DeFazio of Oregon has introduced a version of the bill in the House. The Social Security Administration said the legislation would extend solvency to 2078 and would increase monthly payments by as much as $73.

In a statement released at the time he introduced the legislation, Senator Sanders said, "Social Security has succeeded in keeping millions of senior citizens, widows and orphans and the disabled out of extreme poverty. Before Social Security was developed, about half of our seniors lived in poverty. Today, fewer than 10 percent live in poverty and all of that is done with minimal administrative costs."

Sanders also warned Americans that a bipartisan committee studying ways to cut the national debt was looking at the so-called entitlement.

"Unfortunately," said Sanders, "Republicans in Congress and too many Democrats, have been discussing harmful cuts to Social Security as part of an overall scheme to balance the budget on the backs of the elderly, the sick, the children, and working families."

Social Security is funded by a payroll tax (FICA) as a separate entity, meaning it has no impact, positive or negative, on the deficit. The fund will continue with 100 percent payouts until 2038 and, pending any legislation, could still be counted on for 80 percent of those benefits for decades.

Black Lives Matter

A protest arose as a movement of outrage that had transcended the geography of individual incidents. A blurb on the website for the Aspen Ideas Festival called #BlackLivesMatter "an organization, a movement, and a rallying cry for racial justice. Born online after the not-guilty verdict in the killing of Trayvon Martin, and translated to the streets after the killing of Michael Brown, …young black men are 21 times more likely than their white counterparts to be shot by police…"

In the ensuing confusion and misdirected anger and presidential bluster, BLM has proven to be a lightning rod for hate and anger from a variety of sources. Rather than dealing with the issues of a criminal justice system in serious need of repair, it is important to see where the government has failed to protect these young men.

In the aftermath of Trayvon Martin's death and the acquittal of his assailant, George Zimmerman in 2013, Alicia Garza, Patrisse Cullors, and Opal Tometi gave birth to a movement that asks why so many young black men have died.

In a society where whites see law enforcement as helpful guardians, many bristle defensively when accusations are leveled at those who "serve and protect." Another counter-movement called Blue Lives Matter demands that those who are convicted of killing police be sentenced under hate crimes statutes. Interestingly, cops are feeling under attack from the community. Their culture doesn't allow them to consider weeding out the bad actors. They stand together because a police officer's partner may have to provide backup in a life-and-death situation. When I ran for political office, the Los Angeles Police Protective League, the police union, asked, if elected, would I author a bill to toughen the penalty for shooting a police officer? I said no. "A police officer accepts the position knowing he may put himself in harm's way in the line of duty," I said. I understand the argument: if we as a society get used to the deaths of law enforcement, we are courting anarchy. If police don't have that presumption of authority, confrontations will be more likely to happen and the role of police in society will be undermined. They don't seem to realize they have undermined their own position in society by protecting the bad apples.

Is there a serious problem within the system that metes out justice differently for people of color? The deaths of Tamir Rice, Tanisha Anderson, Mya Hall, Dontre Hamilton, Walter Scott, Sandra Bland, Mike Brown, Eric Garner, and many, many others seem to support this premise.

"He ran." (Walter Scott)

"He refused to cooperate with police." (Dontre Hamilton)

Even if these scenarios are true, or they were confronted during the commission of a crime, there is no reason an unarmed suspect should pay with their lives. Former police officer and Los Angeles City Councilman Dennis Zine once told me, "To protect myself I view every traffic stop as somebody who might try to kill me. That's how I stay alive."

A statement signed by 1800 sociologists in the aftermath of the shooting death of Micheal Brown in Ferguson, Missouri in 2014 was published on countless websites and points to a "climate of suspicion of people of color among police departments and communities. Instead of feeling protected by police, many African Americans are intimidated and live in daily fear that their children will face abuse, arrest, and death at the hands of police officers who may be acting on implicit biases or institutional policies based on stereotypes and assumptions of black criminality."

Of course, these issues divide those of us at the bottom and if we're too busy fighting among ourselves, the one percent continue to play off our fears of each other. Bring back community-based policing.

Medicare

Speaker Paul Ryan was out to gut Medicare for his entire political career. He's gone but the GOP fight to get rid of Medicare continues.

"We're going to have to get back next year at entitlement reform, which is how you tackle the debt and the deficit," Ryan said in various interviews. "... Frankly, it's the healthcare entitlements that are the big drivers of our debt, so we spend more time on the health care entitlements — because that's really where the problem lies, fiscally speaking." He has lied over and over that Medicare is going broke.

What irritates Republicans most is the weaving of Medicare with Obamacare. Medicare stands in the way of repealing the Affordable Care Act; both programs are more popular than Republicans in Washington had realized. Repeated attempt to repeal Obamacare have met with failure. The rising deficit was kicked into overdrive by the president's tax package passed in December 2017, and Democrats are concerned the unprecedented level of the deficit will be the excuse Congress needs to dismantle so-called entitlement programs. The new tax plan is already expected to take health care from 13 million Americans.

Republicans would like to replace traditional Medicare with a privatized plan, despite the efficiency of the current program that guarantees treatment and offers low administrative costs. Before he retired in 2018, Ryan had been pushing "premium support," a voucher system that would subsidize seniors' insurance premiums. But healthcare costs continue to skyrocket and any value of a voucher, a defined benefit of a specific dollar amount, would be eaten up by the commercial carriers, translating to fewer funds for actual treatment. Who would make up the difference? The Kaiser Family Foundation looked into Ryan's plan when he first proposed it in 2011 and predicted, if implemented, premium support would cost seniors over twice as much.

Flint, Michigan

Dr. Mona Hanna-Attisha administers to some of the area's poorest children at a state-funded medical center. She was the pediatrician thrust into the national spotlight when she brought Flint's water crisis to the public's attention. She became alarmed in 2015 at elevated blood-lead levels of children in the area.

The problem began when the source of water for Flint, Michigan was changed in 2014 from treated Detroit Water and Sewerage Department water (sourced from Lake Huron and the Detroit River) to the Flint River and the city failed to apply corrosion inhibitors to the water.

When Dr. Hanna-Attisha began to suspect contamination of the public water supply, she tried to gather data and was rebuffed by officials then given falsified numbers. Her research, obtained through private channels, indicated a dangerous jump in lead levels in the city's water.

Because of the devastating public health implications, Dr. Hanna-Attisha announced her findings at a press conference in September 2015. State officials denied her claims then confirmed her numbers about a week later.

According to reports, several lawsuits have been filed against government officials, and several investigations have been opened. In January 2016, the city was declared to be in a state of emergency by the Governor of Michigan, Rick Snyder, before President Obama escalated the situation to a federal crisis and authorized additional help from the Federal Emergency Management Agency and the Department of Homeland Security less than two weeks later.

Four government officials resigned over the mishandling of the crisis, and one additional staff member was fired. The water crisis has brought about fifteen criminal cases against local and state officials.

Said Dr. Hanna-Attisha, "Government failed Flint miserably. The water crisis was primarily the result of an unforgivable failure of a bungling state government, one that deprioritized public health and the environment since the 1990s. But really, it was decades of deliberate policy, including racism, austerity, regressive tax policy and deindustrialization, by government and business, that resulted in Flint's decades of misery and are arguably the real causes of the crisis."

If we look around, we can all see evidence of government malfeasance, waste and corruption: the Aliso Canyon gas leak and alleged meltdown of a nuclear reactor at the Santa Susanna Laboratories in California, the infamous Love Canal dumping and pollution, Jim Crow laws and lynchings, the indifference of the Bureau of Indian Affairs, and the use of our military against its own citizens... That is why we must all be involved in our government and raise our voices when we see injustice.

Chapter 13

Pension Raiders and Deadbeats

"Greed is the religion of the billionaire class. The Walton family (owners of Wal-mart) is the wealthiest family in America, and pay their employees starvation wages. The Koch brothers are the second wealthiest family, and make huge campaign contributions in order to cut Social Security, Medicare, and Medicaid. A nation based on greed will not survive morally, economically or politically." Senator Bernie Sanders of Vermont

Who is Scott Walker and why does he hate me?

Scott Walker was, at the time of this writing, the 45th governor of Wisconsin and a former candidate for President. He took the unprecedented action of cutting off state employees' bargaining rights. Much hue and cry ensued, but despite a massive effort to recall Walker and three legislators who colluded with him to bring labor to its knees, only one legislator paid for his actions against working people. This victory was due to a major infusion of cash to the state's Republican Party in the days shortly before the recall elections. **Update:** Scott Walker was defeated in the November 2018 elections due in large part to labor's efforts to oust him.

Pensions vs. 401(k)s

Sometime in the late 1980s, Pacific Bell introduced 401(k)s to its employees. As a provision of the Revenue Act of 1978, the 401(k) allowed employees to defer taxes on a percentage of pay diverted into the fund and matched by employers up to a certain percentage. Initially, I didn't buy in; I smelled a rat. Traditionally, employees collected a pension upon retirement. The pension was a sum of money set aside each month by the employer as a monthly stipend to supplement Social Security in the employee's golden years. Some employees, for instance, teachers, rely exclusively on the guaranteed pension that awaits them in retirement. A pension didn't require any of today's money that paid my bills, that I needed *now*, to be inaccessible. "You're a fool not to invest in our 401(k)," a friend said. "It's free money."

In a way, he was right. The company matched me up to 6 percent, but I was free to invest as much as I wanted. Many of my co-workers dove right in. After all, we still had our pensions.

The recent trend in the private business world has been away from pensions and toward a 401(k). An employee has a vested interest in "contributing to the business" aka working harder when the value of their portfolio is affected by their production in the office. Our precursor to a 401(k) plan was the Team Performance Award, a bonus based on "team" performance, meeting or exceeding our numbers on quantity and quality. The bean counters could only explain the formula for determining whether we had reached our goals and had earned our subsequent payouts at the company. We soon found that a stupid management decision, independent of anyone else down the food chain, would and did affect our numbers and our Award. The next year we realized directors and VPs would tell the bean counters what the outcome should be and the results were reverse engineered to avoid any compensation. The Team Performance Award was repackaged as the Team Award then the Special Team Incentive Plan (STIP), but we were no longer buying into a plan that dangled the carrot just out of reach.

That's why many of us held a healthy amount of skepticism for this new 401(k) plan. We were worried about the future of our pensions if the new plan took hold and our fears were confirmed as we saw pensions disappear or appear to verge on insolvency.

There are those in the financial sector that believe a 401(k) can also create a windfall if managed the right way. A 401(k) is also a helluva lot more volatile. How many of us in the working sector can successfully maneuver the vagaries of the stock market? How many of us with our noses to the grindstone have the time/knowledge to build a sustainable nest egg for retirement?

Defined benefit vs. defined contribution

When a defined benefit is contrasted with a defined contribution the topic puts most of us to sleep. The difference in the two terms is crucial in understanding how cost-shifting from employer to employee is happening company by company, industry by industry.

Defined benefit: XYZ Corporation spells out that each employee has a healthcare benefit that will take care of your vision, teeth, hospitalization, everything. Some employees pay a monthly premium and a co-pay. Some have negotiated a better deal in lieu of extra pay or an extra day off: they pay just a co-pay. A pension is also a defined benefit with the risk absorbed by the plan provider.

Defined contribution: XYZ Corporation says, "We're going to give you $10,000 a year for benefits," maybe using the term "cafeteria-style." Pick one benefit from Column A, one from Column B. After the initial $10,000 a year is maxed out, sometimes after meeting a deductible, the employee absorbs any further costs. If your insurance says they will cover life-saving cancer treatment, but suddenly it costs more, guess who pays the difference. Healthcare costs have not been reined in and they're rising yearly, meaning employees are taking on more and more of the burden of healthcare. Whatever bump in wages won at the bargaining table, is quickly eaten up by higher costs in the doctor's office. One of the motives of the Affordable Care Act was to contain and bring down the costs of healthcare. But concessions were made to Big Pharma, another to private insurance companies. This is just one more way that government has failed us and there's plenty of blame to go around. A 401(k) is a defined contribution, subject to the volatility of the stock market.

Big business has successfully turned public sentiment from "I want that, too!" to "Those union folks are spoiled!" Working families haven't grasped that 401(k)s are a poor substitute and much more of a burden on them.

Of course, there are differing opinions. In an article published in the May 15, 2013, issue of *US News and World Report*, David Ning, founder of the financial website MoneyNing, stated emphatically that 401(k)s are better.

1. Only 40 percent of workers had a pension. The other 60 percent had to pay taxes on savings. *Pensions are better for the employee because your contribution is there where you can't touch it.*
2. Funds in a 401(k) are vested much quicker. And those funds move with you when you leave (All too often these days.) *Okay, good point.*
3. You can play with your money to avoid taxes. *The average worker has no clue nor any knowledge on how to shuffle money to avoid taxes.*
4. You can liquidate in an emergency or borrow against it. *The whole point is ensuring you have something to live on in retirement. Man cannot live on Social Security alone.*
5. There's a better chance of leaving money for your heirs. *Before pension buyouts, this made sense, but now you can roll that pension over into a tax-free IRA.*
6. Possible high fees, but yeah, index funds! *The ideal, based on personal experience is a combination of a solid pension with a reputable company that won't bail on their fiduciary responsibility in the fourth quarter, and a 401(k) where an aggressive approach to saving resulting in a loss won't mean game over. Index funds, share the profit between the insurer and the client in a bull market and pay/lose nothing if the market takes a dump.*

Companies and municipalities, however, are reneging on pension payouts that workers were promised a pension in their retirement years.

Pension Reform

Cities and states are staring down the long barrel at mounting pension costs. Managed state pension funds are estimated at over $2 trillion. Part of the problem of unfunded pension liabilities is due to legislatures who have failed to set aside the agreed-upon funds to keep the pension systems of public workers solvent, "borrowing" funds meant for tomorrow to deal with today's budget priorities. Some of the fallout derived from the financial crisis of 2008 when investments of pension funds in toxic assets took a bath, in turn, decimating billions in anticipated tax revenues for states and municipalities. Governments have turned for solutions from the same sources that created the original problem in 2008: Wall Street and the banks. Enter pro-business, anti-union groups to offer pension reforms that shifted costs onto employees.

Rhode Islanders were very impressed with Gina Raimondo, their newly elected state treasurer, a former Rhodes scholar, and venture capitalist. She presented the Rhode Island Retirement Security Act, an aggressive plan to gain control of runaway costs.

Raimondo fooled everyone. Fourteen percent, $1 billion, of the state's pension funds were funneled into hedge funds controlled by New York financiers as a grand experiment spearheaded by John Arnold, a former Enron executive. Raimondo's business associates would skim off tens of millions in yearly fees, and Arnold had found a way to rob public workers legally.

Public pensions weren't subject to the same protections as private pensions, which were regulated under the 1974 Employee Retirement Income Security Act (ERISA). ERISA was designed to protect pensions with oversight on pension investments including the right to sue for any dereliction of fiduciary responsibility.

The 400,000 members of the Central States Pension Fund, many of them truckers, saw a serious depletion of funds after the industry was deregulated and smaller funders filed bankruptcy. It's estimated that the Plan is only receiving $1 for every $3 distributed to retirees. The fund states, "The loss of $2.8 billion per year in retirement income will also harm other local businesses and shrink tax revenue." To save the Plan, benefits may be reduced.

In 2017, the Pittsburgh Gazette reported Teamsters there were looking at draconian benefit cuts. "[The Plan] has about 48 cents for every $1 in benefits it owes to retirees and ... is expected to pay out nearly $129 million in benefits this year but will collect only about $54 million in contributions."

What do former employees do when a contract for pension benefits was bargained in good faith and they're relying on that pension in their golden years?

Pennsylvania, Michigan, and Arizona are examining ways to deal with rising pension debt. For example, Michigan legislators passed one of the most comprehensive pension reforms enacted by any state to-date. The Michigan Public School Employee Retirement System struggled with $29 billion in debt while being 40 percent underfunded. The challenge was to stop the bleeding while ensuring that teachers and retirees receive every penny they were promised.

Their change to the pension structure for future teachers from a defined benefit system to something considered more "flexible," provides new teachers with more retirement options without short-changing their pension savings. The change does not affect pension benefits for current teachers or retirees. Current teachers are paying into a blended pension-401(k) plan. Future teachers will receive a 401(k) only plan. The Michigan Department of Treasury has identified 110 out of 490 local units with underfunded pension liabilities or an unhealthy health care plan or both.

In 2017, the Pennsylvania state Senate came up with options for future public employees, a choice from three retirement savings plans, including two defined benefit/defined contribution hybrid retirement plans and a defined contribution retirement plan aka a 401(k) style option. With more than $70 billion in pension debt from both the state's public employee and teacher pension systems and underfunded by 40 percent, Governor Tom Wolf forecast some relief: these new plans should save the state more than $1 billion and reduce existing unfunded pension liabilities, by some estimates, $10-$20 billion.

And in Arizona, the Public Safety Personnel Retirement System was, according to Arizona's Auditor General's office, "Deteriorating." In a report to employees, three contributing factors to the pension shortfall were listed: underperforming investment returns, unrealistic expectations, and cost of living raises for the prior 29 years. Lawmakers built upon their 2016 pension reform by restructuring the state's corrections officers' retirement plan. Underfunded by 47 percent and looking at $1.4 billion accumulated debt, long-term solvency of the plan loomed. The Libertarian think tank Reason Foundation whipped up support for the reforms. Their overzealous bill passed overwhelmingly, but was ruled unconstitutional because it went after everybody, retirees included, not just future hires. The reforms were promised to ensure the long-term solvency of the pension system while saving the state $500,000 to $1.5 billion over the next 30 years. Common sense tip: If ALEC, the American Legislative Exchange Council's for it, it can't be good.

In Illinois, a similar attempt to cut benefits to those already retired as well as future hires was thrown out by the courts. Writer Aaron Camp identified the culprits working to push a right-wing agenda on workers: The Florida-based leveraged-buyout pioneer John Childs, the private equity investor Sam Zell and Paul Singer, a prominent New York hedge fund manager, and Richard Uihlein, a conservative businessman from the Chicago suburbs. ALEC strikes again!

What caused the problem in the first place? The Economic Policy Institute, as usual, provides some keen insight. "In most cases where there is a genuine problem with the actuarial health of a public pension plan, the problem has nothing to do with accounting assumptions but is instead driven by the employer's failure to make required contributions in full."

Research often reveals the problem is not unrealistic expectations or overgenerous benefits, but politicians who want to spend more and tax less. A 2013 Center for Retirement Research analysis of 32 plans in 15 states, took into account benefit cuts and increased employee contributions, both of which reduced employer costs, as well as employer cost adjustments, found employer costs were almost half of what they were prior to "reform."

According to an Economic Policy Institute (EPI) report, layoffs and pay cuts will tend to inflate pension costs as a percent of payroll, giving the impression that pension costs are a growing burden on taxpayers, making reform that much more attractive.

As usual, in the interest of protecting the taxpayer from looming public pension liabilities, Big Business has sold the public an intentionally inaccurate accounting of all the variables needed to make an informed decision about what's at stake for all parties.

Chapter 14

Unions as Appeasement?

"It is now beyond partisan controversy that it is a fundamental individual right of a worker to associate himself with other workers and to bargain collectively with his employer." FDR, Address at San Diego Exposition, October 2, 1935

The wealthy in the 30s were very concerned that the nation's working class was seriously flirting with socialism and communism. Why did Franklin Delano Roosevelt, one of the ruling class, decide to support unions? Was he forced into appeasing the masses because of a perceived threat to capitalism and thus democracy or did FDR rise above his station in life to champion the common man?

Despite the stock market crash of 1929 and the ensuing Depression, Socialism as a movement seemed to be on the decline in America when Roosevelt was first elected in 1932. An attempt to build an American Labor Party in an alliance with the Socialist Labor Party was racked with infighting. Many of the jailed Socialist objectors to World War I, some of the members and former members of the Industrial Workers of the World, an umbrella union organization, emerged from 20-year prison sentences with signed agreements that ended their rabble-rousing days and any interest in stirring the pot politically.

It was ironic, then, that during the election of 1936 when FDR ran for his second term, Republicans painted him as moving the country toward "creeping Socialism." Citing the New Deal and the administration's robust attempt to get people back to work, they warned that government involvement in production was overreaching and intrusive and "robbed men of their desire to succeed." Labeling Roosevelt as a Socialist bothered both Roosevelt and former Socialist Party presidential candidate Eugene Debs' true socialist successor, Norman Thomas. Both Roosevelt and Thomas agreed that FDR was no socialist. The American people didn't buy the hype; FDR was reelected in a landslide.

In his first run for the Presidency, before he was elected in 1932, the affable, intelligent Roosevelt appealed to almost everybody, though he had detractors on both sides of the political spectrum. Independently wealthy, Roosevelt may have been the only one who could claim not to be beholden to corporate benefactors, but he knew little or nothing about the struggles of the working class.

The early thirties was a time of great tumult; cries for justice came from all corners, voices that must have drawn FDR's attention. The Kingfish, Louisiana Governor and later U.S. Senator, Huey Long, called for a general redistribution of wealth with his "Share Our Wealth" program, echoing the cries of colleagues in the National Union for Social Justice. He had successfully shifted taxes from common folk to business in his state and made corporations nervous.

The National Union for Social Justice or "the Union," as it was later called, was started by Father Charles Coughlin, a Catholic priest with a radio following of 30 million. He had been an earlier supporter of FDR and the New Deal, but he thought the president was too cozy with the banks. Coughlin's accusation was that capitalists in America had made Socialist and Communist ideology too attractive to many Americans. Coughlin deplored both communism *and* capitalism, speaking out against both. He warned, "Let not the workingman be able to say that he is driven into the ranks of socialism by the inordinate and grasping greed of the manufacturer." He called for bank reform, tight reins on Wall Street, the nationalization of major industries and railroads, and protecting the rights of labor.

One of his followers in California, Dr. Francis Townsend, a retired doctor, promoted the idea of an old age pension as a way to keep the elderly from starving and free up jobs for young people. Unfortunately, the Union was not very organized, and Father Coughlin's rants turned virulently anti-Semitic. The Union died in 1938 and Coughlin was forced off the air by the Roosevelt administration in 1939.

But Roosevelt had heard the cries of Townsend and others like him: Social Security, that "old age pension," embraced by the good doctor, was among his list of reforms introduced in 1935. He also regularly listened to, and sought, his wife's viewpoint on issues of the day.

Eleanor Roosevelt was the true motivating factor in FDR's labor largesse. In 1921, FDR was diagnosed with polio and was meeting with a barrage of doctors to determine treatment. Unsure that his affliction would allow Franklin to continue to pursue his political ambitions, Eleanor searched for her own political identity by involving herself with a number of nonpartisan organizations – the League of Women Voters, the Consumers League, and others. In 1922 she joined the Women's Trade Union League, which devoted itself to better working conditions for women and encouraged them to be part of the labor movement. ER, as she was known, became an active member of the New York branch and grew close to outspoken leaders in the League, Margaret Dreier Robins, and Rose Schneiderman. Both women became mentors to Eleanor.

Margaret Robins was a labor leader's labor leader. In 1907, she was elected president of the WTUL and served 15 years as its leader. President Robins organized women into unions, taught women workers how to organize and take on leadership roles and advocated for legislation that would bring dignity and respect to women on the shop floor. She actively supported some well-publicized strikes of the era, including the 1910 International Ladies Garment Worker's strike that drew over 20,000 women to protest the deplorable conditions in sweatshops. In 1915, Illinois Governor Edward F. Dunne appointed her to the state's unemployment commission.

Rose Schneiderman, just two years older than Eleanor, had survived a tough childhood. Her father died when she was ten; she quit school and went to work to help support her family at the age of 13. She formed her first union, the Jewish Socialist United Cloth Hat and Cap Makers' Union, at the age of 21. Her autobiography, *All for One,* describes a life immersed in her relentless pursuit of fair wages, decent hours and safe working conditions for workers – especially those of women.

Schneiderman and ER hit it off; she became a regular guest at Eleanor's scrambled egg dinners with close, intimate friends. She taught ER about the challenges facing women workers, the trade union movement in general, and the confrontational nature of labor-management relations. According to Schneiderman's autobiography, despite a privileged upbringing, ER became "a born trade unionist."

By the mid-1920s, ER brought Franklin into their discussions and invited Schneiderman to the Roosevelt home at Hyde Park, New York, on a regular basis to share her ideas. These conversations helped influence FDR's viewpoint on labor issues and led to the strongest presidential support of workers in history. Though, according to Conrad Black's massive tome, *Franklin Delano Roosevelt: Champion of Freedom,* FDR was more enamored of workers than union leaders:

> In fact, Roosevelt had little use for most of the labor leaders, whom he thought irresponsible demagogues and leaders of mobs. He was well aware that someone had to defend the working population from the rapacities of the American businessman but he believed he could take better care of the workers without the labor leaders.

To show her dedication to the League's cause, ER chaired the WTUL finance committee and contributed her pay from her 1932-1933 radio broadcasts to the League's coffers. At every opportunity, she used her bully pulpit to promote WTUL in her newspaper and magazine columns and speeches. Schneiderman and Robins became ardent Roosevelt allies and, in turn, WTUL and the labor movement gained important access and a powerful voice in the formulation of labor policy in Washington.

From 1933 until the Supreme Court declared the National Recovery Administration unconstitutional in 1935, Rose Schneiderman served as labor's voice on the NRA's (National Recovery Act) advisory board, overseeing a fair distribution of wages and hours in work.

Created in 1933, FDR's first attempt at a National Labor Board came out of the New Deal legislation passed in his first 100 days. The National Industrial Recovery Act, overseen by the NRA, was a Congressional bill designed as "an Act to encourage national industrial recovery, to foster fair competition, and to provide for the construction of certain useful publics, and for other purposes." The Act was meant to revive business and the economy of the nation with some robust support from government and no small amount of oversight. Some in the Roosevelt administration believed that unfettered competition and greed had helped cause the Great Depression. They believed that government should play an activist role in supporting business through national planning, some limited regulation, support for fair trade practices, and help to establish the "democratization of the workplace," a set of legal parameters meant to standardize the work week, hours in a work day, and better working conditions.

Enter another strong female influence for FDR and US labor standards: Frances Perkins. She was a lady of means, though certainly not wealthy when she witnessed the fire and the bodies of women who had jumped to their deaths at the Triangle Shirtwaist Factory. The incident marked her for life and as David Brooks reveals in his book, *The Road to Character,* "Moral indignation set her on a different course." Already involved in a number of causes, she rolled up her sleeves and focused on justice by any means as executive secretary for the Committee on Safety of the City of New York. She served on the New York State Industrial Commission under Governor Al Smith, then as the state's first Commissioner of the New York State Department of Labor appointed by then-Governor Franklin Roosevelt. It was her work and successes as Commissioner that made her FDR's obvious choice for the very first Labor Secretary. Before taking the job in 1933, according to a Department of Labor historical document by Jonathan Grossman, "she told [FDR] that she would accept if she could advocate a law to put a floor under wages and a ceiling over hours of work and to abolish abuses of child labor."

Grossman writes that in the aftermath of New Deal legislation and with Perkins at the helm, "Employers signed more than 2.3 million agreements, covering 16.3 million employees. Signers agreed to a workweek between 35 and 40 hours and a minimum wage of $12 to $15 a week and undertook, with some exceptions, not to employ youths under 16 years of age. Employers who signed the agreement displayed a 'badge of honor,' a blue eagle over the motto 'We do our part.' Patriotic Americans were expected to buy only from 'Blue Eagle' businesses."

The Roosevelt-Perkins alliance also helped solidify prevailing wage for workers whose employers worked under federal government contracts.

Section 7(a) of the National Industrial Recovery Act was meant to provide protected collective bargaining rights for unions, but the ensuing organizing push by the labor movement was met with violence from business. Labor responded by shutting down businesses with strikes, sometimes meeting violence with violence. A legal battle over the treatment of kosher chickens in New York triggered a Supreme Court decision to declare the NRA as unconstitutional; the National Labor Board and its accompanying standards were doomed.

FDR turned to a proposed bill floated by New York Democratic Senator Robert F. Wagner. Wagner was a populist, well known and well loved by the working class. He led the New Deal Coalition, an association of labor unions, community activists and civic reform organizations, much akin to a coalition of many of the same cross-section of society he and colleague Al Smith had assembled in New York state several years before. For Wagner, the idea of building a strong middle class was a labor of love and a love of labor. His support and advocacy were integral in passing the National Labor Relations Act of 1935, the Social Security Act of 1935, and the Public Housing Act of 1937.

When the National Labor Relations Act, also known as the Wagner Act, was passed in 1935, it guaranteed workers the right to bargain collectively and established the Fair Labor Relations Board. The Fair Labor Standards Act of 1938, also called the Wages and Hours Bill, as first proposed, set a minimum wage of 25 cents an hour for most industrial workers and defined and promised a maximum workweek of 40 hours. Another Francis Perkins initiative, the Labor Secretary's FLSA was designed to hold up to challenges by the courts. FDR added the ban on child labor, realizing it would increase the bill's chances because child labor was a hot-button issue in Congress at the time. The Act aimed to correct the "inequality of bargaining power between employees who do not possess full freedom of association or actual liberty of contract and employers who are organized in the corporate or other forms of ownership association."

The Fair Labor Standards Act had started with higher hopes. The bill was introduced with the aim of 40 cents per hour minimum wage, a 40-hour work week, and a minimum working age of 16 except in specific industries outside of mining and manufacturing. The bill also proposed a five-member labor standards board authorized to set still higher wages and shorter hours after a review of some instances. An alliance of Republicans and southern conservative blue dog Democrats objected to the five-member board but agreed to a one- person administrator. After months of wrangling, the five-member board was back in, but with less enforcement power.

Organized labor fought over various facets of the bill. Grossman writes, "With victory within grasp, the bill became a battleground in the war raging between the AFL and the CIO. The AFL accused the Roosevelt Administration of favoring industrial over craft unions and opposed wage-board determination of labor standards for specific industries. Accordingly, the AFL fought for a substitute bill with a flat 40-cent-an-hour minimum wage and a maximum 40-hour week." Despite the crossfire, the bill was signed into law. To appease southern Democrats, the minimum wage had dropped to 25 cents per hour for the first year.

The NLRA gave this National Labor Relations Board more power and more direction: management was legally prohibited from coercing employees; employees had the right to form unions and to bargain in good faith. The NLRB was also granted the right to determine bargaining unit jurisdictions and had a duty to oversee union elections and to certify the election results as legally binding. Management had an obligation to bargain with a duly certified union.

Reaction to the NLRA was swift and vociferous. Big business screamed bloody murder and cried, "Job killer!" They were certain that the

National Labor Relations Act would destroy the American economy, but a look at the numbers shows just the opposite:

Union membership mushroomed from three million members in 1933 to over 14 million in 1945 (about 30 percent of the industrial workforce), wages grew by 65 percent, and unemployment dropped to less than one percent. This growth spurt of prosperity led to the largest baby boom in American history.

Historians argue over the impact of New Deal legislation; many attribute the demands of war as the real factor that created such strong job growth, but the policies adopted by the Roosevelt administration raised the bar for *quality* of life in the middle class.

Other historians believe Roosevelt's progressive policies increased the duration of the Great Depression. Thomas DiLorenzo, a professor of economics at Loyola College in Maryland, wrote, "It was capitalism that finally ended the Great Depression, not FDR's hair-brained cartel, wage-increasing, unionizing, and welfare state expanding policies." Other conservative voices echoed that sentiment in less vitriolic terms.

The NLRA and legislation that reformed Wall Street and the banks, the G.I. Bill that allowed access to higher learning for more of the working class, the Social Security safety net, unemployment insurance and jobs on WPA projects, together with the hardships Americans had endured through the Depression and World War II, gave rise to a new optimism for the future to the emerging and growing middle class. In this day of McJobs that keep workers living paycheck to paycheck and living below the poverty line, it's important to note that these collective actions strengthened the American economy and gave the American worker an opportunity for a better quality of life. The American Dream was unfolding.

ER was alive to see the pushback from business two years after FDR's death when Congress passed the Taft-Hartley Act also known as the Labor Management Relations Act of 1947. The law was meant to check the powers unions had earned under the National Labor Relations Act. Under the NLRA, business had restrictions put on their behavior codified as unfair labor practices (ULPs). Taft-Hartley listed practices that unions were now to adhere to: almost any strike for anything other than an impasse at the bargaining table was considered illegal. Taft-Hartley prohibited strikes over union jurisdiction, wildcat strikes, walk-outs in solidarity with other unions (also called secondary boycotts or sympathy strikes), political strikes, closed shops requiring union membership for a job, and political contributions by unions to federal political campaigns. Union officers were also required to sign affidavits declaring no affiliation with the Communist Party. Union shops, also called agency shops, where a new-hire had to join the union within a certain period of time, were heavily restricted, and states were allowed to pass so-called right-to-work laws that outlawed closed union shops. Taft-Hartley already outlawed closed shops; section 14b meant workers didn't have to pay dues or join the union and would still get the same salary and benefits and representation in grievances, as their union counterparts. These folks, in the pro-labor vernacular, were referred to as "freeloaders." Under Taft-Hartley, the executive branch of the federal government can head off or break a strike with a legal injunction if it looks like an impending or current strike imperils the national health or safety. (Courts have upheld that this clause includes national security.) In the 21st century, several cash-strapped states have enacted "right-to-work" to avoid covering pensions of retired state and municipal employees.

Mrs. Roosevelt, 74 and in poor health at the time of the bill's consideration, objected to Taft-Hartley, pointing out that these laws undermined the NLRA, effectively diminishing human rights in the workplace. When it passed, ER co-chaired the National Council for Industrial Peace to defeat the extension of the right-to-work laws to six more states, declaring that it was time "for all right-thinking citizens, from all walks of life, to join in protecting the nation's economy and the working man's union security from the predatory and misleading campaigns now being waged by the US Chamber of Commerce and the National Association of Manufacturers."

Morton Bahr, former president of the Communications Workers of America, was involved in the first major strike after Taft-Hartley was passed. "I worked for Mackay Radio and Telegraph Co, a subsidiary of

American Cable & Radio, which was owned by ITT. We were members of the American Communications Association, CIO (Congress of Industrial Organizations), and went on strike January 1, 1948. Several weeks into the strike, the company filed with the [National Labor Relations] Board a petition that the union no longer represented the workers. The Board ordered a new election. However, since the officers couldn't or wouldn't sign the non-communist affidavit required by Taft-Hartley, we were decertified. We stayed out several weeks longer and after 95 days went back to work without a union. That situation lasted until April 1954 when CWA won the election and I was elected president of the NY local."

The fight continues. The International Workers of the World, also known as the Wobblies, were suspicious of the vagaries of lawmaking and thought fights for wages, hours and working conditions should be waged at the bargaining table. As we see hard-won victories undermined in Washington and the courts, we might be tempted to agree with their view. But laws can also be challenged and changed for the better.

Congressman Brad Sherman of California has introduced a bill almost every year since his election that would strike section 14b of the Act and abolish right-to-work. Detroit, reeling from the loss of auto manufacturing jobs, pushed Michigan into jumping on the right-to-work bandwagon. Beloved United Auto Workers leader Walter Reuther must be rolling over in his grave.

Chapter 15 Soliders of Fortune 500s

Chapter 15

Soldiers of Fortune 500s

"Corporations have been enthroned and an era of corruption in high places will follow…" Abraham Lincoln, November 21, 1864

"If we really saw war, what war does to young minds and bodies, it would be impossible to embrace the myth of war. If we had to stand over the mangled corpses of schoolchildren killed in Afghanistan and listen to the wails of their parents, we would not be able to repeat clichés we use to justify war… We prefer to celebrate ourselves and our nation by imbibing the myths of glory, honor, patriotism, and heroism, words that in combat become empty and meaningless." Chris Hedges, *Death of the Liberal Class*

On January 27, 1973, my friends and I were thrilled when President Nixon announced the draft for the Vietnam War was over. There hasn't been a draft since because, at least in theory, we *all* serve, and the rich die standing next to poor immigrants. Almost 30 years later, in the aftermath of 9/11, I watched in horror as young men, waving American flags, beat their chests and screamed, "USA, USA!" pumped up on adrenaline and hell-bent on war. There was no time to grieve; it was time to kick some ass. Some of them would come back missing limbs or in a body bag or lie awake fighting off the nightmares. That's what made this war in the Mideast different. Media exposure would be limited and calculated. And these soldiers *wanted* to go.

We now have a 100 percent volunteer army. There were fears poor minorities, looking for a paid education or a path to citizenship, would sign up in droves or be targeted by recruiters. This new volunteer army is composed of young men and women who come from a variety of backgrounds. The common perception of the left paints a picture of a military of 90 percent people of color. NPR recently collected data about who serves. In a comparison between percentages of ethnicities serving and the general US population, the numbers proved fairly proportional:

Military		US Population
White:	66%	64%
Black:	16%	12%
Hispanic:	10%	16%
Asian:	3%	5%
Other:	5%	3%

Findings of the right-wing think tank Heritage Foundation indicate some preconceptions of the left may not be accurate:

- Members of America's volunteer Army are not enlisting because they have no other economic opportunities.
- America's soldiers are less likely than civilians to be high school dropouts.
- Contrary to conventional wisdom, minorities are not overrepresented in military service.

The commonly held belief that people of color were considered so much cannon fodder comes from their prominent place on the battlefield in Vietnam.

The population of California was seven percent Hispanic during the Vietnam War, but fifteen percent of that state's casualties in the war were Hispanic. The state of New Mexico was 27 percent Hispanic, but

Latinos counted for 69 percent of those drafted in the state. Further, one out of every two Hispanics who went to Vietnam served in a combat unit.

In their paper, *The Poverty Draft? Exploring the Role of Socioeconomic Status in U.S. Military Recruitment of Hispanic Students*, authors McGlynn and Monforti examined the pitch to young people of color by military recruiters.

> The education and career benefits of military service were prominent themes heard by potential enlistees… However, over 86% of respondents said military service was never portrayed to them as dangerous. As well, while not presented in a table, we also found that when questioned about the details of military service, it appears that recruiters do not convey much information about jobs and deployment. Less than half of all respondents with military contact said specific positions and job responsibilities within the military were discussed and about half responded that no explanation of the difference between combat and non-combat positions was given.

Charlie Harvey, age 60, joined the military in November 1974 and reported for duty May 9, 1975, when Vietnam was winding down. He enlisted, he said, to learn discipline and serve his country. "I probably wouldn't have made it to 40. I was hot-headed, had no direction," he said. He came from the wrong side of the tracks in a small southern Texas town, a wild problem child who saw a bleak future. "At 17 or 18 life is just starting. It's better to be in harm's way before you have a family, before you're established. Some go in for the right reasons: to travel, to get training or college education, some for the wrong reasons: to escape a bad relationship, to erase a criminal past, to become a citizen." The military life was not what he expected. "We were all brothers, divided up in social situations, but in combat, we were all the same."

The consensus: poor people are more likely to be targeted for recruitment. With fewer opportunities for higher education and few prospects for making a living wage, that demographic is more vulnerable to pitches for adventure and job training.

Enter the Puppet Masters

There was a time when soldiers were assigned KP duty when punishment might include peeling potatoes behind the mess hall. We've seen it in all the old movies. The new reality reveals that much of the "grunt work" is now performed by subcontractors like KBR and DynoCorp. The website DangerZoneJobs.com reports, "There are more than 300 larger companies offering jobs in Afghanistan and Iraq." These include electrical, construction, and the most controversial: security, but there are many, many other positions.

According to the website of US. News & World Report, the top five highest paid security firms in Iraq are:

1. Blackwater Worldwide (awarded $1.21 billion in contracts since 2003)
2. Aegis Defence Forces, Ltd. ($799 million since 2003)
3. DynoCorp International LLC ($691 million)
4. Triple Canopy Inc. ($529 million)
5. EOD Technology Inc. ($329 million)

Keep in mind these figures were published in December 2008, from the website of the Office of the Special Inspector General for Iraq Reconstruction (SIGIR). From 2003 to 2008, the US government had paid almost $3.4 billion to private security contractors!

According to an article entitled, "Twenty-First Century Fascism: Private Military Companies in Service to the Transnational Capitalist Class," located ubiquitously on the internet, the transnational capitalist class or TCC, representing thousands of millionaires and billionaires, the wealthiest top .0001 percent, control governments worldwide through trade agreements and military might.

Writers Peter Phillips, Ray McClintock, Melissa Carneiro, and Jacob Crabtree report:

> When the empire is slow to perform or faced with political resistance, private security firms and private military companies (PMC) increasingly fulfill the TCC's (Transnational Capitalist Class) demands for the protection of their assets. These protection services include personal security for TCC executives and their families, protection of safe residential and work zones, tactical military advisory and training of national police and armed forces, intelligence gathering on democracy movements and opposition groups, weapons acquisitions and weapon systems management, and strike forces for military actions and assassinations.

In her Master's thesis published at the American University at Cairo, Tori Aarseth has determined, "Privatization…reflects empowerment of the capitalist class at the expense of the working class in both the industrialized nations of the global north and third world countries in the south."

Private forces aren't concerned for the whole civilian population. They're hired to look after their corporate sponsors and their property.

Aarseth references a previous work on the subject that defines some of the roles private companies take on in war zones:

> Military Provider Firms are those closest to the tip of the spear, engaging in actual fighting and command of field units in battle. Sandline and Executive Outcomes are two examples. Military Consultant Firms engage in advising and training of military or police units, exemplified by MPRI, Vinnell, and Dyncorp. Military Support Firms provide "non-lethal aid and assistance" such as supply, logistics, and intelligence. Firms in this category include Brown & Root (now KBR) and SAIC.

In September 2007, 17 Iraqis were killed when guards who worked for Blackwater, (a security company founded by ex-Navy seal Erik Prince, brother of President Trump's Secretary of Education, Betsy De Vos), opened fire in Nisour Square, in Baghdad while protecting a convoy of US diplomats. The five Blackwater employees said they were fired upon first, but, according to a report from the Brookings Institution, "Iraqi police and witnesses report that the contractors opened fire first, shooting at a small car driven by a couple with their child that did not get out of the convoy's way as traffic slowed."

The company was involved in almost 200 shootings between 2005-2009, and this appeared to be the last straw for Iraq's government. The interior ministry revoked Blackwater's license after the shooting and threatened to prosecute the contractors involved and expel all its employees, but the US ignored the order and renewed the company's contract the following April. In 2007, the number of private military forces deployed in Iraq was 160,000, about the same amount and better paid than their armed forces counterparts, both on Uncle Sam's payroll. Since 2009, the ratio of contractors to troops in war zones has increased from 1 to 1 to about 3 to 1.

Peter Singer sums it up an article for the Brookings Institution, "The massive outsourcing of military operations has created a dependency on private firms like Blackwater that has given rise to dangerous vulnerabilities. Our dependency on military contractors shows all the signs of the last downward spirals of an addiction."

So, why is this a problem? Wouldn't we prefer to have someone else fight out battles and leave our soldiers out of harm's way?

These mercenaries work for approximately 147 corporations that control approximately 40 percent of the wealth within a global network of corporations. While we make the false assumption that we are maintaining our borders and sovereignty, these networks ignore them as they focus on foreign direct investment, cross-border mergers and acquisitions, overlapping boards of directors; joint ventures and strategic alliances of all sorts; appearing on stock exchanges trading partners' shares while increasing global outsourcing and subcontracting networks: Capitalism gone global.

Fifteen million people across the globe are part of the $200 billion a year private security industry. G4S, a British multinational security company, was founded in 2004 when an English company merged with a Danish business.

According to Project Censored:

> G4S is the largest PMC in the world with 625,000 employees spanning five continents in more than 120 countries. Nine of the largest money management firms in the world have holdings in G4S. Some of its more important contractors are the governments of the UK, the US, Israel, and Australia. In the private sector G4S has worked with corporations such as Chrysler, Apple, and Bank of America. In Nigeria, Chevron contracts with G4S for counter-insurgency operations including fast-response mercenaries. G4S undertakes similar operations in South Sudan and has provided surveillance equipment for checkpoints and prisons in Israel and security for Jewish settlements in Palestine.

Blackwater is still around, renamed Xe Services in 2009, renamed again in 2011 as Academi and, after an acquisition, became part of Constellis Holdings. Together with Triple Canopy, (employing over 5,000 Special Ops, Special Forces, Rangers, SEALs, and "select" law enforcement officers), they have contracts with the State Department and the CIA, but offer services to foreign governments, multinational corporations, and international organizations. Constellis has a collective force of 20,000 and is managed by an all male board of directors including John Ashcroft, the former attorney general and seven other members with backgrounds in Fortune 500 companies. Among the four member international advisory board is Jose A. Rodriguez, Jr., a 31-year veteran of the CIA and Zalmay Khalilzad, surprisingly a Muslim American, former US Ambassador to Afghanistan, Iraq, and the United Nations under George W. Bush. Another member is Jason Pinson, CEO of Ursus Holdings, LLC, whose portfolio of companies covers artificial intelligence, pharmaceuticals, nanotechnology infused armor systems and canine training and deployment. If all of this doesn't scare you, it should.

What does this proliferation of private military contractors (PMCs) mean for us? According to *Project Censored*:

The 99 percent of us without wealth and private police power face the looming threat of overt repression and complete loss of human rights and legal protections. There are signs: daily police killings (now close to a hundred per month in the US), warrantless electronic spying, mass incarceration, random traffic checkpoints, airport security/no-fly lists, and Homeland Security compilations of databases on suspected resisters, heightened insecurity and the specter of downward mobility. Far-right forces pursue militarism, a racist mobilization against scapegoats, and shifts from social welfare to social control states, bolstered by mystifying ideologies rooted in race/culture supremacy and an idealized past. Neo-fascist culture normalizes--even glamorizes--war, social violence, and domination.

According to *Time*, these are the companies profiting the most from war:

- General Dynamics. > Arms sales 2012: $20.9 billion. > Total sales 2012: $31.5 billion
- Raytheon. > Arms sales 2012: $22.5 billion. Total sales 2012: $24.4 billion
- BAE Systems. > Arms sales 2012: $26.9 billion. Total sales 2012: $28.3 billion
- Boeing. > Arm sales 2012: $27.6 billion. Total sales 2012: $81.7 billion
- Lockheed Martin. > Arms sales 2012: $36 billion. Total sales 2012: $47.2 billion

The War Hawks are winning. President Trump has signed an executive order authorizing $610 billion to upgrade the Armed Forces with new weapons, including the "modernization" of US nukes, and planes and ships.

Of course, beefing up our military reallocates funds spent on important research and the agencies that provide oversight on healthcare, education, the environment, housing, and transportation and much-needed repairs to our crumbling infrastructure.

Weapons manufacturers would insist they put Americans to work with high wages and benefits. Communities become dependent on these jobs as well as the military bases that house them and efforts to create a "peace dividend" are discarded before they're even considered. Both parties are guilty of what President Eisenhower warned us, "In the councils of government, we must guard against the acquisition of unwarranted influence, whether sought or unsought, by the military-industrial complex. The potential for the disastrous rise of misplaced power exists and will persist."

From *Truthout* website March 22, 2012:

In an article entitled, *Lockheed: The Ultimate Pay-to-Play Contractor* by Dina Rosor, Lockheed Martin's close ties to every end of the supply chain position it for maximum profit.

James Courter, a former lobbyist for Lockheed, founded the nonprofit Lexington Institute, a think tank that endorses defense contractors and believes in a strong military and defends those funds as necessary. The Lexington Institute receives funding from Pentagon defense contractors. Loren Thompson, the chief operating officer for the Institute, is also CEO of Source Associates, a for-profit that advises defense contractors. His opinion pieces for AOL Defense are also posted on the Lexington Institute website.

2012 Profits by Corporation:

Boeing:	$ 3.9 billion
Lockheed Martin:	$ 2.7 billion
BAE Systems:	$ 2.6 billion
Raytheon:	$ 1.9 billion
General Dynamics:	$332 million
Total	$114.3 billion

These are the latest figures available online (2012). The wars and military spending have continued unabated for the last six years and, with President Trump's insistence, have expanded.

Drones

The use of drones in the battlefield is well documented. The rapid growth in the use of drones domestically has stymied local law enforcement and emboldened them. The FAA has claimed authority to regulate all air space and has stated that as long as privately operated drones do not harm or endanger individuals and are not used for nefarious or criminal uses, they can legally fly and hover above all private property. However, there are no current federal laws that specifically address this issue; non-commercial drones are bound by FAA guidelines, but are subject to local and state statutes. As of December 2015, the FAA requires that all drones weighing between .55 and 55 pounds be registered by their owners, and that a paper or electronic certificate be in the operator's possession when flying the drone. Failure to attain a license ($15 for a minimum 3-year commitment for hobbyists) can result in civil sanctions of up to $27,500 and/or criminal penalties including imprisonment for up to three years and/or a fine of up to $250,000. In California, an attempt to make flying a drone less than 350 feet above private property without consent criminal trespass was vetoed by Governor Jerry Brown, a clear win by paparazzi. However, they and others were tripped up by *Civil Code Section 1708.8*, which prohibits the use of drones to capture video and/or a sound recording of another person without their consent (invasion of privacy). Violators are liable for up to three times the amount of damages related to the violation, and a civil fine of between $5,000 and $50,000. Thirty states are apparently still studying the issue.

Law enforcement has always been eager to put military products and programs to use in the community. Cops and border patrols around the country have used drones to collect evidence and conduct surveillance.

Agencies can also use drones, sometimes referred to as Unmanned Aerial Vehicles (UAVs), to photograph traffic crash scenes, monitor jails and prisons, track prison escapees, control crowds, and more. In 2015, the Illinois State Police began using drones to monitor accidents, reporting overhead surveillance helps them get traffic moving again. In March 2016, a drone helped an Ohio police department track down an inmate forty minutes after he escaped. The Fremont Police Department plans to continue using drones to track suspects, find missing people, and map crime scenes.

In a 2011 report from the ACLU, the implications of regular drone deployment are ominous:

> "What would be the effect on our public spaces, and our society as a whole, if everyone felt the keen eye of the government on their backs whenever they ventured outdoors?"

> "Video surveillance is susceptible to individual abuse, including voyeurism." They cited a case of an NYPD helicopter that filmed a copulating couple on a rooftop using night vision.

> Profiling: "In Great Britain, camera operators have been found to focus disproportionately on people of color."

> Stifling the right of peaceful assembly: "...We are seeing an upsurge in spying against peaceful political protesters across America."

> "Drones are part of a trend toward automated law enforcement, in which cameras and other technologies are used to mete out justice with little or no human intervention."

All of these concerns should give us pause and a reason to proceed cautiously. Criminal justice enters a gray area between community safety and our right to privacy.

The militarization of local police

In the United States, the 1033 Program legally requires the Department of Defense to make various items of equipment available to local law enforcement.

The previously named 1208 program stemmed from the failed War on Drugs when, in 1990, the DOD was authorized by Congress to pass along military gear to federal and state agencies specifically "for use in counter-drug activities." In 1996, President Clinton expanded the purview of the program to include counter-terrorism efforts.

Boys with their toys, kids in a candy store. Pick your analogy; the race was on among law enforcement agencies to get the biggest, baddest weaponry available.

The Department of Defense transferred $5.1 billion in military hardware, most of it new, into local law enforcement agencies from 1997 until 2014. Many of the items requested were cost prohibitive for the budgets of smaller police departments. The most common article received from the 1033 program was ammunition, cold weather clothing, sandbags, medical supplies, sleeping bags, flashlights, and electrical wiring. The agency also offered tactical and armored vehicles, weapons, including grenade launchers, watercraft, and aircraft to help local law enforcement fight the drug war and flush out terrorists.

As of September 2014 more than twenty school districts received military-grade equipment through the program. The San Diego school district came under fire for purchasing a military surplus vehicle. The Los Angeles Unified School Police Department acquired 61 assault rifles, three grenade launchers, and a Mine Resistant Ambush Protected vehicle (MRAP). Ten School Police Departments in Texas received 25 automatic pistols, 64 M16 assault rifles, 18 M14 assault rifles, 15 vehicles, and tactical vests through the 1033 program.

The Department of Defense has provided a variety of military and police equipment to both private and public universities across the country. Institutions of higher education that participated in the program included local community colleges, state universities, and Ivy League university Yale. Equipment allocated has ranged from gauze, trousers, and other basic supplies, to armored vehicles, grenade launchers, and M-16 rifles.

In 2013, Ohio State University, the school where four students were gunned down by National Guard troops in 1970, received an MRAP vehicle equipped with a machine gun turret, becoming the first campus in the U.S. to incorporate military-grade equipment into the arsenal of the campus police department. Florida State University acquired a Humvee, Central Washington University also received an armored truck through the program, but the most popular military equipment acquired by colleges and universities through the 1033 program is the M-16. Campus police at the Arizona State University obtained 70 M-16's and Florida International University, and the University of Maryland received 50 each. Many college and university representatives pointed to the Virginia Tech shooting as reason for concern and increased militarization of campus police departments.

Colleges and universities that received military equipment cited cost savings as the primary motivation for enrolling in the 1003 program. And they were getting a pretty sweet deal. Participating campuses paid only for delivery and maintenance of their acquired military supplies. The University of Louisiana at Monroe paid only $507.43 for about 12 M-16 rifles.

In January 2015, in the wake of unrest in Ferguson, Missouri, a White House executive order created the "Task Force on 21st Century Policing." The working group released a 116-page document of recommendations regarding the use of military-grade equipment. They recommended two lists: One list identified "prohibited equipment" that could no longer be distributed to police and the other, "controlled equipment," could only be provided for a demonstrated need.

The "prohibited equipment" tracked armored vehicles, weaponized aircraft, vessels and vehicles of any kind, bayonets, grenade launchers, firearms and ammunition of .50-caliber or higher and some camouflage uniforms. The "controlled equipment" included tactical and armored vehicles, aircraft, Unmanned Aerial Vehicles (drones), explosives, specialized firearms, and riot equipment, would be transferred only if local police provide additional certification and assurances that the gear would be used responsibly. In 2016, the government began recalling surplus gear that had been placed on the prohibited equipment list.

President Trump issued an executive order on August 28, 2017, that rescinded the previous bans. Attorney General Jeff Sessions justified the change to the Fraternal Order of Police on the same day, citing "an increase in violent crime, a rise in vicious gangs, an opioid epidemic, threats from terrorism, combined with a culture in which family and discipline seem to be eroding further and a disturbing respect for the rule of law." The specter of terrorism was raised again, but the original justification for the program, the War on Drugs, was not included in the AG's address.

At about the same time as President Obama was writing his executive order to curtail the militarization of police, Senator Paul Rand wrote about the issue for *Time:*

> When you couple this militarization of law enforcement with an erosion of civil liberties and due process that allows the police to become judge and jury—national security letters, no-knock searches, broad general warrants, pre-conviction forfeiture—we begin to have a very serious problem on our hands.

Although cities and campuses across the nation that have been involved in the 1003 program and probably will be again, vow that these weapons and equipment will only be used in a campus shooting or other terrorist scenario, the temptation to use them to put down protests may prove to be more than they can resist. As in the Kent State Massacre, innocent bystanders may be hurt or killed. At the very least, our civil rights may be threatened.

Chapter 16

Third World Incursion: Bring Back Our Jobs!

"Our nation was built by pioneers – pioneers who accepted untold risks in pursuit of freedom, not by pioneers seeking offshore profits at the expense of American workers here at home." Ted Strickland

"Like a lot of business owners out there, I don't desire to face the continual flogging from government regulators who push burdensome and confusing state tax and employment laws on the business. It creates an unnecessary risk when, as an owner, I can just take it offshore." Brandon Webb

In the race for governor in Wisconsin in 2014, the issue of outsourcing created heat in both camps. Gov. Scott Walker took his Democratic challenger to task because Mary Burke's family had outsourced bicycle production for their company, Trek Bicycles, to China. Burke responded by pointing to Walker's new job creation agency that incentivized companies with big tax breaks only to see them later outsource jobs.

There's some quibbling over the terms "outsourcing" versus "offshoring" as though the minor difference between them makes a difference to the worker who lost his job. *Somebody* is doing the work that he used to do. Often the two are used interchangeably because that particular job was outsourced offshore. If a company moves work overseas but hires under the company banner, the work has been offshored, but not outsourced.

We had some of both at SBC. As I mentioned in a previous chapter, in 2002, I walked in as a new union president of the Communications Workers of America, to the largest layoff in the company's history, at least under SBC. SBC, the saying went, stood for Surplussed by Christmas, the term and excuse the company used for the layoff: too many "surplus" people. My local lost 20 percent of our membership in the last months of 2002. Those jobs either disappeared or were consolidated into other, right to work, low wage states like Texas. Many of our members downgraded their title, pay, and ambitions. The jobs they might have transitioned to were no longer there. Call center operations were consolidated and much of the IT work, the so-called jobs of the future, was outsourced *and* offshored to India and the Philippines.

In negotiations in 2004, we were told that the company had agreed to bring call center jobs home. Now there's an effort to make the request a demand. According to the communications Workers of America:

Congress can pass H.R.1300 and S.515, common sense legislation that

> Requires that U.S. callers be told the location of the call center to which they are speaking.
- Offers callers the opportunity to be connected to a U.S.-based call center.
- Makes U.S. companies who offshore their call center jobs ineligible for certain federal grants and taxpayer-funded loans.

Senate Republicans filibustered the Bring Jobs Home Act in 2014, killing the legislation on a procedural vote. U.S. Senator Sheldon Whitehouse (D-RI), a cosponsor of the bill, released the statement below regarding the failed vote:

> Today Senate Republicans voted to preserve a tax loophole that rewards companies for sending jobs overseas and declined to support companies that bring jobs back to America. That might make their big business allies in the Chamber of Commerce happy, but it's not going to help American workers. I fought for the Bring Jobs Home Act because tax policy should encourage job creation in America, not overseas. Rhode Island taxpayers shouldn't be footing the bill to send jobs to other countries. I'm disappointed that my Republican colleagues don't agree.

At present companies are allowed to deduct the expenses of moving operations to other countries. The Bring Jobs Home Act would have ended that loophole and would have also offered companies a tax credit equal to 20 percent of the cost of bringing jobs back to America.

President Trump's threats to rewrite NAFTA and the immense tax cuts offered to big business have created an atmosphere of appeasement with an announcement from Fiat Chrysler that they are moving production of their Ram pickups from Mexico to Michigan. Other manufacturers are said to be considering a move "home."

The competitive advantage companies look for when establishing an office or a factory overseas is not just about lower wages in a third world country. The costs of operations may also weigh into the decision to offshore. Items such as power, rent, lax health and safety and environmental laws may offset the added costs with shipping.

Most American companies say they offshore because there's a shortage of skilled domestic employees and not because it's cheaper. Show of hands: who believes this? Nevertheless, we will examine the impact of work visas for this country.

Most Popular Companies That Outsource Jobs

Writer Jenny Jordan's article of the same name seemed to be an innocuous listing of major corporations who take some of their work elsewhere, (Microsoft, 3M, Google), but suddenly played apologist for corporate giant, AT&T. "As the second largest mobile service provider in the country, AT&T requires so much manpower that they *have no choice* (my emphasis) but to outsource to other countries. The kinds of positions they outsource tend to be the typical jobs normally associated with call center work, such as tech support, customer assistance, and billing." Of course, she used the term "outsource" without ever offering the term "offshoring."

Economists use something resembling math when they study the impact of market forces on sectors of the nation. Sometimes the profound and sometimes the obvious are buried in pie charts, graphs, tables, complicated formulas, and footnotes. In a paper in the Chicago Journals, authors Daron Acemoglu, David Autor, David Dorn, Gordon H. Hanson, and Brendan Price pin significant employment losses on the US decision to confer Most Favored Nation status on China by Bill Clinton in 1998. "The value of annual US goods imports from China increased by a staggering 1,156 percent from 1991 to 2007. Our central estimates suggest job losses from rising Chinese import competition over 1999–2011 in the range of 2.0–2.4 million."

Three of the same authors suggest in another paper titled, *The China Syndrome: Local Labor Market Effects of Import Competition in the United States*, that China's export growth is driven by their changing policies internally and by the rest of the world. "China's export growth ... appears to be strongly related to factors that are specific to China ... The growth of Chinese exports is largely the result of reform-induced changes within China: rising productivity, greater investment in labor-intensive export sectors, and a lowering of trade barriers," the paper stated.

The demand for imports from Mexico and Central America are directly related to US demand for products that were outsourced to the region in the first place and are now blowing back across the border to buyers in the US.

A number of studies have examined the effects of imports from a specific geographic origin on domestic labor markets. Imports from low-wage countries can undercut prices and may doom US plants in the same product category.

Geoffrey James of MoneyWatch has listed the top 10 reasons offshoring is bad for business:

- REASON #1: You can lose control of your intellectual property.
- REASON #2: It can result in low quality, brand-damaging products.
- REASON #3: You may be supporting slave labor and child labor.
- REASON #4: You might create massive environmental degradation
- REASON #5: You may not get access to local markets.
- REASON #6: You may be empowering political thugs.
- REASON #7: It makes you vulnerable to energy spikes.
- REASON #8: Your product might end up killing people.
- REASON #9: You're helping to destroy your own country.
- REASON #10: Everyone is doing it.

The Duh Factor

Offshoring to low-wage countries is associated with reductions in US employment in the same industry.

Relief

The U.S. Department of Labor has implemented Trade Adjustment Assistance (TAA) since 1962 and little used until it was expanded it in 1974 to include training and reemployment. Ronald Reagan gutted the program in 1981, but in 2002, the Trade Adjustment Assistance Reform Act (TAARA for those in Congress) expanded the original program and added the trade adjustment program defined in the North American Free Trade Agreement (NAFTA). As always, Congress modified the program several times in the last 16 years.

According to the TAA website, they are:

TRANSITIONING WORKERS TO TOMORROW'S CAREERS

The TAA Program seeks to provide adversely affected workers with opportunities to obtain the skills, credentials, resources, and support necessary to (re)build skills for future jobs. The TAA Program invests $450 million in training funds annually to serve more workers impacted by foreign trade and gets those eligible for TAA ready to work by providing them with tailored training for new skills that create pathways to well-paying middle-class jobs.

TAA Helps

- Up to two years of tuition-free training
- Wage supplements for older workers
- Job Search allowances
- Income support while in training
- Health Coverage Tax Credit
- Relocation allowances

According to the agency, in FY 2016, an estimated 126,844 workers were negatively affected by trade and became eligible for TAA benefits and services. The cause listed for the vast majority of these TAA recipients was "Shift in Production to a Foreign Country." The agency approved 1,192 petitions filed on behalf of affected workers, 673 of those came from the manufacturing sector, (about 83,664 workers). Of the almost 127,000 workers impacted nationwide, 45,814 (36 percent) received assistance. Over 53 percent (approximately 24,282) of those participants received training during the year, (21,532 who didn't), and over 93 percent of those who completed training received a credential. Almost 76 percent of TAA participants were hired within six months of completing the program. For those who had earned some credential in the program, 77 percent found employment within six months with over 79 percent of everybody who got jobs changing industry sectors. Clearly, they perceived their previous employment as a job in a dying or rapidly changing industry and with their new skills went looking for a more secure future.

TAA participants were predominately male (67 percent) and white (70 percent) 50 years old with a high school diploma, GED or less.

What happened to the other 81,180 (64 percent), who had jobs before free trade ruined their livelihoods and drove a truck through their dreams? Were they offered training and turned it down? Were they eligible to retire or did they give up? Another 60,871 workers had petitioned for TAA consideration and had been denied. What happened to them? Of the recipients of new skills and certifications, what kind of jobs did they land? How did their pay compare to their previous job?

The agency reported that over four thousand retrained workers ended up in manufacturing, most of them probably for the second time though the work might be different. Other "popular" occupations included such broad categories as administrative support and waste management and remedial services and health care and social assistance. Whether displaced workers went through training or not, their wages after their job loss were about 80 percent of what they had been before.

A contractor contacted me for a county training and employment program about nine months after I was laid off by AT&T in 2011. They said I was eligible and offered me a menu of training choices. By the time I chose one, the list had drastically dwindled. I ended up being pushed into classes in building databases, something for which I had little interest and even less aptitude. I received two certifications and would have achieved others, but I felt hustled for my training dollars and shrugged off any further "assistance."

The TAA program reported spending $391.45 million in FY2016. The top five recipient states were Texas at $25.3 million, Pennsylvania ($22 million), New York ($12.4 million), Minnesota (just shy of $12 million) and Michigan ($11.7 million).

Coming to America

My union, the National Writers Union, UAW Local 1981, writes letters for lawyers so their candidates may receive an H-1B visa. My initial reaction when we first considered helping foreign workers attain a visa was adamant opposition. "We've got people in this country who can do this work," I said.

The Immigration Act of 1990 created the H-1B program, a program that helps American employers hire foreign workers with specialized skills that they claim they can't find in the United States. By law, employers promised to pay visa workers the area's prevailing wage for their position to diminish the incentive to hire them as cheap replacements for the current workforce.

65,000 H-1B visas are up for grabs in a lottery system every year. More than 40,500 companies sponsored workers for H-1B visas in fiscal 2017. A total of 345,262 H-1B petitions were approved in fiscal 2016, including 230,759 extension requests, and the applications continue to grow each year.

The rules are simple: The visa is good for three years with renewals and extensions possible. The incoming worker must have at least a Bachelor's degree. Employers must pay a minimum of $60,000 a year. Employers must confirm that the wages and working conditions of American workers will not be disadvantaged by the hiring of an H-1B worker.

Who is profiting from these highly skilled workers? The Migration Policy Institute, an independent, nonpartisan, nonprofit think tank in Washington, DC, has found:

- Almost one-third of all approved H-1B petitions in fiscal 2017 went to just 20 companies, even as 40,645 firms were approved to sponsor H-1B visas that year. The top employers are either foreign consulting firms, some accused of using the visa to outsource U.S. jobs, or U.S. high-tech giants such as Amazon, Apple, and Google.
- Among the top 20 firms, those with the highest share of H-1Bs pay less and employ fewer workers with advanced degrees, compared to companies that are less dependent on an H-1B workforce. Workers at H-1B dependent employers in the top 20 earned an average $82,788 in fiscal 2017, as compared to $110,511 for H-1B workers in top firms that are not dependent.

And just 27 percent of H-1B workers in the dependent firms had a Master's degree or higher, as compared to 55 percent working for employers who are not H-1B dependent.
- About 71,000 spouses of H-1B visa holders have received work authorization under a 2015 policy that the Trump administration has signaled it plans to end.
- The share of H-1B workers in computer-related occupations has risen from an average of 47 percent between fiscal 2000-2009 to a high of 69 percent in fiscal 2016.

Walt Disney World fired more than 200 IT workers in 2015 and hired an outsourcing company to replace them with workers on H-1B visas, a clear violation of the intent of the program. Southern California Edison, California's largest utility company based in the Los Angeles area, laid off more than 400 IT workers, some of whom trained their replacements, Indian workers with H-1B visas. And using the same outsourcing company that worked so well for Disney, the University of California, San Francisco, signed a $50 million contract to lay off 80 IT workers and outsource much of their work to India. The school claims it will save $30 million in five years, but the deal cost UCSF $50 million.

Once again, this is an example of corporate exploitation and a law that was meant to supplement the American workforce rather than supplant them. Some companies are creating a pool of cheap labor, paying H-1B workers lower salaries than they would pay Americans to do the same job. American companies are using the system to ship jobs overseas or importing workers who are overjoyed to have a job in the Land of Plenty even if they have to work for less than their American counterparts.

The law has been amended to deal with concerns that companies are exploiting the system to undermine American workers. Under the amended law, companies who use more than 15 percent of their workforce with H-1B workers will raise a red flag when applying for additional visas. These companies will have to avow that their H-1B workers won't replace American employees at their own company, or be used as to replace employees at firms that the company had contracts with.

There's some additional job security for American workers, but there's an exemption in the "fine print" in the new law that turns previous rules on their head. H-1B dependent companies can ignore the requirements for protecting American jobs if they hire a foreign worker at the same $60k a year minimum but with a master's degree.

According to the Economic Policy Institute:

> The Essential Worker Immigration Coalition (EWIC)—a lobbying group representing the interests of employers—claims that it is "concerned with the shortage of *both semi-skilled and unskilled* ('essential worker') labor" and thus "supports policies that facilitate the employment of essential workers by U.S. companies that are unable to find American workers."

The H-2B visa program allows employers to hire *both semi-skilled and unskilled* foreign workers to come temporarily to the **United States** and perform temporary nonagricultural services or labor on a one-time, seasonal, peak load or intermittent basis. The office of US Citizenship and Immigration Services is awarding the H-2B visa to 66,000 foreign workers biannually for fiscal year 2018.

President Trump ordered a review of the H-1B and other visa programs shortly after his election in 2016. In April 2017, he issued a "Buy American, Hire American" executive order, putting matters into motion that would capitalize on that theme. Interestingly, the first lady can thank the H-1B visa for allowing her to stay in the United States with her highly desirable, technical skills as a model.

The United States Citizen and Immigration Services, the federal agency that approves visa petitions, was directed to tighten its oversight. Last year, the agency issued 45 percent more challenges or requests for more evidence, slowing the processing of visas, and creating an uptick in denials.

Agency fraud teams began conducting surprise visits where large numbers of H-1B workers are employed. In a policy memo, the agency is also expanding its assessment of H1-B workers at third-party worksites, asking about the nature of the work, wages, and why a foreigner is required.

The motive behind the rules is suspect. Is it xenophobia? On the campaign trail, he had said all the right things about protecting American jobs, but reality was proving that he was pushing issues from a business point of view: removing roadblocks like health and safety and environmental regulations, and putting millionaires and billionaires on his cabinet to chip away at agencies and laws that form the safety net for workers, the disabled and the poor. His vocal disdain for NAFTA and the Trans-Pacific Partnership got him elected.

Some of the president's business allies have reacted in alarm; they thought they would have carte blanche, ruling the marketplace with an iron hand with his blessings and, more importantly, his support. Over and over again, he proves he has no understanding of the consequences of his actions. His naiveté has enhanced his gullibility, but occasionally he accidentally saves American jobs and jeopardizes his connections with business and the Republican Party. He may be holding business' fevered pitch for more cheap labor in check.

Let's take a look at the roles of the bank and Wall Street in the fleecing of America.

Chapter 17

Bankers, Stockbrokers and Money

"It is well enough that the people of this nation do not understand our banking and monetary system, for if they did, I believe, there would be a revolution before tomorrow morning." Henry Ford

"A business that makes nothing but money is a poor kind of business." Henry Ford

"The liberty of a democracy is not safe if the people tolerate the growth of private power to a point where it becomes stronger than their democratic state itself. That, in its essence, is fascism." FDR

There are at least three theories that try to explain why the wealthy and corporations have an undue influence on politics. According to Thomas Ferguson in his book *Golden Rule: the Investment Theory of Party Competition and the Logic of Money-driven Political Systems*, who credits the insights of **investment theory** to Anthony Downs who presented the concept in his 1957 work, *An Economic Theory of Democracy*. One of the reasons corporations can influence politics, both authors state, is the cost of much of the politically relevant information we all need that comes naturally to businesses in the course of their daily operations.

An example might include international banks whose business contacts constitute "a first-rate foreign policy network."

Economies of scale -- the larger the corporation, the lower the cost -- give businesses an advantage over ordinary citizens. For example, large investors and corporations routinely consult with lawyers, public relations advisors, lobbyists, and political consultants before acting, experts that ordinary citizens, unions and non-profits couldn't afford.

Although the Investment Theory recognizes the importance of financial contributions to political parties, direct cash contributions "are probably not the most important way in which truly top business figures act politically." Investors are also likely to act as sources of contacts, fundraisers, and as sources of legitimation for candidates, particularly through endorsements in the media. Contrary to commonly held beliefs, elections aren't always won by the party or candidate that spends the most money. Instead, those funds can be used to acquire information and other essential resources to win, but Ferguson says it's not just about the money.

Voter Realignment Theory, on the other hand, has proposed since 1955 that parties and policymaking change in swift, dramatic shifts. Indeed, in 2016 voters expressed a desire for iconoclasts Bernie Sanders and Donald Trump, both candidates that promoted bold, innovative action. The *Washington Post* reported the day after the 2016 election that 194 of the 207 counties that voted for Barack Obama in either 2008 and 2012 had shifted to Trump. Those who had supported Obama in both elections still gave Trump 209 of 676. 331 counties voted for Bush in 2004 than voted for Obama in 2008. The jury is still out on whether these results indicate a realignment. Those who announced a realignment in 2008 were disappointed by results in 2012 when Obama won only 22% of counties nationwide. Those who had predicted a realignment in 2008 were apoplectic with 2016 results.

I can point to 1932 when FDR was elected and 1981 with the election of Ronald Reagan as pivotal moments in economic policy and political realignment.

The 1929 **Median Voter Theorem** observes that one issue can make the difference in an election and that the voter in the middle has all the power. That's why primary campaigns, all fire and brimstone and very partisan in their pitch, suddenly move to the middle and mainstream their rhetoric on the way to the general election.

Trump was elected, in significant part, to campaign promises to the working class: he would renegotiate NAFTA, save jobs and remove other roadblocks to American business. Political writer Tom Frank said that Trump was swept into the Oval Office on a wave of fake populism. The first two years of his first term indicate that assessment was accurate.

In 2008, facing a cataclysm in the housing market that swept through the suburbs, overturning mortgages and the fortunes of many homeowners in the subprime debacle, Obama turned, inexplicably to many, to the culprits of the crises for a way out. Former supporters were disenchanted with Obama's message of change and hope when they saw Larry Summers and Tim Geithner, fresh from Wall Street, presented as our saviors.

The banks were, and still are, a big part of the problem, but Wall Street shares the blame for careless disregard for common people's money. In the last several years, attempts have been made to put Social Security funds at risk by putting those funds into the hands of stockbrokers, a move that has been spun to convince us that we can decide better than the government how that money should be invested.

I firmly believe in the common sense of the American people, but I think we all realize that some of us are clueless about the stock market; some of us think we know the market. Then there are those who are willing to let all our money ride on some get rich quick scheme. And, of course, there's a small percentage of us who would invest wisely and frugally and have more than enough money to ride into the sunset and even leave some for the kids.

> "There are known knowns. These are things we know that we know. There are known unknowns. That is to say, there

are things that we know we don't know. But there are also unknown unknowns. There are things we don't know we don't know." - Donald Rumsfeld

P.T. Barnum said it best: "There's a sucker born every minute and two to take him." Nowhere is that more evident than in the financial sector. As President Obama bluntly stated to members of the American Association of Retired Persons (AARP) about retirement investing, "There are a lot of very fine financial advisers out there, but there are also financial advisers who receive backdoor payments or hidden fees for steering people into bad retirement investments that have high fees and low returns."

Why is that?

"Right now, there are no uniform rules of the road that require retirement advisers to act in the best interests of their clients, and that's hurting millions of working and middle-class families," said the President.

His appearance before the members of AARP with Senator Elizabeth Warren of Massachusetts was meant to send a strong message that, despite the fact he has been a friend of Wall Street for the previous seven years, he now was going to do something about the fleecing of the American public.

Unfortunately, while I admire this president's rhetoric, his actions sent an entirely different message. Beginning with his appointments right after he was elected, Obama brought on Larry Summers, etc. and other former Wall Street players. Of course, we had a scary recession in 2008, and it looks like the president was convinced that if Wall Street and the banks caused it, then they were the ones who could fix it.

To date, no one has gone to jail over the sale of toxic assets, except in Iceland, where 29 bankers were sentenced up to five years for market manipulation and breach of fiduciary duties. I didn't understand the term "toxic asset" at the time and the passage of years hasn't cleared it up much for working folks. What we do know: From about 2005 to 2008 houses were being sold willy-nilly to folks who couldn't possibly cover the nut over time. Realtors claim they were pressured to get more Americans into homes. Adjustable Rate Mortgages lost value after the housing bubble burst. Houses were declared "underwater" because they weren't worth the mortgage payment anymore. Homeowners bailed and walked away.

Some of us knew the bubble couldn't last. Back in 2006, I asked on the NPR Motley Fool investment program when the housing bubble would burst. The Fools didn't have an answer. Not that I was in the market as a buyer or seller; a relationship had gone south; when we sold our house that was, foolishly, in her name only, my investment disappeared with her. I only asked the question of the Fools to see if I would ever be able to afford a house again in my lifetime.

By the time we were ready to buy in 2009, realtors and banks were no longer make deals that were too good to be true.

Finding a house to buy in the first place was an ordeal. Many of the homes in our $200,000 - $300,000 range were what we referred to as "clown" houses where the tenants or owners had kept building onto the original structure to accommodate expanding families and/or friends and cousins new to the country that just needed a room. I know that $200k is a lot to pay for a house just about anywhere other than LA or New York. Here in LA, it ain't much.

When my new girlfriend and I found a house we liked and made an offer, we invariably found that a house-flipper was offering cash. They would buy the house, fix all the bugs, and put it back on the market for a dandy profit. How could we with our 10 percent down ever hope to compete with that?

Against the advice of our realtor, she made a call to the owner. "I'm a single parent and I'm trying to find a home for us," she tearfully told him. He understood; he had a daughter he was trying to provide for.

"If it's in my power," he promised her. "You'll get the house."

The housing market continues to be a seller's market. Though they're not as strict as they were when we bought our place five years ago, the banks are still making the loan process agonizing. Thinking back on our short-sale purchase, I realize our home was one of those toxic assets.

Owing more than the house was worth, the owner and the bank lost money on the transaction. The owner owed about $500k and it was sold to us for $290k, a good deal for an 1100 square foot home in the San Fernando Valley. Good news: the value of the property has risen 200%!

Small businesses have reported that they're finding it equally challenging to attain loans. The effects of the Great Recession continue to rumble through the Middle Class long after the banks started to teeter from the initial economic tremor.

So, where's the money?

Bernie Sanders said that there are 18,857 U.S. corporations registered at the Ugland House, a five-story building in George Town, Cayman Islands. He appeared on Facebook to announce the discovery of millions of files that reveal how corporations and the one percent juggle offshore accounts to avoid paying their fair share of taxes. The revelation follows a similar one brought to light in 2015.

That pales in comparison to the protection provided domestically in Wilmington, Delaware. The Corporation Trust Center is home to about 285,000 resident agents. What's a resident agent? Under corporate law, corporations are required to have somebody in the office to receive summons and process official paperwork from government entities or forward those documents to the appropriate party in the corporation.

Why Delaware? The state charges NO INCOME TAX on corporations not operating in the state. According to the state of Delaware, "more than one million business entities have made Delaware their legal home." That statistic includes more than 66 percent of publicly traded companies, including 66+ percent of the Fortune 500. Google parks it here, as does Apple, Wal-mart, and American Airlines. Both Donald Trump and Hillary Clinton have companies registered here.

Panama Papers

400,000 journalists are investigating 214,000 offshore companies, scouring 11.5 million anonymously leaked files involving corporations, political leaders and wealthy individuals in 80 countries. So far, governments have issued 150 audits, investigations, prosecutions and arrests. Documents indicate Mossack Fonseca in criminal activity including fraud, tax evasion and circumventing international sanctions against states. The outcome has resulted in an estimated $135 billion being wiped off the value of nearly 400 companies and the recuperation of over $110 million worth of unpaid taxes.

Paradise Papers

The Paradise Papers expose´ came from 13.4 million files leaked from two offshore service providers and 19 tax havens' company registries. A law firm called Appleby, which has branches in Bermuda, the Cayman Islands, the British Virgin Islands, the Isle of Man, Jersey, Mauritius, Seychelles, and Guernsey, manages tax shelters for corporations, banks and the very wealthy. Unlike Mossack Fonseca, and despite the obvious revelation that once again corporations and the wealthy have avoided paying into the system that rewards such dereliction, Appelby's transactions and oversight appear to have operated within the law.

Among other high-profile individuals, the private estate of Great Britain's Queen Elizabeth II has been implicated with millions of pounds invested through the Cayman Islands in a company called BrightHouse. Britain's largest rent-to-own retailer, BrightHouse supplies TVs and home appliances to families under a high-cost credit scheme. Earlier this year Britain's exchequer said the company had not acted as a "responsible lender" and ordered it to pay the equivalent of $19 million to about 250,000 customers. It seems that Stephen Bronfman, the chief fundraiser to Canada's Prime Minister Justin Trudeau might have moved millions of dollars between offshore accounts to legally avoid paying taxes in the U.S., Canada, and Israel. The investigation has also taken note of the involvement of Secretary of Commerce Wilbur Ross in the shipping firm Navigator. That business connection puts him within arm's length of Putin and his son-in-law, Kirill Shamalov and provides yet another tie to Russia.

In the power grab for the presidency in 2012, the Republicans were twisting arms and calling in favors from Corporate America, excuse me, Multinational Corporations who seem to be sitting on large caches of cash. The L.A. Times reported that Apple Corps had socked away millions and nobody was hiring or getting raises.

President Trump used the banks' reluctance to loan money to businesses as an excuse to dismantle, or at least hobble, the 2010 Dodd-Frank Wall Street Reform and Consumer Protection Act. Dodd-Frank, passed in response to the financial meltdown of 2008, established financial reform passed by the Obama administration. Named after sponsors Senator Chris Dodd and Representative Barney Frank, provisions of the act were designed to protect consumers and the financial markets from some of the risks in the system. New government agencies were created to manage those changes to avoid creating other, new issues. Some provisions were intended to be rolled out over several years to allow for a low, cautious transition to more robust oversight.

From all the information garnered, Dodd-Frank has helped rather than hindered business expansion. But, Trump sees all regulation as an impediment to business. In May 22, 2018, Congress voted along partisan lines to roll back some of Dodd-Frank. Banks had been chafing at the increased oversight and regulation. The impact of these changes may not be seen right away.

In article after article immediately following the initial implementation of Dodd-Frank regulations, word was banks were reluctant to give out loans. Big banks were gobbling up community banks and holding onto their cash, not lending to small businesses. If you own a small business, there was an 80 percent chance your loan request would be denied. According to website BPlans.com, several factors were driving this behavior.

With fewer community banks and their friendlier terms, small businesses were forced to approach large banks like B of A, Chase, and others for loans. The Big Boys weren't realizing profits from small business that made the risk worth loaning money to a company that may not be around in a few years, small businesses are more susceptible to ups and downs in the economy and have fewer assets to offer as collateral. The banks were also complaining that regulation was tying their hands.

This loan reluctance by banks may explain President Trump's belated attempts to "fix" the system, but he is working with outdated info. According to Forbes.com, "loan approval rates at big banks increased to a post-recession high in July 2017, while approval rates at small banks also rose to 48.9 percent, and are now inching to the 50 percent benchmark." Alternative sources of loans priced themselves out of business or were forced to adjust rates to remain competitive, unemployment numbers look good and business owners are feeling confident.

Credit Reporting Agencies

When you and I want a credit card or a bank loan, institutions look at credit scores. The Brookings Institution said Washington needs to examine the way credit is reported:

> Policy makers need to resist the headlines and focus on the real problem that directly harms millions of Americans: the astounding number of errors in the credit reports that are the result of misaligned economic and legal incentives.

Twenty percent of us have some error in our report that means credit denied or a higher interest rate. The FICO score that credit reporting agencies publish is determined by information collected from banks, mortgage servicers, debt collectors and other credit providers.

Equifax explains away inaccuracies as unavoidable, part of the collection of massive amounts of information:

> Each of the major bureaus has over 200 million credit files that, on average, contain 13 past and current credit obligations, resulting in 2.6 billion pieces of data. Each month, more than 1 billion pieces of data are updated, requiring a speedy system. With so much data coming from so many sources, so quickly, errors are inevitable.

Who is responsible for clearing up these little discrepancies? You. If you dispute an item on your credit report, and there were eight million such disputes in 2016 according to Equifax, the only legal obligation the credit bureau has is to check with the debt collector to confirm your unpaid debt obligation. As long as they say you owe money, that ding stays on your credit report.

Morning Consult, a technological research firm, found consumers then turned to the Consumer Financial Protection Bureau with about 281,100 credit report complaints since the creation of the CFPB in 2011. Only debt collection and mortgages generated more criticism. About 40 percent of consumers had their problem fixed in 2017.

Now that the CFPB is in the hands of those who serve the banks and Wall Street and who fought the formation of the agency, much of the consumer oversight will be retooled to make it more business-friendly.

Payday Loan Companies

I had a girlfriend who pawned her jewelry when she was strapped for cash, buying it back by the shop's deadline. Now she has another option:

If you can't get a bank loan or just need $300 until Friday's paycheck, payday loan companies are a controversial solution. Payday lenders, or "small-dollar loan providers" as they refer to themselves, serve more than 12 million American households, about 10 percent in 35 states, according to the Community Financial Services Association of America, the industry's trade group.

Community Financial Services Association CEO Dennis Shaul told Congress in 2016 that as many as 76 percent of Americans live paycheck to paycheck, with no means to deal with unexpected expenses. Elevate Credit, which offers small loans often with triple-digit annualized interest rates, identified a growing 'New Middle Class' "with little to no savings, urgent credit needs and limited options."

Pew Charitable Trusts found the typical payday-lending customer is a white woman age 25 to 44. The small-dollar loan providers claim that curtailing or eliminating their services could cause financial ruin for some, "incurring overdraft charges and extraneous bank fees by bouncing more checks, seeking out illegal, offshore, or unregulated lenders, or [motivating consumers into] filing for Chapter 7 bankruptcy."

Under a proposed CFPB rule, lenders were required to verify that borrowers had the ability to pay off a requested loan before receiving money and would have capped the number of times borrowers can take out consecutive loans. That rule, set to take effect in August 2018, has been dropped. The Community Financial Services Association of America, seeing a sharp reduction in customers and revenue, sued and explored their options.

Now payday lenders have diversified into products that aren't under the same scrutiny as paycheck advances. Bloomberg reported when revenues began to trend downward, two companies, Enova International Inc. and Curo Group Holdings Corp. have seen a significant uptick in earnings. What are they selling? Enova offers installment loans and lines of credit. Curo, too, offers installment loans and some gold-buying, check-cashing and money transfers.

Payday loans were designed to be paid back in a single payment, but many of the new products are paid back in installments, over time at APRs ranging from 100 percent to 450 percent.

These predatory lenders have been widely criticized for allegedly creating debt traps where paying off the debt becomes increasingly impossible due to ever-increasing fees and loan renewals.

The Consumer Financial Protection Bureau, before it was seized in a hostile takeover, said that grievances against debt collectors are the most common type of complaint it received.

A CFPB national survey of 2,000 borrowers released in 2017 revealed about 25 percent of consumers said they felt threatened when contacted by a debt collector. Nearly 40 percent of consumers reported calls from a collector four or more times a week, and a majority reported the debt collector had bad information: the amount was wrong, or they weren't the "Joe Smith" who owed the money.

Sometimes this bad debt is sold off to another debt collector for pennies on the dollar, and the borrower gets harassed by a new, more aggressive operation. The CFPB under the honorable Richard Cordray reported that some 70 million people have a debt in collection or have been contacted about one.

We will discuss the country's fastest-growing debt crisis, student debt and its soul-crushing weight over graduates, in our chapter on education.

Chapter 18 The Gig Economy and Universal Basic Income

Chapter 18

The Gig Economy

"Is the Sharing Economy over yet?" Brad Parker

"Many Americans are making extra money renting out a spare room, designing websites, or even driving their own car. This on-demand or so-called gig economy is creating exciting opportunities and unleashing innovation. But it's also raising hard questions about workplace protections and what a good job will look like in the future." Hillary Clinton, 2016 Presidential candidate

Uber and Lyft, GrubHub and Postmates, Freelancers.com and Air BnB are all part of the so-called gig or shared economy. A gig is defined as a short-term contract with a company, not as an employee with regular pay or benefits like a 401(k), medical and paid vacations, but as a free agent with flexible hours and no boss. The doling out of assignments is typically handled through an app or a website.

The gig economy would have looked very familiar to my folks. When we were kids, my mother would wash and iron the clothes of other people to make ends meet. As a customer, I have tried Uber and Lyft in California and New York and again in the Netherlands. I always ask drivers how they like working these types of jobs and almost always get positive responses.

"I work when I want to."

"I don't have a boss. Nobody's looking over my shoulder."

Gig workers aren't just millennials; they're retirees or workers with a 9 to 5 job just trying to get ahead financially. One driver told me he had a wife and newborn and was saving up to buy a house. Another driver from Sri Lanka used the extra money that Uber brought him to visit home once a year.

The US Bureau of Labor Statistics identifies gig workers:

> Some gigs may be very brief, such as answering a 5-minute survey. Others are much longer but still of limited duration, such as an 18-month database management project. When one gig is over, workers who earn a steady income this way must find another. And sometimes that means juggling multiple jobs at once.
>
> For example, TyKecia Hayes is a freelance filmmaker in Los Angeles, California. When she's between filmmaking projects, Hayes picks up gigs that include working as a personal assistant, helping people move, and making deliveries. "I'm able to work when I need money and take off when I need to," she says. "That's the beauty of it."

Then there is the other side of the coin. Jonathan F. complained on Facebook:

"I picked up an order today in Encino and delivered it to Pacific Palisades; by the time I finished the delivery, Postmates said I took too long to complete it and made me log out for 3 hours. I completed the delivery in about 30 minutes and got stuck way out in West LA. For those of you who aren't familiar with LA, Encino and Pacific Palisades are at least 30 minutes away from each other. I've only made about $500 my first week. I have about $1,000 in basic weekly living expenses. I have a political science degree with an almost perfect GPA, and I can't even earn enough money to live."

He realizes he sounds bitter and makes no apology. "It's 4th of July weekend, and I'm running around doing deliveries for about minimum wage and spending my own money on gas." Hourly wages before tips are usually in the $8-$9 range; figuring in the average tip brings the total up to about $12 an hour minus gas money.

I can't make it in this country. (Jonathan was born and raised in the U.S.) About 80 percent of the people living here are living in fucked up conditions so that the remaining 20 percent can have everything, especially the wealthiest one percent. Donald Trump is trying to take my health care away from me (which is shitty anyway) as well as my right to vote, by investigating non-existent voter fraud. What are we supposed to be celebrating? Independence? Democracy? We have a system that gives the elite class in this country ... everything on a silver platter and people like me who are trying have no opportunities at all."

Jonathan earns most of his living collecting signatures for ballot initiatives in California and considers his signature gathering part of the gig economy. "It should be," he states emphatically. "As a deadline approaches for an initiative to be eligible for the ballot, the price per signature goes up. If I were a 9-to-5 employee, that rate would never increase beyond probably a dollar a signature." He would also have to push every initiative whether he liked them or not. At present, he has the option to refuse any ballot initiative he opposes, though it limits his income. "In 2015, I made about $28,000 for the year. In 2016, there were a lot of issues I could support, and I cleared about $75,000 before taxes."

Data from the Bureau of Labor Statistics on this growing segment of the working population dates back to 2005 when this group of "contingent" workers accounted for roughly 2 to 4 percent of all workers. About 7 percent of workers were independent contractors, the most common alternative employment arrangement. The BLS has more recent data but admits there's no separate category for gig workers. "Gig workers may be included in counts of workers who are part-time, self-employed, or hold multiple jobs. But these counts also include workers who are not part of the gig workforce."

Meanwhile, the numbers grow. The BLS looks to census data for a more accurate picture of gig workers. Meanwhile, Wired magazine reveals the English are considering suggestions recently laid out in the Taylor Review, a significant report of the UK's work life that focuses on three areas: addressing worker exploitation, increasing clarity in employment laws, and making laws fit with the UK's industrial strategy that looks to retool the country's economy post-Brexit.

The Review recommended a designation of "dependent contractor" for gig workers, with a guaranteed minimum wage for people with contracts with no minimum guarantee of hours and/or the right to request a fixed number of working hours from employers with permanent contracts.

Shannon Liss-Riordan, an attorney whose firm maintains offices in both Boston and San Francisco, sued Uber stating the ride service was misclassifying its drivers as independent contractors. Class-action lawsuits in California and Massachusetts have given drivers more rights, but they're still classified as independent contractors. At this time, a judge has thrown out the judgment that awarded $100 million to drivers for expenses and tips they never received, calling it "not fair, adequate and reasonable."

More often than not, Travis Kalanick, the former CEO of Uber was described as a callous and ruthless capitalist, the kind of guy who jacks up prices during natural disasters and his company has been labeled by some as "the most ethically challenged company in Silicon Valley."

A lawsuit filed by Liss-Riordan against Lyft was settled out of court and netted the drivers $12.25 million while curbing their ability for future class actions. They're also still designated independent contractors.

All of these lawsuits may ultimately pay out, but technology in the form of driverless cars may make the victory short-lived and bittersweet.

Teaching at colleges and universities have created adjunct professors, and now 31 percent of part-time faculty live at or near the poverty line and 51 percent of college professors are categorized as adjunct. Very often that means no benefits, no union representation.

The Department of Labor has determined that 34 percent of all workers are already part of the gig economy; a study by Intuit predicts that 40 percent of the workforce will ultimately be working within the gig economy.

Companies are trying to avoid works comp, unemployment and benefits. The state of Pennsylvania calculated they were losing $6 million a year in workers comp revenue and even more in unfunded mandates like pensions.

Who or what determines how much money you make? Are wages dependent on an industry standard, adhered to in an effort to avoid employee churn? In most companies, salaries are determined through a third-party compensation service that has compared other jobs like it in that field and has arrived at a wage range for that position.

In a gig economy, there are no wage comparisons around the water cooler, no union to negotiate those rates. In my retirement years, I have considered the gig economy and have even participated in it to a limited extent. I thought about uber, but I can't keep my car clean. I have tried freelancing assignments for writing and photography. I wrote for an online magazine that actually pays its writers a decent story rate (for the internet). It took me nine months to get paid! I had tried diplomacy, humor, empathy and finally got mad. "If you can't pay me in the next couple days, I have no choice but to go to my union, the National Writers Union," I informed the editor. I was paid that day but was blackballed from ever working for them again. I encountered the same delayed pay issue when I took some photos for a client.

Now there's AI Writer offering "Content creation made efficient." This website promises, "Just feed our AI author a headline, and it will do all the research and writing work for you." (I think I'll look into what it would cost me for the rest of this book.) While we artists guffaw at the thought, Uber drivers are looking over their shoulders at a scene from the horror flick *Christine* and a driverless car bearing down on them. "AI technology might be able to 'take away' from the market on the shallow end," explained Fabian Langer, German creator of AI Writer, "...However, it will augment writers and be used as a tool by them in order to produce content more efficiently. Instead of being a threat for them, it will be 'just another tool' in their toolbox."

Reports indicate the gig workplace may not be the safest work environment. Many workers are "encouraged" to sign waivers that absolve their employer of liability if they're injured in the line of work. With no workers' compensation, sick leave, or health care, they may be out of a job of any kind for a long time or forever. At least with the Affordable Care Act in full force, there was a very good chance an Uber or Lyft driver could get medical attention. It's a possibility, though, they went without a plan because of the lingering high costs of healthcare. That's a subject for another chapter.

Driving for a living is one of the most dangerous jobs in the country. The National Employment Law Project reports taxi drivers and chauffeurs are killed on the job at a rate five times higher than other workers. Drivers incurred the highest number of fatal injuries in 2016, according to the Bureau of Labor Statistics. Their workplace, American roads, and highways saw an increase of 2,054 in 2015 to 2,083 in 2016 in "transportation incidents." Together, roadway collisions with another vehicle and other roadway incidents account for about 60 percent of fatal work-related transportation injuries.

Is Seasonal Work considered part of the Gig Economy?

The Brookings Institution has two terms when referring to these short-lived, "contingent work arrangements." They call these jobs "online gig" or "on-demand." There has been, according to BI, "increased policy interest" without identifying who is generating that increased interest. And, yes, many workers may be part of the "shared" workforce: independent contractors, subcontractors, temps, part-timers, and seasonal. The line is blurred when all workers receive their tasks for the day via the internet or an app.

Workers in the early throes of attraction may agree with customers and their never-seen supervisor that the arrangement works for everyone. The employee has flexible hours and supplemental income, customers receive low-cost services that range from grocery delivery to housecleaning at the door, and the employer doesn't deal with benefits, pensions, training, or pesky safety laws.

What may lead gig workers to an uprising is the realization that many of those traditional benefits – health care, training, pensions, and robust government oversight – have been replaced by a laissez-faire policy and almost Herbert Hoover-like faith in capitalism. Those of us down here at the bottom realize we weren't quite at the bottom yet; we've got much further to sink in living standards and sacrifices so that entrepreneurship may thrive.

What's the answer?

In a policy analysis from the Libertarian think tank, the Cato Institute, Michael Tanner compared the pro and cons of what they refer to as a "Guaranteed National Income."

Tanner examined three options: a Negative Income Tax, wage supplements and a Universal Basic Income.

A favorite of Milton Friedman, Negative Income Tax provides financial assistance to those below the poverty line, everyone is eligible, and there is no work requirement. Payouts under negative income tax can be adjusted so that benefits are phased out as earned income rises or modified to accommodate every member of the growing or shrinking household.

Wage supplements would make up the difference between a worker's wages and an established minimum. Not everyone qualifies; only people who have earned some level of income would be eligible. Suddenly everyone is paying poverty wages, and the taxpayer foots the bill to make up the difference. This plan lets low wage employers off the hook.

Some countries, such as Finland, Canada, the Netherlands, Scotland, and Iran, and some US cities, Stockton, California, for example, have been experimenting with Universal Basic Income (UBI), but the subject is an old one. In Speenhamland, England, during a grain shortage in 1795, prices soared, and incomes didn't. The government's solution was to raise household incomes to cover the cost of living, enough to buy about 25 pounds of bread a week for a family of five. In return, some men worked for a little extra cash to live on, but others received the bread and didn't work. People on all sides of the political spectrum hated the concept. Karl Marx accused it of keeping wages low. Others complained that it was a handout.

Reverend Martin Luther King, Jr. spoke of a "guaranteed minimum income for all people" in a 1967 speech. Former speaker Daniel P. Moynihan in his 1973 tome *The Politics of a Guaranteed Income* reported that Nixon considered a similar plan in the late sixties, referred to as the Family Assistance Plan.

Nixon's plan would have put $1600 a year (about $11,000 in today's dollars) and food stamps into the hands of penniless families of at least four members. After learning of the folly of Speenhamland, he realized that if there were no work requirement, his Republican colleagues would call it welfare for all on their way to oppose the bill. The plan died a quick and decisive death in the Senate. Writers of future plans would include a work requirement because Congress wants the poor to "earn" the government's help through a clearly demonstrated work ethic.

Experiments and passionate conversations have revived consideration of UBI. The relentless advance of technology, the loss of good-paying union jobs, and staggering student loan debt have created their own incentives. Further, some say it would be good for the economy. A study by the Roosevelt Institute found that giving $1,000 cash to all adults would grow the economy by 12.56 percent after eight years, about $2.5 trillion by 2025. The larger the universal basic income, the greater the benefit to the economy, according to the report.

Living in California, I investigated the city of Stockton's efforts at UBI funded with the financial assistance of Facebook co-founder Chris Hughes. In *Fair Shot: Rethinking Inequality and How We Earn*, Hughes intends to "put cash in the hands of those who need it most."

> An income floor of $500 per month for every working adult whose family makes less than $50,000 would improve the

lives of 90 million Americans and lift 20 million people out of poverty overnight.

The Economic Security Project reports the Stockton Economic Empowerment Demonstration (SEED), will partner with the city to give 100 residents $500 a month for 18 months and will monitor the results. The website states, "The housing bust turned Stockton into an epicenter of a national foreclosure disaster and plunged the city into bankruptcy." Nearly one in four live below the poverty level.

Captains of industry, known innovators, want us to consider the impact of technology and Artificial Intelligence they're unleashing upon the globe. Facebook's Mark Zuckerberg is on board with UBI. In a commencement address last year to the 2017 graduating class at Harvard, Zuckerberg said UBI would "make sure that everyone has a cushion to try new ideas." "There is a pretty good chance we end up with a universal basic income, or something like that, due to automation," Musk said in a 2017 interview. Richard Branson stated in a blog post, "A lot of exciting innovations are going to be created, which will generate a lot of opportunities and a lot of wealth, but there is a real danger it could also reduce the number of jobs. This will make experimenting with ideas like basic income even more important in the years to come."

Chris Hughes thinks we're at one of humanity's major forks in the road and should act accordingly.

> I believe we live at the beginning of a tumultuous era, similar to the turn of the last century when railroad and shipping tycoons amassed historic fortunes. We need to be as open to creative, new ideas as the most forward-thinking leaders of the Progressive-era were then. They created an income tax, enacted direct elections for senators, banned corporate contributions to political campaigns, enfranchised women, and laid the groundwork for labor protections like the minimum wage and old age pensions. We need to be equally bold today.

Chapter 19

Environment vs. Economy

"Michigan Governor Rick Snyder ignored warnings about lead in the drinking water of Flint, a town that is poor and black. Since the effect of lead poisoning of black kids will have harmful effects over many years, some observers have been calling Flint a case of 'environmental racism.'" Peter Temin, *The Vanishing Middle Class*

"Trade unions were the very first environmentalists. It was the diseases of workers, more than anything … that triggered concerns about environmental chemicals." Brian Kohler Director - Health, Safety and Sustainability, IndustriALL Global Union

"…The way capitalism has evolved has compromised the ecology and environment of this planet." Dr. Richard Wolff

In an article entitled, "A New Economic System for a World in Rapid Disintegration" by Lily Sage and C.J. Polychroniou for Truthout, the writers stated the case against growth as a sustainable model for living and livelihoods. We are all now looking at a concept called sustainability:

> The so-called Golden Age of capitalism ended decades ago and the system has now run into a brick wall, as it appears

to have reached a point where it is no longer capable of sustaining a constant momentum of growth to keep the economy reproducing itself at a pace that generates higher standards of living for the next generation.

Indeed, the productivity rates in the advanced industrialized regions of the world (such as the US, Europe and Japan) since the eruption of the financial crisis of 2007-08 are far slower than those of previous decades, thereby confirming the claims of various experts who argue that we have reached the end of the age of growth.

Labor unions have come down hard on both sides of environmental issues. While agreeing in principle that coal use is contributing to global warming, coal miners are concerned that the best-paying jobs in the region are under attack from environmental groups. "Coal mining has been in the family for generations," they say. "We don't know anything else." That unflinching loyalty to that particular fossil fuel cost Hillary Clinton hundreds of votes in West Virginia.

Everyone over thirty remembers the battle between environmentalists and labor over the future of the spotted owl.

In 1986, after a steep decline of spotted owls in Oregon and California, a concerned environmentalist group petitioned the US Fish and Game Service to list the owl as an endangered species. The timber industry threatened to take the government to court for denying them their God-given right to cut down trees. In June 1990, after years of heated negotiations and litigation among the government, environmentalists, and the timber industry, the northern spotted owl was declared a threatened species. Under the designation, timber companies are required by law to leave at least 40% of old-growth forests intact within a 1.3-mile radius of any spotted owl nest or activity area. The timber industry complained it would mean the loss of 30,000 jobs in logging and mill work. Logging companies ignored the order until the government enforced their decision and shut down logging in 17 national forests. The timber industry blamed the moratorium for 130 mill closures and a local unemployment rate of 25%. A study at the University of Wisconsin-Madison attributed most of those losses to increased automation and argued that lumber industry jobs had been in steady decline before the passage of the 1964 Wilderness Act, a law that was credited with saving 51,000 jobs in the following 30 years.

Many in labor have found that it's possible to create jobs without destroying or even compromising the environment by working with employers. Despite the fact that the American labor movement and working families have been under attack since the Reagan era, a coalition has been formed that chooses sustainability over mindless growth. Thanks to the efforts of our local unions and coalitions like the Labor Network for Sustainability, workers in the US have also built successful coalitions with groups in Europe and globally, including IndustriALL Global Union and Trade Union Actions. European unions have not suffered the same attacks by business hell-bent on their annihilation, so they have been able to focus on improving the lot of workers. But it was an American in the early 90s, Tony Mazzocchi of the Oil, Chemical and Atomic Workers, who came up with the idea of a "Superfund for Workers" for workers whose livelihoods were threatened by needed environmental bans. Why should workers who made tetraethyl lead, for example, have to pay 100 percent of the cost of getting society off the stuff - for the benefit of society? IndustriALL Global Union calls it a Just Transition:

> Our first choice is always to protect present-day workers by making existing jobs sustainable. When this is not possible, then there must be a socially just way to shift workers to new jobs while keeping them whole. It is simply unfair and socially unsustainable to ask the workers who made today's society possible to pay the full cost of changes that society now requires. There will be opportunities as well as risks as the economy is transformed. However, we cannot rely on the free market to build a greener economy, or at least not a just one – governments must step in with sustainable industrial policies. Moving towards a low-carbon economy requires planning, not luck.

Mazzocchi also published the first newsletter in the labor movement on global warming in about 1988, called "Global Warming Watch."

"It soon became apparent that the only way to have an intelligent conversation with workers on big issues like climate change, was to talk to them first about a Just Transition, said Brian Kohler Director - Health, Safety and Sustainability, for the IndustriALL Global Union based in Geneva, Switzerland.

He drafted the first-ever trade union resolution on Just Transition and got it passed at his national union congress - the then Communications, Energy and Paperworkers' Union of Canada.

"We then passed very progressive energy policies and pulled the Canadian Labor Congress along with us. Remember, we were a union of oil workers, chemical workers, paper workers, and even some coal miners. Not exactly a group you would expect to be thrilled by the concept of global warming. But we presented the facts - we were honest with our members, and they accepted the truth."

These environmental/labor organizations have realized the impact of a sustainable, environmentally conscious paradigm shift and have intervened on behalf of workers who might be the victims of this shift. Workers have said, "I'm in favor of a cleaner world for my children, but what happens to me?" By addressing these concerns and raising awareness, these coalitions are hoping to protect workers and put a positive spin on an unknown future. According to the International Labor Office, their Workers' Education and Environment project, in cooperation with the Norwegian government and coming to a head at about the same time as the spotted owl controversy in the US, was designed to empower those industries which are most affected:

> One objective of the project was to put the cooperating trade unions in a position to participate in the formulation and implementation of national environmental and sustainable development policies which reflect the particular needs and concerns of the workers and their organizations. The other major goal of the Project was to increase trade union

representation on relevant environmental advisory and decision-making bodies at the bi- and tripartite level. Since the beginning of the Project, trade unions have become involved in formulating and implementing environmental and sustainable development policies at all levels.

This is a silver lining to this storm cloud: A report from the Worker Institute at Cornell University finds dealing with global warming has opened up the possibility of job creation.

Numerous studies have shown that there is significant job creation potential from tackling the climate crisis, reducing greenhouse gas emissions, and transitioning to a low-carbon, sustainable economy. Moving toward a low-carbon or zero-carbon economy requires substantial improvement and expansion of public transportation systems, the manufacture and deployment of renewable energy sources like solar and wind, modernization of electricity, water and gas infrastructure, comprehensive energy efficiency retrofits of residential, commercial and industrial buildings, and the development of more sustainable food, waste and agricultural systems.

As the gap between the 1% and the 99% widens, groups representing the working class grow more militant. "The huge amount of security surrounding this year's G20 meeting shows that governments are failing and people are angry," said IndustriALL Global Union General Secretary, Valter Sanches. "The disparities of wealth and opportunity have continued to grow on the back of an economic model that is broken. The G20 leaders can no longer ignore the calls for a more equal society."

"The 1940s asbestos strike in Canada was largely about concerns for healthier working conditions," said Brian Kohler of the IndustriALL Global Union.

Occupational health and safety (OH&S) pioneers in the trade union movement moved their concerns to the forefront and a central demand in collective bargaining in the 1960s and 1970s. "Unions demanded health and safety rights for workers: to KNOW about the hazards of work (especially chemical agents), to REFUSE unsafe work without fear of discipline or discharge, and to PARTICIPATE in OH&S policies, programs and procedures in workplaces primarily through OH&S representatives and Joint Health and Safety Committees. Workers fought for these ideas in workplaces and on picket lines like the Shell strike of 1973. That strike was mainly about these rights; they were not simply given to us." said Kohler.

The Global Carbon Project, according to their website, "was formed to assist the international science community to establish a common, mutually agreed knowledge base supporting policy debate and action to slow the rate of increase of greenhouse gases in the atmosphere." Composed of international environmental organizations exploring the science behind global warming, the Project measures carbon dioxide, (CO_2) emissions worldwide. The organization is attempting to measure the amount of carbon pollution outsourced by developed nations. By estimating "production emissions" (that is, the CO_2 produced within a country's borders) and "consumption emissions" (the CO_2 emitted around the world in the course of manufacturing goods for that country) they have found wealthy nations "consume" a fair bit more CO_2 than they actually emit within their own borders. Garbage dumps and the poor typically coexist in urban areas; carbon dumping extends that indignity to a global scale.

This may explain why US corporations continue to deny global warming. Workers in this country should take up the gauntlet.

Brian Kohler explains:

> It is one of the missed opportunities of the US labor movement that it never fully embraced the idea of Just Transition, leaving the AFL-CIO fumbling for how to speak the truth to its members about global warming. It was mostly mute on the Kyoto Accord, for example. Because of the failure of the AFL-CIO to take a clear stand, the US labor movement has been bitterly divided on the questions of Keystone and Dakota Access [pipelines].

A Green New Deal

Voters in the state of Washington rejected Initiative 1631, a bold attempt to confront both climate change and economic inequity in the state. Much like IndustriALL's Just Transition, this ballot measure would provide both job retraining and wage, and benefit protections for workers in fossil-fuel-reliant industries as those industries are phased out over a generation. The University of Massachusetts' Political Economy Research Institute created a plan that would commit the state to massive reductions in CO_2 emissions: 20 million tons per year, which, by 2035, would be 40 percent lower than they were in 2014. A carbon-emissions fee on big polluters would generate billions of dollars in revenue for investments in clean energy and water. The money would be directed to employers with a high-wage, labor-protection model, to be spent on the economic, environmental, and health-care revitalization of communities on the front lines of global warming and energy assistance programs for low-income households as well as workers whose jobs were eliminated during the transition.

The $15 per-ton fee on CO_2 emissions (starting in 2020 and rising thereafter), creates a path to full retirement for fossil-fuel-industry workers within five years of retiring. Those with one to five years would receive a year of guaranteed income, health care, and retirement contributions for every year of service. For those in the industry for more than five years, a wage-insurance program would make up whatever income difference there might be between their old wages in the fossil-fuel industry and their new ones in non-fossil-fuel sectors for up to five years.

The rest of the world isn't waiting for the US to catch up. Kohler addresses global efforts:

> In 1992 the first "Earth Summit" was held in Rio. Trade unions fought for a place in those discussions as part of "civil society" and won - and we've been involved in all of the subsequent UN summits and climate talks on the international stage, since. It is due to our efforts that the

Paris Agreement has Just Transition embedded in it. I am proud to say I've played a role in all of this.

Also in the 1990s, the environmental justice movement (as distinct from pure environmentalism) began to grow in the US and other places. The problem was/is that toxic industries and waste sites are overwhelmingly sited in poor neighborhoods and communities of color. ... Globally, in a 1991 memo Lawrence Summers, then Chief Economist of the World Bank made the argument that the developing world was "underpolluted". Although he later claimed he was being sarcastic rather than serious, it is this kind of thinking that leads to environmental atrocities like those of the Nigerian oil industry. Again, the Just Transition movement linked arms with the Environmental Justice movement with some effect. All of this is historical background to where we are now.

By withdrawing from the Paris Agreement, the US will no longer be committed to the Paris Agreement's expectations that governments create a Just Transition for affected workers in coal mining communities. This administration will weaken the ability of trade unions to negotiate good deals for affected workers when faced with the industrial transformations that are inevitable – Trump, or no Trump.

In short: no new jobs; and less protection for workers.

"Predatory casino capitalism may yet render the entire planet uninhabitable," states Kohler.

There is hope. Before Washington's bill was crafted, California had implemented cap-and-trade. Companies pay penalties if they exceed the cap, which gets stricter over time. The trade part is a market for companies to buy and sell allowances that permit them to emit only a certain amount. Trading gives companies a strong incentive to save money by cutting emissions.

California passed Assembly Bill 32, the California Global Warming Solutions Act of 2006. This law requires California to reduce its greenhouse gas emissions to 1990 levels by 2020 — a reduction of approximately 15 percent below "business as usual." According to the California Air Resources Board, "The full implementation of AB 32 will help mitigate risks associated with climate change, while improving energy efficiency, expanding the use of renewable energy resources, cleaner transportation, and reducing waste."

Senate Bill 350, the Clean Energy and Pollution Reduction Act, signed into law in 2015, mandates the state of California increase electricity consumption from renewable sources from 33 percent to 50 percent.

In 2016, the California Federation of Labor officially came out in support of curbing global warming and the policies that have led to climate change with a resolution:

CLIMATE CHANGE, CLEAN ENERGY, AND UNION JOBS PRESENTED BY: EXECUTIVE COUNCIL

WHEREAS climate change poses an immediate and long-term threat to all working people, our communities and our economic security; and

WHEREAS workers, communities of color, and low-income Californians suffer disproportionately from environmental degradation and climate change through polluted air, water, and land and drought; and

WHEREAS California's unions have worked for decades to transition union industries to be safer, cleaner and more sustainable and also to maintain labor standards and union density through this transition; and

WHEREAS AB 32 and SB 350 must both be implemented to ensure adequate worker protections and the preservation and creation of family-sustaining and safe jobs; and

WHEREAS there is work to be done by every union to combat climate change, protect and prepare our communities for the impact of climate change and actively engage in the fight for policy changes that promote sustainability, environmental protection, and good job creation.

THEREFORE, BE IT RESOLVED that the executive council of the California Labor Federation will prioritize climate change policy to ensure that issues of good jobs, union jobs, worker safety, prevailing wages, and project labor agreements, where appropriate, are always present in climate change policy setting and that California Labor's policy agenda addresses climate change and environmental justice issues that impact workers, communities, and unions, and

THEREFORE, BE IT FURTHER RESOLVED that the California Labor Federation will educate our members and our policymakers about the ways union members and workers are impacted by climate change and the importance of ensuring good jobs as we transition our economy, and

FINALLY, BE IT FURTHER RESOLVED that the California Labor Federation will engage in the passage and implementation of key environmental policies with a focus on ensuring good job creation and environmental sustainability.

In these days of an increasingly ineffective, eviscerated Environmental Protection Agency, we must look to ourselves and each other for all the small ways we can compensate for corporate and bureaucratic climate change deniers.

Magali Delmas, an economist at the UCLA Anderson School of Management, recently addressed the issue in a book she co-wrote called *The Green Bundle: Pairing the Market with the Planet* and in a talk entitled, "Does Environmentalism Need to Make Peace with Capitalism?" at Zocalo Public Square in Los Angeles.

Delmas suggested a move from conspicuous consumption to conspicuous conservation. "A lot of us consume to show what we have so with conspicuous conservation we show who we are through our consumption. We show that we can conserve. That would be a way to incentivize though who want to show they're greener, that they're doing the right thing."

> There are five categories of these personal incentives: increased quality, which encourages consumers to pay a premium for, say, an expensive but eco-friendly cleaning product; products that leverage peer pressure, for example, by using Hollywood stars to promote the Toyota Prius at the Academy Awards; linking a product with personal health benefits; showing how using a product can result in either short- or long-term monetary savings; and by crafting marketing narratives that stimulate empathy and persuade a consumer that her or his personal choices will make a tangible difference to the environment.

This shift in consumerism, the "coolness" factor in buying organic, suggests a significant change in the way Americans think of consumption. But without growth or with controlled growth governed by sustainability factors, what kind of work will we do? What will be the jobs of the future?

Chapter 20 Education – Right or Privilege

Chapter 20

Education: Right or Privilege?

"Widespread public access to knowledge, like public education, is one of the pillars of our democracy, a guarantee that we can maintain a well-informed citizenry." Scott Turow

"A rich, robust, well-resourced public education is one of the best routes out of poverty and a pathway to prosperity." Randi Weingarten

Ignorance is Bliss. Or is it?

Growing up in a small Texas town with parents who dropped out with ninth grade educations, it would be safe to say that "book learning" was undervalued and viewed with suspicion. My dad, endeavoring to expose me to the hard, cold facts of life, said, "I don't know why you read and write so much. You will always be poor, so you need to learn how to work with your hands."

I always had my nose in a book from the age of five when my maternal grandmother taught me to read. I think learning to read at an early age made school fun. Despite living in abject poverty and being bullied by schoolmates almost daily, I found reading and learning freed my mind. But that environment could have beaten me down eventually if I hadn't been offered the chance to leave that dead-end little town with its small-minded folks. Many have fled and never looked back. The sign at the outskirts of town when I lived there said Population: 4,510. It now states Population: 3,676.

I witnessed the disparity of education firsthand in Palacios. We had one school for white and brown kids, another for black children. "Separate but equal" schools, separate but not equal, were first upheld by the US Supreme Court in 1896, overturned by the Supreme Court in 1954, but not fully integrated until 1968. In Texas, the enlightenment arrived in the Fall of 1966 when I was 11.

The reaction to integration: lots of angry poor southern whites. They went from next-to-last on the totem pole, able to look down on "colored folk," to what they perceived as dead last after blacks got a hand up. Poor southern whites blamed their new ranking not on the system that seemed to change overnight, but on gummint and these uppity Negroes who no longer had to bow and scrape and get called "boy." To my dad who had grown up here, it was just another affront.

One advantage to overt racism: it can be addressed overtly, but when you're considered poor white trash, prejudice is a much more subtle thing. That kind of prejudice is related to poverty: hand-me-downs, bad haircuts, and poor hygiene. We and our black neighbors situated on the wrong side of the tracks were suddenly equals, still held down by a system governed by access to opportunity and that access was, ultimately, tied to money. Truth was, there were no opportunities for any of us, no way out. The future in our cards was much like my dad had laid it out for me: working for the county for a pittance, knocking up one of my classmates at 18, raising four screaming brats just a few years later. And the cycle would repeat. Dad knew because he had experienced it.

My grandmother, safely entrenched in the middle class, drove down from Colorado and looked around in disgust. She decided to rescue me from my dismal to middling future. Shamefully, I left behind my family with scarcely a second thought.

I knew I was lucky and the statistics bear me out: even today twenty-two percent of the nation's children live in poverty. Of the 35 wealthiest countries, the US is second only to Romania for the highest rate of child poverty. That's worth repeating: *the US is second only to Romania for the highest rate of child poverty.* 2.8 million kids are living in extreme poverty, and it's getting worse. Between 2007 and 2010, the median net worth of Americans fell 39 percent. The scenario is much, much worse for people of color.

I moved to Denver and an endless opportunity to expand my education, but most of my counselors and teachers decided I wasn't college material. Nobody talked to me about grants or scholarships. I was involved in extracurricular activities; my grades were high Bs and low As for the most part, but I wore my hair to my shoulders, smoked pot and hung out with the school outcasts. I was never aware that I was a finalist my junior year for a scholarship from Junior Achievement until it was awarded to someone else at their annual banquet. My grandmother who had been footing the bill for me so far had retired and was disappointed she couldn't further my education. College didn't seem to be in the cards for me. (I mention all this because it was pretty typical scenario for my age group.) Was I going to end up at a dead-end job at 18 with several kids after all? Was this my destiny?

Again, I was a living, breathing statistic, though present statistics paint a bleaker picture: National efforts to equalize college opportunities have been losing ground for the past 15 years. In 1994 a student from a high-income family was ten times more likely than a low-income student to have earned a degree by age 24. The reasons for this?

1. Skyrocketing tuition has made college less affordable.
2. The share of family income required to pay for college has increased.
3. Student financial aid has failed to close the gap.
4. Shifts in student aid policies make eligibility a more drawn-out process.
5. We've seen a move from a grant-based to a loan-based system. (Ah, capitalism!)

College: the great equalizer, last-chance opportunity for those of us born without advantage to rise above our station in life.

Right after graduation, I was hired at Mountain Bell where I started my 37-year career in telecommunications. In those days, when asked about my interest in college, I proudly stated, "I don't need college. I'm a graduate of the School of Hard Knocks." I knew I was making more money than many college graduates and I felt real life experience was more valuable than book learning. And you don't always know what you don't know.

I transferred to AT&T in California in 1980. The "phone company" had never been enough for me; I was taking occasional writing classes at UCLA and Pierce, my local community college. A friend talked me into auditioning for plays at Pierce by pointing out I was getting college credit in case I decided to pursue a degree. He hired me as the copy editor for his fledgling graphics arts company, and even as I made money as a professional writer, I was lamenting the lack of legitimacy from that little piece of paper.

When Pacific Bell offered tuition aid, I jumped at the chance to get a degree. I spent two years at Pierce taking journalism classes and the accelerated Associate of Arts degree curriculum while acting in the occasional play. I was also working full time and had been elected to the executive board of my union, the Communications Workers of America Local 9503 where I represented 2500 of my fellow employees.

I transferred two years later to California State, Northridge, a "commuter college" so designated because many of their students were coming back to college from the workforce to attain an advanced degree. I liked the atmosphere at CSUN, but though I was convinced by those around me that I would have had more opportunity at UCLA or USC, CSUN was what I could afford. With some financial effort, I could buy my books and get reimbursed for my tuition as long as I stayed on top of the paperwork *and* my school work, and my job and my executive board duties. In 1992, I received my Bachelor's degree in journalism. I had missed the bonding experience of a fraternity with all its implied networking opportunities and, with my age and blue-collar experiences and focus, I knew life and my salary wouldn't change much. At least I had no nasty student debt following me for the rest of my career.

Already in the early 90s the cost of getting a college education was almost out of reach, even with tuition aid with payment due upfront. This was also the point where I left my former classmates behind. Few of my friends, if any, in either Texas or Colorado went to college. I was 33 years old, attending in my "spare" time with too many responsibilities and no time for forging the connections that might have advanced my career.

I often wonder who I would be if, like most, I had pursued my degree right after high school. My friends and I were distracted. They were thrust, like me, off the couch and into the working world. We were partly victims of the times. The nation was dealing with an OPEC-led gas shortage, the tail-end of the Vietnam War, Watergate. Before Nixon ended the draft in January of 1973, I had toyed with applying to the Air Force Academy in Colorado Springs. Like many who join the military, I was looking for a "free" college education that might not be able to keep me out of Vietnam, but wouldn't plunk me into the middle of a rice paddy in harm's way. Timing is everything. I missed both the Vietnam War and college as a formative experience, but I think my detour into real life gave me insights I might have missed if I had started college directly from high school.

I was no slacker in high school: I played in the marching band. I worked on the yearbook and learned sign language through my own initiative with our school's deaf students during my homeroom period. What marked me as different, as a lost cause? I wonder if a counselor would have gambled on me if I had been on the varsity football team or if my grandmother had been a presence with money to throw around.

I wish I had known about grants and the steps to prepare for college. Those of us who come from a level of poverty, who are the first in their family to consider higher education, have no mentors to guide us. We can only hope that someone spots our promise and has the time and resources and *desire* to show us the way.

I first met Augie when he was 13, a bright Latino kid considered at risk in the Van Nuys neighborhood he called home. I was his mentor through a Big Brother-type organization called the Fulfillment Fund and I was supposed to provide guidance, a little wisdom and a gentle push toward college. His father was in prison; his mother cleaned other people's houses. I could relate; my mother had washed and ironed other people's clothes and had cleaned fleabag hotel rooms. We attended FF functions together, toured college campuses, were taught how to fill out FAFSA forms. He was practically guaranteed a scholarship.

As graduation neared, Augie seemed restless. I think he was afraid of the responsibilities facing him, a pressure many immigrants feel from parents or children not to succeed, but not to *fail*. I could hear doors of opportunity slammed as he lowered his expectations. He trained to be a massage therapist, gave a half-hearted effort to find work and moved on to something else. He went to school to be a long-haul trucker and now sells houses. In between these gigs, he did go to college and eked out an Associate of Arts degree.

There was a time in California's history when a community college tuition was free and that time was relatively recent. In fact, the state first instituted a fee of $5 per unit in the Fall semester of 1984.

In the election of 2016, Vermont Senator Bernie Sanders had offered to help students get a college education through free tuition. Many scoffed at his idea of "free" college, but Californians knew it was possible.

Many educators recommend the following:

1. Restore a needs-based standard.
2. Find alternative financing for at-risk students.
3. Restore the value of Pell Grants.
4. Expand pre-college outreach.
5. Focus on student success rather than student access.

Horror film director Jamie Brown said college was a disappointment for him. "Kids are bombarded with this idea that going to college will ensure they make $100k a year when the truth is, the only $100k guarantee they get is indentured servitude paying off those loans while working McJob's for $10-$20 an hour.

The house has rigged the deck, and as long as you go to college for the four years of bad decisions, drunken theme parties and the occasional class that teaches you something, then you won't be disappointed, but in this day and age everyone should be working towards a phony piece of paper in something that makes them happy and a side trade that will allow them to buy a house."

Student Loan Debt

Recent reports indicate that student loan debt is second to only mortgage debt in this country and the crisis is worse than initially reported. In the *Evolllution* newspaper, Erin Dunlop Velez from RTI International, a not-for-profit research organization, analyzed information attained from the U.S Department of Education and debunked several myths about student loan debt, looking back along a 20-year timeframe for students who enrolled in college in 1995-96.

For instance, there has been a commonly held belief that most student loans are paid off within ten years:

> ...Even among those who borrowed only for their undergraduate education (and not for graduate school), *only half of students* had paid off all their federal student loans 20 years after beginning college in 1995–96. The average borrower in this group *still owed approximately $10,000* in principle and interest, about half of what was initially borrowed, 20 years after beginning college.

It has also been believed that graduates default on loans within three years of entering the workforce. Not true.

> Among 1995–96 beginning students, however, *more than half* of students who defaulted within 20 years of beginning college were in repayment for more than three years before they defaulted. The average time between students entering repayment and their first default was 4.9 years. The percentage of those defaulting was about 25 percent. Later

graduates (with higher student debt) reached the 25 percent default rate within 12 years.

But wait! Those higher defaults aren't due to higher debt.

> Students who obtained a bachelor's degree borrow more than their counterparts who earn an Associate's degree or certificate. Those who drop out of college borrow less, on average than those who attain a Bachelor's or Associate's degree, but more than those who attain a certificate.

But those with bachelor's degrees are less likely to default. "These data suggest that whether a degree is completed, and the type of degree may be more important factors related to the increasing default rate than the amount students borrow," the organization reports.

What about K-12?

Education Secretary Betsy DeVos had endorsed H.R. 610. The bill was a giant step backward. According to congress.gov, *Choices in Education Act of 2017* would have repealed the Elementary and Secondary Education Act of 1965 and limits the authority of the Department of Education (ED) such that ED was authorized only to award block grants to qualified states.

To be eligible to receive a block grant, a state must: (1) comply with education voucher program requirements, and (2) make it lawful for parents of an eligible child to elect to enroll their child in any public or private elementary or secondary school in the state or to home-school their child.

The bill would have repealed certain nutrition standards for the national school lunch and breakfast programs. Current standards require schools to increase the availability of fruits, vegetables, whole grains, and low-fat or fat-free milk in school meals and reduce the levels of sodium, saturated fat, and trans-fat in school meals with an eye on calories.

If the bill had passed, (and it's mentioned here because a form of this bill could reappear), it would have undermined the Department of Education's authority and could have diverted funding for public school to pay for vouchers given to students for private schooling, or homeschooling, according to the *San Diego Union-Tribune*. The bill would have resulted in confusion and chaos, at the very least.

Education? It's location, location, location!

The World Economic Forum states "In the current era of global value chains, many companies are locating different job functions and categories in different geographic locations to take advantage of the specific strengths of particular local labor markets."

They're not just looking for a geographical advantage for locating in a particular market; they're casting a wide net for recent graduates who have the skills they need.

As children in inner-city Houston, S. Shankar writes about her students of color who had grown up in segregated urban neighborhoods, a term called "graphic exclusion." I now have a term to categorize what I felt when I walked to school every day. Harassed, beat up and beat down affected dad, too. When the scoutmaster forgot to award me a merit badge, I was forced to resign from Cub Scouts. I shudder to consider how much worse it is for people of color. Shankar again:

> Many took on unpayable student loan debt for college, then struggled to stay in school while juggling work and family pressures, often without a support system.
>
> Several students also contrasted their cramped downtown campus—with its parking problems, limited dining options, and lack of after-hours cultural life—with the university's swankier main digs. Others would point out the jail across from the University of Houston-Downtown with bleak humor, invoking the school-to-prison pipeline.

The gap in opportunity and exposure to a quality education start early. Black, Hispanic, and low-income children attend lower quality elementary and secondary schools, as measured on a number of essential criteria including test scores and teacher experience. Racial differences in attendance and completion at the pre-secondary level, persist at the post-secondary level and continue into college.

Assessing the quality of a college is far from simple; teachers matter, declared majors matter. A good starting point to determine the quality of a school is to look at the financial successes and stresses of alumni.

Consider three such quality measures:

1. graduation rate
2. earnings after attendance
3. default rate on federal student loans

On each of these measures, black, Hispanic, and low-income students attend colleges with significantly worse outcomes than white, Asian-American, and international students.

- Parental background (income and education) is becoming less important as a predictor of college attendance;

Federal data from the Department of Education and College Scorecard shows that students are increasingly likely to borrow from the federal government (up from 38 percent in 2000 to 47 percent in 2012), and that federal borrowers are increasingly likely to be first-generation students (from 15 percent in 1997 to about 37 percent in 2013). Taken together, these trends strongly suggest that students from families in which no parent went to college make up an increasingly large share of all college students.

- But race gaps in attendance and completion are holding steady or even increasing:

Among adults aged 25 to 30, 80 percent of Asians and 72 percent of whites have attended college, compared to just 58 percent of blacks and 45 percent of Hispanics. Over the last quarter of a century, gaps in attendance have remained unchanged for blacks, and have widened for Hispanics.

- Gaps in college quality have not decreased in recent years, with black and first-generation students seeing little improvement in terms of quality.

What about teachers?

The answer in the north to school integration was busing. That created "white flight," as parents tried to distance themselves from what they perceived as forced integration. They didn't see integration as new opportunities for black kids, or maybe they did but saw it more as their child mingling with dangerous gangsters who would introduce them to drugs and violence. My wife, when she was a single mom, decided that she would send her daughter to a private parochial school because they were more strict. I think Mikaela would have excelled at any school because she is bright and her mother was attentive and supportive.

In the Texas town where I was born, integration created a win-win for students at Palacios Jr. High and a black teacher named Larry Deadrick. He taught American History when I was in the ninth grade and made it more interesting with his cool swagger and tons of facts about the African-American experience. Looking back, there was so much more he could have told us, but we thought we were learning something controversial when we heard about Crispus Attucks. I made straight As in his class, aced every test. Thanks, Mr. Deadrick!

Are public schools and teachers getting a bad rap? According to Noah Karvelis, one of the teachers who led a statewide strike in Arizona in 2018 that resulted in a 20 percent pay raise, a list of roadblocks to success for teachers includes:

- Resources
- Class sizes
- Debt for advanced degrees and limited financial incentive to pursue those degrees

- Respect
- Healthcare
- Time restrictions/demands

"And very few counselors/social workers, so you end up performing a lot of those jobs as well for your students," said Karvelis, who teaches music at Littleton Elementary in Avondale, Arizona.

"It all essentially revolves around funding. Our teachers don't have the resources they need such as textbooks that go beyond W. Bush or enough chairs in the class for all of the students due to huge class sizes," said Karvelis. "For many teachers, they take on tens of thousands of dollars in debt to pursue a master's degree and then are only given a small pay increase. Say, $500 or $800, in some cases. It takes years to break even on that investment. Yet many teachers do it to hone their craft and teach more efficiently.

"We have abysmal health care. Many teachers can't afford to insure their own families and, because of the costs, have paychecks with $700 [net] even though they have 20 years of experience and a Master's degree.

"As for counselors, we have an incredibly high student-to-counselor ratio which negatively impacts students in any number of ways. Ultimately, the teacher then has to essentially provide that service to their students."

Vouchers and some charter schools siphon off public money to private schools which are often for-profit companies. Public education is part of the covenant with the American people and pulling those resources from those who can't afford private schooling is not living up to that promise.

When schools lose students, they have to reduce services, and that usually means cuts to "non-essential" staff, with music and art programs absorbing much of the blow. And schools, like other brick and mortar establishments, can't reduce associated operating expenses. Remaining students still need heat, lights, clean classrooms, and meals.

The Network for Public Education, a concerned party opposed to vouchers and so-called education reform, had statistics to support their position:

> In Nashville, TN, an independent research firm MGT of America estimated the net negative fiscal impact of charter school growth on the district's public schools result in more than $300 million in direct costs to public schools over a five-year period.
>
> Another study by MGT in Los Angeles, CA found district public schools lost $591 million due to dropping enrollment rates among students who leave and go to charters.
>
> A research study of school districts in Michigan found that choice policies significantly contribute to the financial problems of Michigan's most hard-pressed districts. When the percent of students attending charter schools approaches 20 percent, there are sizeable adverse impacts on district finances.
>
> In New York, a study found that in just one academic year the Albany school district lost $23.6 – $26.1 million and the Buffalo district lost $57.3 – $76.8 million to charter schools. Because charters in both districts had smaller percentages of limited English proficient students, and charters in Albany enrolled fewer students with disabilities, the affected public schools were unable to reduce spending on English as Second Language and special education services.

If the neighborhood public school is to stay open, then homeowners could see a rise in taxes. The *Washington Post* reported, "Direct and disguised vouchers to private schools and other public school alternatives start small and then expand, increasing the burden on taxpayers. Additional administrative costs coupled with a lack of transparency waste taxpayer dollars and open the door to excessive legal and fraudulent personal gain."

It appears that efforts to privatize our schools, much like efforts to privatize our prison system, leave public education susceptible to abuse, divert much-needed funding to for-profit private business, and lack transparency and accountability. It should be obvious that government cannot be operated as a business.

Chapter 21 No Justice! No Peace!

Chapter 21

No Justice! No Peace!

"Well, the terrible thing right now, and I don't know the statistics, but there's a growing concern in some communities about how rapidly people are sent from school to jail, how quickly they're put into the criminal justice system. And, of course, the rapidly growing number of brown people, both men and women, in prison." Anna Deavere Smith

"What does labor want? We want more schoolhouses and fewer jails…" Samuel Gompers

"Anyone who thinks that race does not still … skew the application of criminal justice in this country is just not paying close enough attention. Our prisons are full of black and brown men and women who are serving inappropriately long and harsh sentences for non-violent mistakes in their youth." – Rand Paul

In the months between high school graduation and going to work for Ma Bell, I was caught in an amusement park carrying 60 amphetamines, enough for a long night of test prep in a very small frat house. I was arrested and escorted in handcuffs to a patrol car past startled patrons. I was 18, scared and in serious denial that this was even happening. My grandmother borrowed against her house for the $10,000 bail and

I was released the next day. I was assigned a public defender, and for two months I wondered what the future held for me.

It was expedient, my public defender assured me, to plead guilty. I did, though I insisted I was innocent. I was lucky. Young and white, with no prior record, I was given six months deferred prosecution. The lenient judgment meant my present charges would be dropped after six months but would compound a penalty for any future offense. How would I have fared at another time or place, say Texas in the sixties? Or as a person of color?

The answer these days comes down to one question: What kind of justice can you afford? Yes, lack of money can make a difference between a good defense and a travesty of justice for the accused. The Prison Policy Initiative reports that most bail amounts are equivalent to eight months salary for many defendants.

I was proud when my state, California, was the first state to eliminate money bail when a California appellate court declared the state's cash bail system as unconstitutional. The California legislature passed the Money Bail Reform Act in 2018. Washington, D.C. instituted a moneyless bail system first, but one might argue the impact of the Golden States legislation will impact many more.

"Today, California reforms its bail system, so that rich and poor alike are treated fairly," Governor Jerry Brown declared after signing the bill. The new law goes into effect in October 2019. The judicial system through the local courts will decide who will be released while they await trial. Those decisions will be based on an algorithm created by the courts in each jurisdiction, with defendants scored on how likely they are to show up for their court date and the seriousness of their crime. In most nonviolent misdemeanor cases, defendants would be released within 12 hours.

This issue of money bail, like the issue of same-sex marriage, is toppling like a row of dominoes, state by state. The *Houston News* reports U.S. District Judge Lee Rosenthal has determined that Harris County's bail policy violates constitutional guarantees of due process and equal protection even in Texas. The judge ordered the county to start releasing those arrested for misdemeanors who haven't been able to meet bail in a mid-May pending trial.

Putting away the "bad guys."

Prison populations ballooned in the 1970s and climbed steadily through 2009. A quarter of the world's prisoners are behind bars in U.S. jails, even though we make up only five percent of the world's population. According to the Prison Policy Initiative, the American criminal justice system holds almost 2.3 million people in 1,719 state prisons, 102 federal prisons, 1,852 juvenile correctional facilities, 3,163 local jails, and 80 Indian Country jails as well as in military prisons, immigration detention facilities, civil commitment centers, state psychiatric hospitals, and prisons in the U.S. territories. Every year 626,000 walk out of *prison* gates, but people go to *jail* 10.6 million times each year. Jail populations are high because jails are meant to be temporary, and most of our jails are full of people who have not been tried, much less convicted, of any crime. Some have just been arrested and will make bail in the next few hours or days, and others are too poor to make bail and they will be behind bars until their trial.

Reagan pushed for tough drugs laws, George HW Bush pushed harder. Things got worse for those convicted in the 1980s and 1990s. America was on a get-tough agenda. Prison populations more than quadrupled. By early 1994, 31 states and DC had mandatory minimum sentences.

President Bill Clinton was a "successful" Democratic president because he co-opted the Republican agenda. The Prison Population Initiative pointed to Clinton-era legislation that led to mass incarceration:

- 1994: Violent Crime Control and Law Enforcement Act put 100,000 more police on the streets and created federal economic incentives for states to make their own laws more punitive. The 1994 crime bill broadened "three strikes," funded more prison construction, and vastly expanded the death penalty. Under this law low-income, incarcerated people were no longer eligible for Pell Grants to pay for higher education courses.

- 1996: The Prison Litigation Reform Act made it harder for incarcerated people to use the federal courts to protect their civil rights and made it easier for prisons and jails to escape oversight of their operations.
- 1996: The Anti-terrorism and Effective Death Penalty Act made it harder for wrongly convicted people to prove their innocence by limiting their access to habeas corpus, legal challenges to the court that kept many on death row alive and frustrated prosecutors. AEDPA may well have caused the death of innocent people who were executed because of the absence of due process.
- 1996: Megan's Law required states to share law enforcement's databases of people who have committed sex offenses with the public. While no doubt well-intended, there is no evidence — despite years of scholarly effort — to indicate that these laws reduce sex offender recidivism. They seem increasingly likely to be exasperating it while wasting resources and time that could be spent on other, more effective law enforcement activities.
- 1996: The Personal Responsibility and Work Opportunity Reconciliation Act, aka the bill to "end welfare as we know it," also included provisions that banned, for life, people with drug felony convictions from ever receiving food stamps.
- 1997: The Adoption and Safe Families Act required states to move more quickly to terminate parental rights and place children who are in foster homes up for adoption. One side effect of this law is it made it more likely that any incarcerated parent with a sentence of at least 15 months — even if their crime did not involve their children — could lose their children forever.
- 1998: The Higher Education Amendments of 1998 delayed or denied federal financial aid for college to anyone with a misdemeanor or felony drug conviction.

There have been attempts to undo most of the damage of these Clinton-driven initiatives. At the federal level, judges have been given more discretion in sentencing. At the state level, 29 states have taken steps to roll back sentences, but most are not retroactive.

The system we have continues to breed racism and fear on both sides, though to argue that young black men aren't on the losing side, is to ignore the statistics. "You just look at our prisons and jails," said Carol Steiker, Henry J. Friendly Professor of Law at Harvard Law School, "and they are overwhelmingly filled with poor people and people of color."

In a Slate article, writers Andrew Kahn and Chris Kirk attempted to explain What It's Like to Be Black in the Criminal Justice System:

1. Black Americans are more likely to have their cars searched.
2. Black Americans are more likely to be arrested for drug use.
3. Black Americans are more likely to be jailed while awaiting trial.
4. Black Americans are more likely to be offered a plea deal that includes prison time.
5. Black Americans may be excluded from juries because of their race.
6. Black Americans are more likely to serve longer sentences than white Americans for the same offense.
7. Black Americans are more likely to be disenfranchised because of a felony conviction.
8. Black Americans are more likely to have their probation revoked.

According to "The New Jim Crow: Mass Incarceration in the Age of Colorblindness" by Michelle Alexander:

> The rhetoric of "law and order," first used by Southern segregationists, became more attractive as Americans increasingly came to reject outright racial discrimination. Coded racial messages became the staple of the Republican strategy in the coming decades. As Nixon advisor, H. R. Haldeman described, "He [President Nixon] emphasized that you have to face the fact that the whole problem is really the blacks. The key is to devise a system that recognizes this while not appearing to."

After Jim Crow, Alexander opines that Martin Luther King Jr.'s poor people's campaign was another opportunity to unite poor whites and Blacks, but the criminal justice system provided a way to keep us divided. In 2010, 74 percent of drug offenders convicted under mandatory minimums were black and brown.

Being locked up is just part of the picture in the power structure that makes up correctional control. Those working to change an unjust system need to consider the others toiling to pay their "debt to society," some 840,000 people on parole and 3.7 million people on probation. Sometimes the alternatives to incarceration, including mental health programs that deal with issues like drug and alcohol abuse, may look preferable, but come with their own set of rules that prolong the journey back into mainstream society.

Fortunately, for us, some organizations are attempting to turn back the tide to a more reasonable approach to criminal justice. One such organization just appeared on the horizon, the Fair Trial and Penalty Equitable Initiative, founded by Terry Dean Brooks. The fledgling organization is targeting nine areas of reform:

1. Controlled Substance Act
2. Juvenile Justice and Delinquency Prevention Act
3. Foster and Adoption Services
4. Universal Background Checks
5. Mental Health Solvency and Resilience Act

    This would allocate federal funds to states and require them to distribute the funds to local mental health branches and related agencies by direct deposit

6. IMAGINE Act (Immigration/Migration and Growth in New Economy Act)

    Would exempt Dreamer youth, provide a pathway to citizenship, provide economic growth in urban and rural immigrant communities, and ensure access to higher education

7. Strengthen violent crime and sexual predator registries
8. Pass Violence Against Women and Exploitation Resiliency Act

9. Pass Community Enforcement Service Act which would institute state mandates in police protocols

Private Prisons

Private prisons are taking over where state coffers haven't been able or willing to keep up with burgeoning prison populations, and it has proven to be a profitable enterprise. CoreCivic and GEO Group, the country's largest private prison contractors, earned $4 billion between them in fiscal year 2017. Both companies operate immigration detention centers; these administration immigration policies have ensured their continued success.

According to the Justice Policy Institute, "private prisons have increased the number of people held in private federal facilities by approximately 120 percent since 1990, while the number held in private state facilities increased roughly 33 percent.

"During this same period, the total number of people in prison increased less than 16 percent. Meanwhile, spending on corrections has increased 72 percent since 1997, to $74 billion in 2007."

Anti-immigrant legislation implemented in Arizona and other states that require expanded incarceration and housing of immigrants has provided quite the windfall for Corrections Corporation of America (CCA). The Justice Policy Institute reported that in 2010, CCA operated 66 correctional and detention facilities, 45 of which they owned with contracts in 19 states, the District of Columbia and with the three federal detention agencies.

It appears CCA might have contributed significantly to their own financial success as part of the American Legislative Executive Council's (ALEC's) Criminal Justice Task Force, creating templates for private prison contractors interested in developing their own anti-immigration legislation. (CCA has stated that, after years of steering the Task Force, they are no longer affiliated with ALEC.)

So, turning our prisons over to the private sector is a win-win, right? They assume all the costs of incarceration and we taxpayers get a break.

But private prisons are corporations out to maximize profits. Private prison companies and their subcontractors that provide health care and food cut corners. They're creating hostile environments that are more violent and undermine sincere rehabilitation efforts. Serious oversight is desperately needed.

Follow the money.

Figures from the Prison Policy Initiative point to a system that we are subsidizing in the absence of real prison reform:

> In 2014, the two largest private prison companies in the U.S., Corrections Corporation of America (CCA) and GEO Group, spent at least $5.9 million on lobbying and campaign contributions.

> Private prison contractors earn their money from government contracts, which means we taxpayers pay for these companies to lobby and throw campaign contributions around. CCA and GEO Group are using our money to grow their businesses.

> During the 2013 and 2014 election years, the corrections industry contributed more than $2.5 million to 360 candidates running for state offices.

> In 2014, out of the 30 governors, lieutenant governors, controllers, attorney generals, and legislators that received individual contributions of $5,000 or greater from the corrections industry, 27 won their races.

> During the 2014 election cycle, CCA contributed to 23 senators and 25 representatives in the House and GEO Group contributed to 10 senators and 28 representatives.

> In 2014, out of the 17 senators and representatives that received contributions of $5,000 or greater from CCA or GEO Group, 14 won their races.

In 2015, CCA hired 102 lobbyists in 25 states, and GEO Group hired 79 lobbyists in 15 states.

Community Education Centers (CEC), Corizon Correctional Healthcare, Global Tel*Link (GTL), and MHM Services—companies that provide services to the criminal justice system—likely hired more than 150 lobbyists at the state level.

In 2015, CCA and GEO Group hired 20 lobbyists in Washington, D.C., paying them a combined $1.6 million.

Seventy percent of their lobbyists had previously worked in congressional offices.

Education behind bars

Education as an integral part of rehabilitation is making a comeback. The organization Corrections to College has issued a report on recent successes:

> In three years, California has gone from offering face-to-face college in one prison to full-credit degree-building college courses in 34 of 35 prisons at all security levels. Almost 4,500 students are enrolled in these face-to-face college pathways each semester, and they consistently outperform students on campus. Critically, more than 95 percent of those in prison and jail will come home, but recidivism rates remain high, with more than 60 percent rearrested within two years. Students in prison who participate in correctional education have 43 percent lower odds of heading back to prison after release than those who do not. The numbers improve even more for college courses: incarcerated students in college programs have 51 percent lower odds of ending up back in prison as compared to those in other education.
>
> Reentry college programs for these new students have expanded from one to nine California State University

> campuses, and from fewer than ten to almost 40 community colleges.
>
> In California, over eight million residents are estimated to be living in the community with an arrest or conviction record. We have 35 prisons and 58 county jails, and approximately 700,000 Californians are estimated to be in prison, in jail, or under criminal justice supervision on any given day. The system is enormous, but it has met its match: our public higher education system, with 114 community colleges serving over two million students, 10 University of California (UC) campuses, and 23 California State University (CSU) campuses, is equally immense.

Students in prison who receive an education are more likely to find employment upon release, transforming them from "offenders" into taxpayers and community leaders. Of course, these efforts fail when students – incarcerated or otherwise – can't find jobs that provide decent wages.

The Final Deterrent?

The ACLU has been a long-time opponent of the death penalty:

> Death sentences are predicted not by the heinousness of the crime but by the poor quality of the defense lawyers, the race of the accused or the victim, and the county and state in which the crime occurred. From 1976 to 2015, 1,392 executions occurred in the United States, and 995 of them took place in the South. Time and time again, we have proven that the criminal justice system fails to protect the innocent and persons with severe mental disabilities and illnesses from execution. Between 1973 and 2015, 148 innocent death-row prisoners in 26 different states were exonerated and released.

In a 2015 *Time* article entitled "The Death of the Death Penalty," writer David Von Drehle points out that the tide is turning: "Change is not coming quickly or easily. Americans have stuck with grim determination to the idea of the ultimate penalty even as other Western democracies have turned against it. On this issue, our peer group is not Britain and France; it's Iran and China."

Nebraska's legislature abolished the death penalty in May 2015, despite an attempted veto by its governor. Other states like Pennsylvania and Illinois have declared a moratorium on capital punishment. Even Texas courts are no longer handing out death penalties. "There, as elsewhere, prosecutors, judges, and jurors are concluding that the modern death penalty is a failed experiment," writes Von Drehle.

Are we as a nation finally building a system of justice that treats everyone equally? Hardly. But efforts by the ACLU, Death Penalty Focus, Prison Policy Initiative, the Innocence Project and the Fair Trial and Penalty Equitable Initiative have produced results and moved the ball forward.

The Innocence Project's mission, according to their website, "is to free the staggering number of innocent people who remain incarcerated, and to bring reform to the system responsible for their unjust imprisonment."

Rodney was wrongfully accused, prosecuted and convicted of rape and kidnapping he did not commit. In 1996, a 17-year-old victim of a sexual assault incorrectly identified him out of a photo line-up. Rodney's lawyer warned him he could get a life sentence for the crime if he took the case to trial and counseled him to plead guilty. He also suggested to Rodney that he would likely serve only two of the seven years.

Rodney explained: "I couldn't go against the system and I thought to get home to my son and to salvage my life, the best thing I could do was to plead guilty and to fight it once I got home."

One of the most egregious offenses is an inadequate defense. According to the Innocence Project, in some of the worst cases, lawyers have:

- slept in the courtroom during a trial
- been disbarred shortly after finishing a death penalty case
- failed to investigate alibis

- failed to call or consult experts on forensic issues
- failed to show up for hearings

> System failures include incentivized informants who are trying to make a deal for themselves, false confessions or admissions, misidentification by eyewitnesses, misapplication of forensic science that causes errors in testing or misinterpretation of the evidence, and government misconduct resulting in coerced confessions and withholding of evidence that could often exonerate a defendant.

It's the money.

Thousands end up in the civil court system each year over family disputes, domestic violence, eviction, foreclosure, denied wages, and discrimination on the job, and have no right to a court-appointed attorney. If they can't afford a lawyer, they're on their own to face a system that is often confusing and riddled with fees. For poorer citizens, the cost of seeking justice often becomes so prohibitive they give up.

That is especially true in David v Goliath scenarios in medical malpractice cases against hospitals or disputes with banks and other large corporations. Most of us realize that corporate lawyers have the resources to draw out a case indefinitely and will prevail eventually, leaving the aggrieved broke and left holding the bag.

It's no wonder civil cases escalate into criminal. The sheer frustration of battling an arcane system is enough to tempt a wronged individual into taking matters into their own hands, with often disastrous results.

In conclusion…

I have failed even to scratch the surface of this issue. To do so would require another separate book. What I have attempted to do, as with all previous chapters, is provoke thought and conversation, some ideas and ultimately some new ideas and new legislation.

Let's consider the financial divide in healthcare.

Chapter 22 Healthcare Haves and Have-nots

Chapter 22

Healthcare Haves and Have-nots

"Let us be the ones who say we do not accept that a child dies every three seconds simply because he does not have the drugs you and I have. Let us be the ones to say that we are not satisfied that your place of birth determines your right for life. Let us be outraged, let us be loud, let us be bold."
Brad Pitt

"Everyone should have health insurance? I say everyone should have health care. I'm not selling insurance." Dennis Kucinich

"Virtually every other developed country has embraced a single-payer system that's far more efficient than ours. Those nations treat health care as a fundamental human right. It's time to stop wasting our money on elaborate efforts to deny people care. Instead, let's devote our resources to providing affordable quality care to every American whenever they need it. - Cathy Glasson, RN, President of SEIU Local 199

At this time, I'm 63 years old. I discovered I had asthma in 1982. I have had a bit of trouble with my eyes: a detached retina in 2000, cataracts and glaucoma. I was diagnosed with colon cancer in 2010 and, knock on wood, have been declared cancer-free every year since. Four years ago I was told I have Parkinson's Disease, an affliction without a cure. "I feel like I have an expiration date stamped on my forehead," I said to my regular doctor. I mention all of this to show that I know what to expect from my healthcare provider, Kaiser Permanente of Southern California.

I have heard a lot of criticisms about Kaiser, the first non-profit healthcare system in California. But I have stayed with Kaiser since the 1980s because they have gained my trust. At the urging of a partner, I tried another plan for a year because it gave me access to doctors and staff at UCLA Medical Center. They were competent for the most part, dealing with my detached retina and other issues. I lost my sense of smell when a cocky surgeon performed a rhinoplasty, removing excess cartilage in my sinus cavity. He left to practice in another state shortly after that. I went back to Kaiser.

Dr. Bill Honigman, a proponent of Single Payer, has educated himself well on the ins and outs of our current healthcare system.

"Kaiser is a nice intermediate provider model between what is commonly referred to as care given by 'committed versus committee' providers. A committed provider would be your longtime family doctor, trusted, tried and true, but admittedly not necessarily up on all the latest greatest methodologies perhaps. A committee would be your UCLA or Mayo Clinic, all evidence-based but not necessarily personal and attentive to your own needs, often with student physicians as your frontline provider with a regular turnover within just a couple of years. Kaiser falls in the middle of the spectrum between the two." explained Honigman. "It is a large group model interdisciplinary practice, with providers who often stay for their entire career, and enthusiastically participate in multi-specialty committees like for a drug formulary to decide on best practices, specifically with 'health maintenance' in mind for their patients. Of course, that's primarily on the provider side.

"Kaiser is also an insurance company and unfortunately allows business practices like selling faulty 'financial products' to influence decisions regarding the availability of resources to its providers. For example, within the last 10 to 15 years, Kaiser has introduced so-called 'skinny plans' that have deductibles and higher co-pays to capture market share from large employer groups. This, of course, undermines efforts by its providers who may think specific tests and treatments are needed only to have their patients refuse them due to untoward out-of-pocket costs. It's a complicated mixed bag, that again a Single Payer system of Universal Healthcare where patients can freely choose providers or provider groups would resolve. "

I'm not saying I received better healthcare at Kaiser or worse at UCLA. They were comparable. The difference was the atmosphere in which I received my care.

Kaiser Permanente in Panorama City, California, as its other medical centers, draws its patients from the surrounding community, a wide diversity of incomes, nations of origin, ages and cultures. Kaiser has invested and grown the campus over the years and has focused on improving care and developing a computer system that brings up health history at the push of a button. Their egalitarian "we'll take everybody" facilities and the diversity of their staff, doctors and patients say, "socialized medicine." But that's okay. I appreciate them though, like all large, unwieldy bureaucracies, it's easy to grow frustrated.

The UCLA Medical Center campus is situated in opulent West Los Angeles adjacent to Beverly Hills. Their patients are also probably from the surrounding neighborhoods, most very affluent while retaining the diversity of LA. I felt, though admitting a year is not long enough to give an accurate assessment, that these folks in their business attire were probably receiving more attention, thus more care, than my neighbors over the hill in the San Fernando Valley. I have nothing to validate the truth of that feeling, the hushed corridors and vaulted ceilings of UCLA buildings notwithstanding.

A study by the Journal of the American Medical Association suggests that geography has a lot to do with your state of health and life expectancy. Living in an affluent county and having a college education could add 20 years to your life. The study indicated that haves can focus on lifestyle choices and prevention; the have-nots can't afford the better "platinum" healthcare plans and will sometimes forgo health insurance in an attempt to balance other household costs.

In a *Washington Examiner* article exploring the issue, cardiologist Dr. Kevin Campbell, interpreted the JAMA study that looked at differences in "socioeconomic and race/ethnicity factors, behavioral and metabolic risk factor, and health care factors" from 1980 to 2014 and suggested several solutions (in bold) that had a tenuous connection to the study's data:

Tort reform: a favorite bugaboo of physicians who complain about the high costs of malpractice insurance, Dr. Campbell stated that doctors are practicing "defensive medicine" which leads to expensive and "unnecessary" tests to avoid patient lawsuits. "The best tort reform would be Universal Healthcare. Countries around the world who have it, have half the malpractice claims that we do per capita for two reasons. First, when patients leave the hospital, there's no bill, so there are no personal losses to recover, other than for genuine bad outcomes. And secondly, if you have no limits on how often you can see your doctor, you are way less likely to sue them if something goes wrong. They have built a time-honored trust, a real patient-doctor relationship, something we have long given up to insurance company rationing of provider visits," that's according to Dr. Honigman, a physician in California.

Allow insurers to compete across state lines: Dr. Campbell believes that increased competition, especially in areas where patients have zero or a single healthcare choice (estimated to be 20-25 percent of U.S counties), will "force insurers to compete with one another for our business and allowing them to cross state lines is likely to lower costs, improve care and improve choice."

Place limits on drug prices: Pointing to the well-documented fact that Big Pharma charges U.S. consumers more than anyone else in the world, Dr. Campbell suggested, "How can we expect patients to improve their health status if they cannot follow their treatment plan due to a lack of financial resources? ... We must hold big pharma accountable IF they are found to be price gouging." If? If they aren't price gouging, then we are subsidizing the industry's largesse for the rest of the globe.

Individual responsibility: "Treating diseases is a team effort. Doctor and patient must work together, but we must be allowed to collaborate without government interference in the exam room."

Neither Dr. Campbell nor the study deals with the high costs of specialists, tests that aren't administered because insurers want to avoid additional charges or the concept of standardized prices for common practices or substances that include everything from an IV drip to an aspirin. All of these would address the concerns of patient healthcare inequality and life expectancies mentioned in the JAMA study.

The Patient Protection and Affordable Care Act aka Obamacare was passed on March 23, 2010. The Affordable Care Act provided health care coverage to an additional 20 million, permitted children to remain under parents' plans until age 26, and prohibited insurers from charging more to those with pre-existing conditions.

In many ways, however, the ACA was a sellout to Big Pharma and insurance companies. States and insurers weren't allowed to negotiate better drug prices, and a hoped-for option or Single Payer system were not part of the national plan passed by Congress. The most popular form of Single Payer has been called Medicare for All, a public option would be an alternative to other, more costly plans. Republicans are adamantly opposed to both any type of Single Payer plan would include robust government involvement, anathema to a free market model. Studies from the Congressional Budget Office have concluded that a public plan would cost consumers substantially less and would allow negotiated lower drug prices.

Let's look a little closer at Obamacare. Is the plan the great equalizer, the panacea for healthcare inequality?

An article from the website of California's ACA Plan called Covered California has dealt with misinformation that has made the rounds since the Affordable Care Act was first passed. Death Panels? There was discussion during the design stage to include free coverage for doctor's appointments to deal with end-of-life issues. The idea was scrapped, but many think it's still part of the ACA.

Are immigrants getting free healthcare? Nope. Immigrants in the country illegally are prohibited from getting Obamacare. They can get preventive care at community health clinics. That is supposed to lower health care costs for the rest of us and keep infectious diseases from spreading. As before the ACA, emergency rooms must treat everyone. When more people in the country illegally use community health clinics, there are fewer expensive emergency room bills.

Medicare benefits haven't been cut. The ACA cuts *funding* for Medicare by $716 billion over ten years. Hospitals are paid for better results rather than for every test and procedure. Under the ACA, hospitals lose $260 billion. ACA restrictions on cost increases mean Medicare Advantage insurance providers are collecting $156 billion less. Medicare Advantage plans rose 5.9 percent a year over the last five years. The ACA limits cost increases to just one percent above economic growth rate, a confusing formula of GDP, unemployment, and inflation. The rest of the cuts to Medicare funding affect home health care, hospice, and skilled nursing services.

According to writer Kimberly Amadeo and thebalance.com, the ACA actually increased Medicare benefits. "Medicare now includes free preventive care, like physicals and mammograms. In 2020, beneficiaries will receive 100 percent funding for the Part D "doughnut hole" prescription drug costs."

My brothers and sisters in the Teamsters union were enraged when they learned of the so-called Cadillac tax due to be implemented against their negotiated benefits beginning in 2020. The 40 percent excise tax will probably also hit workers with high health care costs due to employer plans that exceed $10,200 in premiums per year for individuals and $27,500 for families. The tax will look at employer and employee premium contributions, contributions to health savings accounts (HSAs), Archer medical savings accounts (MSAs), flexible spending accounts (FSAs), and health reimbursement accounts (HRAs).

A Koch Brothers-funded working paper released by the Mercatus Center at George Mason has inadvertently made a case for a Medicare-for-All Single Payer system. Former Speaker of the House Paul Ryan praised the study before discovering the facts: Current healthcare system cost: $49 trillion. Medicare for all cost: $32 trillion. We save $17 trillion and thousands of lives by covering everyone.

Conservative states still try austerity, withholding healthcare or selling it to the highest bidder. In Iowa, poor constituents are feeling the brunt of healthcare cuts. Cathy Glasson is a Registered Nurse (RN) and President of SEIU Local 199 representing 5,000 Iowa healthcare workers and public employees. She was a Democratic candidate for governor, finishing second in the 2018 primary. In California, with its "top two" election process, she could have found herself in a race against another Democrat, and we might have seen just how progressive Iowa is. Glasson wrote an op-ed about the state's health care system for the Des Moines Register. "About 600,000 poor or disabled Iowans have their health care covered by Medicaid, which has been managed by for-profit companies since 2016," she wrote, "and Iowa state government continues to hand oversight to private companies.

"...All of Iowa's hospitals are being squeezed in a fiscal vise. Ever since former Gov. Terry Branstad privatized the management of Iowa's Medicaid system in 2016, the for-profit providers that run it have been refusing to reimburse hospitals for millions of dollars in care. Last year, charity care — care for which hospitals aren't paid — jumped 17.4 percent."

Costs are once again climbing as are the numbers of uninsured. Glasson pointed to an oft-repeated statistic: our percentage of GDP being eaten up in health care costs, (17.2 percent), close to double the costs anywhere else on the planet. Single payer is the answer, she wrote, "let's devote our resources to providing affordable quality care to every American whenever they need it."

The bill languishing in the Republican-controlled Congress that would provide a Single Payer system is HR 676. It would become Medicare For All, provided to every resident in the country.

Under HR 676 patients could choose their own doctors and hospitals. This healthcare model would cover every person for all necessary medical care including prescription drugs, hospital, surgical, outpatient services, primary and preventive care, emergency services, dental (including oral surgery, periodontics, and endodontics), mental health, home health, physical therapy, rehabilitation (including substance abuse), vision care and correction, hearing services including hearing aids, chiropractic, durable medical equipment, palliative care, podiatric care, and long-term care.

HR 676 ends deductibles and co-payments. How would we pay for it? We would save hundreds of billions annually by cutting out the middleman, the one trained to say, "No." We could eliminate the high overhead and profits of the private health insurance industry.

Remember AEC, the American Legislative Exchange Council?

Health insurance companies such as Humana and Golden Rule Insurance (United Healthcare), profit directly from pro-business ALEC model bills, such as the Health Savings Account bill that passed in Wisconsin and has now spread across the country. Americans aren't saving enough to cover emergency medical expenses because they don't have extra disposable income to fund an HSA. So they're putting off necessary medical procedures. According to the Employee Benefit Research Institute, there are high deductibles and more than likely 87 percent would not have enough to deal with a catastrophic illness.

Pharmaceutical firms such as Bayer (which now owns Monsanto) and Johnson and Johnson benefit directly from ALEC's so-called tort reform that makes it hard er to sue when injured by dangerous products and reduces the damages they can recover.

Tort reform may affect the ability to sue for medical malpractice. The topic was an important one with Consumer Attorneys when I ran for California State Assembly in 2008. Lawyers were proposing changes to the state's Medical Injury Compensation Reform Act (MICRA) of 1975. Pain and suffering damages were capped at $250,000 and have never changed.

According to attorney Thom Peters: "Most California residents do not realize that they are limited by caps on medical malpractice lawsuits until a physician or medical care provider injure them. At that point, they might also discover they are unable to find an attorney to represent them, or that their recovery in court is insufficient to compensate them for their damages."

Many of the corporate representatives on ALEC's Private Enterprise Advisory Council are lobbyists representing corporations such as AT&T, Pfizer, Koch Companies, Exxon, and the U.S. Chamber of Commerce.

Just three health plans control the lion's share of the California market: Blue Shield, Health Net, and Kaiser Permanente. When health plans merge, consolidation is likely to result in fewer choices and higher prices for millions.

A bill in the California State Assembly, AB 595 by Assemblymember Jim Wood, promises stronger oversight and accountability with proposed health plan mergers by strengthening the Department of Managed Health Care's ability to scrutinize them and determine the impact on consumers. Governor Jerry Brown signed the bill into law in September, 2018.

Despite the insurance industry's claims, bigger is not necessarily better for consumers, and the state must thoroughly review proposed mergers, provide the public with the opportunity to voice concerns, and require health plans to put patients and the public first.

In the absence of a federal Single Payer system, states are exploring their options. In California, SB 562 would have provided such a system, but the bill was provocative and controversial. First introduced by Senator Ricardo Lara, his jaded colleagues accused him of grandstanding in his bid for state Insurance Commissioner. His bill contained no verbiage on funding, but pundits said Obamacare federal funds would help pay for it, money that's no longer a sure thing under the Trump Administration. Speaker of the Assembly Anthony Rendon took all the heat by sitting on the bill.

Interestingly, former State Senator Sheila Kuehl had managed to get a similar bill all the way to the governor's desk, where Governor Arnold Schwarzenegger promptly vetoed it and did so again when both houses passed the bill for a second time two years later. Kuehl's legislation, according to a non-partisan analysis, would have saved California $8 billion in the first year and $344 billion over ten years.

The wealthy have never worried that one healthcare catastrophe would mean bankruptcy. They pay a substantial amount for their health care coverage, but it is the best in the world. The NY Times explored the Shlain Private Medical Group in a June 3, 2017 article entitled, "The Doctor is in. Co-pay? $40,000." The article reveals that a price tag of $40,000 to $80,000 per family is the going rate for the kind of care these doctors offer. Doctors limits themselves to 50 patients, make home, work and airport visits, and "will locate the top specialists nationally, secure appointments with them immediately and accompany the patient on the visit, even if it is on the opposite coast."

Lenox Hill Hospital in New York hired a former executive of Louis Vuitton and Nordstrom to cater to V.I.P. patients and make them forget they were in a hospital and feel like they were visiting a luxury hotel. The Park Avenue Suite in the maternity ward costs $2,400 per night and overlooks the famed boulevard. The suite includes a separate sitting room for family members, a kitchenette and a full wardrobe closet. Slightly less grand, other private rooms in Lenox Hill's maternity ward range from $630 to $1,700 per night. Who wouldn't want that kind of care? Other families still share an old-fashioned room divided by a curtain.

Doesn't Congress get their healthcare for free? Almost. Their Obamacare Gold Plan is 72 percent subsidized and, while in Washington, they're entitled to free medical outpatient care at military facilities in the D.C. area as well as "free or low-cost care" through the Office of the Attending Physician. That's not a little clinic located in the basement of the Capitol. ABC News reported in 2009 that the Office of the Attending Physician includes physicals, routine examinations, on-site X-rays and lab work, physical therapy and referrals to medical specialists from military hospitals and private medical practices. According to congressional budget records, the office is staffed by at least four Navy doctors as well as at least a dozen medical and X-ray technicians, nurses and a pharmacist. When specialists are needed, they're brought to the capitol, usually at no cost to the member.

Members of Congress do not pay for individual services they receive at the OAP, nor do they submit claims through their federal health insurance. Instead, they pay a flat, annual fee of $503 for all the care they receive. The rest of the cost of their care, sources said, is subsidized by taxpayers. Did someone say "entitlements?"

All of this excess at a time when the average person has to wait months to be seen by a doctor. A 2017 study by Merritt Hawkins reports that in 15 of the largest US cities it takes about 24 days for a new patient to book an appointment with a family physician, about six days longer than reported just three years prior.

> Boston is experiencing the longest average physician appointment wait times of the 15 metro markets examined in the survey: 109 days to see a family physician, 52 days to see a dermatologist, 45 days to see an obstetrician/gynecologist, 45 days to see a cardiologist and 11 days to see an orthopedic surgeon. On average, it takes 52 days to schedule a physician appointment in Boston, according to the survey.

Other countries have universal healthcare. Why don't we?

In 1906, the American Association of Labor Legislation (AALL), a progressive organization formed to make capitalism work for everyone. In 1912, they created a social welfare committee and decided to concentrate on health insurance for poor families with income under $1200 a year. The proposal included physicians, nurses, hospital care, sick pay, and maternity care. The proposal also called for a $50 death benefit.

In 1914, the American Medical Association (AMA) offered support for the AALL proposal. "Your plans are so entirely in line with our own that we want to be of every possible assistance." By 1916, the

AMA and AALL formed a united front on behalf of health insurance. "In 1917, the AMA House of Delegates favored compulsory health insurance as proposed by the AALL, but many state medical societies opposed it," says Karen S. Palmer, who presented this history of healthcare to Physicians for a National Health Program in 1999. "There was disagreement on the method of paying physicians, and it was not long before the AMA leadership denied it had ever favored the measure."

Meanwhile Samuel Gompers, the president of the American Federation of Labor, apparently worried that a government-based insurance system would weaken unions by usurping their role in providing social benefits, repeatedly criticized compulsory health insurance as a system of state supervision over people's health. In the decades before collective bargaining was legally recognized, unions were concerned with any effort that seemed to undermine their efforts on behalf of workers.

Health care costs also began to rise during the 1920's, mostly because the middle class began using hospital services and expenses started to gr ow. By the 1930s, medical expenses were considered a more serious problem than wage loss from sickness.

Concerns over the management of medical care led to the formation of the Committee on the Cost of Medical Care (CCMC). The CCMC was created and funded by eight philanthropic organizations including the Rockefeller, Millbank, and Rosenwald foundations and hosted a think tank of fifty economists, physicians, public health specialists, and major interest groups. Their research determined that there was a need for more medical care for everyone, and they published these findings in 26 research volumes and 15 smaller reports over a 5-year period. The AMA treated their published findings as heresy, calling it socialized medicine and "an incitement to revolution."

FDR could have included a healthcare plan in the Social Security bill introduced in 1935, but he knew the AMA opposed it and, at the time, its inclusion took a backseat to getting people back to work and creating old age benefits that eventually became Social Security. FDR's administration formed the Tactical Committee on Health Care in 1937 and introduced the National Health Act of 1939. Efforts to move that forward were killed by newly-elected conservatives and events that led up to World War II.

In 1944, the Committee for the Nation's Health, a group of representatives of organized labor, progressive farmers, and liberal physicians who were the principal lobbying group for the Wagner-Murray-Dingell Bill, called for compulsory national health insurance and a payroll tax.

Accusations said that that one of the committee's key policy analysts, I.S. Falk, was a Socialist tool and conduit between the International Labor Organization (ILO) in Switzerland and the United States government. The ILO, it was claimed, was "an awesome political machine bent on world domination." The bill was reintroduced every at every session of Congress for the next 14 years but never passed.

Harry Truman was firmly committed to passing a single universal, comprehensive health insurance plan, but in a climate of red-baiting, anything that even hinted at socialized medicine was immediately suspect. Senior Republican Senator Taft declared, "I consider it socialism. It is to my mind the most socialistic measure this Congress has ever had before it." Taft suggested that compulsory health insurance came right out of the Soviet constitution and stormed out of the hearings. Those who opposed it were those who would be most affected by it: the AMA. The urgency of a universal health care plan was also thwarted by success at the bargaining table.

In the 1960s, Medicare and Medicaid became law, ambitious efforts to cover the elderly and the indigent.

In the 1970s, universal health care again became a hot topic with congressional hearings and several bills in the hoppers. In February, Representative Martha Griffiths, a Democrat from Michigan, introduced a national health insurance bill developed with the AFL–CIO. In April, Senator Jacob Javits, a Republican from New York, introduced a bill to extend Medicare to all that would include existing Medicare cost sharing and coverage limits.

Senator Ted Kennedy, Democrat from Massachusetts, picked up the gauntlet after the two previous attempts failed. In August, 1970, Kennedy introduced a bipartisan national health insurance bill—without any cost sharing—developed with the Committee for National Health Insurance founded by United Auto Workers (UAW) president Walter Reuther, with a corresponding bill introduced in the House the following month by Representative James Corman, a Democrat from the San Fernando Valley in California. That bill also failed due to intense lobbying by the AMA.

In January 1971, Kennedy was appointed as chairman of the Health subcommittee of the Senate Labor and Public Welfare Committee and served as its chair for the next ten years. He introduced a reconciled bipartisan Kennedy–Griffiths bill proposing universal national health insurance. That bill's failure was followed by six frustrating years under Republican administrations that vowed to veto any national health care bill that might land on the president's desk.

In 1977, Kennedy tried to pass a bill under a Democratic president, Jimmy Carter. In December 1977, President Carter told Kennedy his bill must include a significant role for private insurance companies, minimize federal spending, and be phased-in to avoid rocking the federal budget. Kennedy and organized labor compromised and made the requested changes, but parted ways with Carter in July 1978 when he wouldn't commit.

First Lady Hillary Clinton worked with healthcare experts to give the nation the 1993 Clinton health care plan. The Clinton plan included mandatory enrollment in a health insurance plan, subsidies to guarantee affordability across all income ranges, and the establishment of health alliances in each state. Every citizen or permanent resident would thus be guaranteed medical care. Republicans were concerned that, if passed, the landmark legislation would be a PR nightmare for the GOP, with the Democratic Party painted as the heroes of the middle class. The bill was not passed.

The issue of universal health care continues to be raised, and a public option was included for state implementation under the Affordable

Care Act. Concerted efforts on a number of fronts: labor, organizations like Physicians for a National Healthcare Program, Democratic Party progressives and state legislation have signaled that Medicare for All is cost-effective, comprehensive and a genuine solution for curbing rising costs for healthcare and medicine.

What other ways is the middle class on life support? Let's look at housing and homelessness.

Chapter 23 Housing and Homelessness

Chapter 23

Housing and Homelessness

"When our economy is truly healthy, and everyone rises with the tide of prosperity, then issues such as the lack of affordable housing, homelessness, and hunger are greatly diminished." David Ige

"The suburbs cater to a social structure that is on its way out, a middle America that no longer exists." Doug Casey

"I live in a very low-income area. I can't drive more than a half mile in any direction without driving past a jail. One of those jails is conveniently two buildings away from the homeless shelter. This is strong evidence that the only crime directly enforced is poverty." Araxia Incitar, Florida

The effects of the Great Recession rumbled through the Middle Class long after the banks recovered, long after bankers and stockbrokers were fined and sentenced to long prison terms for dealing in toxic assets and hitting us with the bill. Oh, wait. NOBODY was charged, so nobody was found guilty. Let me remind you:

In the two years following the events of 2008, more than eight million Americans lost their jobs, the banks foreclosed on almost four million homes, 2.5 million businesses closed their doors, and more than 500 banks failed. Ten years later, we are finally climbing out of the hole that opened up and swallowed us in 2008.

The worth of my $290 thousand home has now climbed to about $560k. It's still a cracker box, but it's more than many of the next generation will be able to afford.

CFPB Mortgage Complaints

The Consumer Financial Protection Bureau, in its oversight role, has kept a running tally on homeowners' financial issues with negotiating mortgages:

> Trouble during the payment process
> Struggling to pay the mortgage
> Applying for a mortgage or refinancing an existing mortgage
> Closing on a mortgage
> Problem with a credit report or credit score

Some consumers can't reach their mortgage company on the phone. Consumers complained their mortgage company provided inaccurate or incomplete information or could not answer questions about their accounts. Consumers described a range of challenges when attempting to modify their mortgage.

When homeowners teetered on the brink of foreclosure, companies requested the same information over and over again and offered terms that were unaffordable.

The management of escrow accounts continues to be a challenge. Unexpected changes in monthly payments sometimes lead to overdrafts, oftentimes turning into a "difficult and protracted" dispute over automatic payments for the incorrect amounts.

Some consumers were confused when their loan was transferred to a new company. Some consumers had difficulty reconciling account balances or obtaining information related to their loan terms, including information about their Home Equity Loan or Home Equity Line of

Credit. Their loan account balance was inconsistent with the balance before the transfer, or information didn't match with their account history.

Older consumers described their nightmares with reverse mortgages. Many found it difficult to navigate the process of retaining property after the death of the borrower. Some non-borrowing spouses complained that after submitting requests to remain in the property following the death of a borrower, the process moved slowly, sometimes held up by multiple requests for the same documentation. Sometimes delays resulted in foreclosure proceedings. Successors in interest weren't able to buy or sell the property after providing proof of authority to act on behalf of the borrower's estate.

Over 30 percent of homeowners (26 percent white, 36 percent families of color) are what Prosperity Now calls "cost-burdened" — they spend more than 30% of their income on housing costs and are at risk of eviction or homelessness if the family suffers a decline in income.

Renters are faring much worse. Roughly half of renters (46 percent of white renters and 54 percent of renters of color) are cost-burdened and have been in this predicament since at least 2007 when Prosperity Now began collecting data. "You need four minimum wage jobs to afford the rent in LA. That lowers their ability to save to buy a home," said Larry Gross, Director for the Coalition for Economic Survival. "The homeownership figure in America has not really moved."

"Most of the single-family rentals are now Wall Street entities such as Blackstone Homes, the biggest owner and renter of single-family homes in California," said Gross. "At this point, if you have five single-family dwellings or more, you should be under rent control because [these entities] are totally exploiting their renters. They're not making any repairs. They're raising the rent. They're putting more and more of the things landlords normally provide: water, maintenance, lawn care on the tenants as extra costs. Even with rental control, it's clear it's rigged," said Gross.

"It's the most extreme version of power politics, landlord and tenant. Probably more so than worker and boss, because you can't hide. It's your home. For many people, they're living in fear, fear they're going to get evicted, fear that if they complain, the rent's going to go up. Because without rent control, a landlord can raise the rent as much as they want, as many times a year as they want, and can evict without reason. Tenants without that protection are extremely vulnerable."

That's why voters recently voted on an initiative that would repeal the Costa-Hawkins Act in California. Passed by the California legislature in 1995, Costa-Hawkins limits the use of rent control in California. Costa-Hawkins prohibits cities from implementing rent control on (a) housing first occupied after February 1, 1995, and (b) housing units where the title is separate from connected units, such as condominiums and townhouses. Costa-Hawkins also provided that landlords have a right to increase rent prices to market rates when a tenant moves out, meaning a rent-controlled apartment is no longer available for low-income renters. Before the passage of Costa-Hawkins, local governments were permitted to enact rent control, provided that landlords would receive just and reasonable returns on their rental properties.

Polls on the measure showed initial support for the measure, especially from renters, but "We're up against upwards of $100 million from landlords trying to defeat it," said CES' Larry Gross.

"A lot of the east coast rent control laws have been eliminated. They had rent control laws in Boston, Washington, D.C., and Miami, Florida at one point and eventually, the real estate industry and others were able to get rid of those laws. Here in California, we have the most rent control laws. In addition to LA, West Hollywood, Santa Monica, and up in the Bay Area, we have over 100 jurisdictions with mobile home rent control laws. While you own the mobile home, you're renting the space, so you're both a homeowner and a renter. If you get evicted or get a rent increase you can't afford, you can't put your mobile home on your back and find some other space. And there's been a big push to convert those mobile home parks to higher use and evict. These parks are a big source of affordable housing for seniors."

"Housing and homelessness are directly related," Gross stated. "Our role is trying to prevent homelessness. If we're housing existing homeless people, we'll never have enough housing, but if we're continually adding to those numbers, we're just spinning our wheels. We're never going to build our way out of the affordable housing crisis we have. As part of the effort to deal with homelessness, you also have to deal with preserving the existing affordable housing, keeping those tenants in their homes and not adding to the numbers. That's the role we play, trying to keep the roof over the heads of tenants who now have one."

California voters defeated Prop 10, the measure to allow local cities to reinstate rent control. The motion was defeated by 61 percent of the voters.

Homelessness

Just before dawn on January 17, 1994, we were shaken awake in the San Fernando Valley by a 6.8 magnitude earthquake that made my whole apartment building wobble and sway. Off in the distance, I heard terrified screams. My girlfriend and I grabbed the dog and felt our way down two dark flights of stairs. I had a vacation scheduled to begin that day, but I knew I would be needed at my job just down the street because I lived the closest.

I worked for 13 hours keeping telephone service flowing in and out of the Valley that day, occasionally diving under a desk as another aftershock rattled through. When I arrived home late that night, my girlfriend informed me that our building had been red-tagged by the fire department and we were to vacate immediately because the building wasn't considered safe. We had nowhere to go and I was tired and reluctant to leave, but a fireman making the rounds of the building again demanded we leave.

The first night was spent in the back of my SUV. Morning brought the realization that we had to find a place to live pronto. The next two days passed in a numb haze and despair as I came to grips that we were homeless. We had just the clothes on our backs, and my paycheck was off in an unknown future. I'm embarrassed to call my brief freefall homelessness, but I think if someone who took a roof over their heads for granted experienced a similar scenario, there would be more compassion and empathy for those who have ended up on the street.

Let's talk about homelessness.

The meeting was advertised as an opportunity to discuss the city's homelessness crisis in a "town hall" setting. I had not kept up with the Valley VOTE organization nor attended a meeting since 2013 when I was running for State Assembly. ValleyVOTE was founded in the heat of a secession movement in 2002 by Dr. Keith Richman, a conservative who felt the Valley was not receiving its fair share of city services.

The organization has retained its conservative roots as I discovered when perennial candidate/ValleyVOTE President Susan Shelley called the meeting to order. There were a handful of compassionate Progressives scattered throughout the room. In her opening remarks, Shelley asked the question, "How can we protect ourselves [against the homeless]?"

According to the National Coalition for the Homeless, there are 22 empty houses for every homeless person in America. Comedian George Carlin offered a housing plan that would provide prime real estate and also get rid of a pet peeve of his. "I know where they can build housing for the homeless. Golf courses! Just what we need: plenty of good land in nice neighborhoods, land that is currently being wasted on a meaningless, mindless activity engaged in primarily by white, well-to-do, male businessmen who use the game to get together to make deals to carve this country up a little finer among themselves."

Putting a face on the homeless.

I have known "Tom" for about ten years. Most of that time he was living with another friend in a strictly platonic relationship: she managed apartments, and he was the handyman. He's a nice guy who will do anything for a friend, but he has anger issues. I suppose, if I had experienced homelessness multiple times in my life, (now being one of them), I might be given to drinking a little too much and hiding white-hot anger just under the surface. That said, I talked to Terry about how he got to this point.

"I was about 20 or 21 the first time; I lost the place where I was staying in the [San Francisco] Bay area. I had a job, so that kept me afloat for a little while. I was in motels for a short time, then stayed with a friend. Then I was on the street. It's kind of a Catch-22: when you get into a motel, even if you've got a full-time job, 90 percent of your pay is going directly to the motel room, and you have ten percent to live on. You're juggling everything to try to have food, survive, and still have a roof over your head. You have nothing to put away to get out of the hole." Three months later, he was on the street.

"The trip out of the gutter was a long, stressful run as well. I was homeless for almost two years. I scrimped and saved and worked on something so I could get somewhere else. I went to jail during that time. While I was in jail things changed on the street. When I got out of jail, I was finally able to get up enough funds to get me into a better place, one rung of the ladder at a time."

"I stole a motorcycle," Tom explained. "I stole it, but I kept it for myself. If I had sold it like everything else I stole at the time, I would have had money to live on and wouldn't have got busted." He said he wasn't aware that the system was rigged against him until he "hit bottom. I went through the jail system and saw that end of it. I found out how many different laws were against homeless people: whether or not you could sleep on the sidewalk, different vagrancy laws, laws about whether or not you're sanitary. If you smell like piss and you're all dirty, they can take you off the street on that, or whether or not you've got any money in your pocket. They can take you off the street for just about anything and put you in jail. And then you're in the system.

Once you're in the system, you either become institutionalized and you're always going back into the system, or you get out, graduate and you don't go back to that school."

Ten years later, he found himself in a similar spot. In 2002 in LA, he was going to college, taking classes in visual arts. "My first year I got into student housing and that went well for a while. They told me it would cost me $40,000 for three years of school to get my bachelor's degree. It cost me $34,000 the first year. They really screwed with the numbers, and I wasn't prepared for it. At the end of my second year, I couldn't get student loans without paying some of what I owed, so my housing went away, and I was homeless in my pickup at that time." It lasted just a few months.

"I went back up north to my mom's place and took some classes to take care of some of the general education courses I needed for my bachelor's degree. My student loans went into collections. I now owe $92,000. I still have three classes to go, and I can't get into college without my transcript, and I can't get my transcript without setting up a payment program with a minimum down payment of $10,000."

How do those on the street cope? They hide in fear behind a façade of toughness. Women act deranged to keep predators at bay. There is drug and alcohol abuse, but some have survival skills that come in handy.

"Santa Monica has 67 laws on the books against homelessness. It's at the discretion of the officer whether or not to enforce it. At that point you're at the mercy of that officer who decides whether or not you're going to jail for 60, 90 days or just for the weekend, hitting the drunk tank for a little while."

The homeless who are on their own can be as young as 13 up to 70 years old. According to the *Los Angeles Times,* the number of those living in the streets and shelters of the city of L.A. and most of the county surged 75 percent — to roughly 55,000 from about 32,000 — in the last six years.

Tom again: "There are kids and families on the street as well. There are several different levels of street life. Some families live in their car and are traveling from shelter to shelter, trying to keep their kids safe and fed and warm and alive. They're the ones who need help the most. The people who don't need it the most take part of that away from them. Certain shelters only take single men, certain shelters take families – women, and children. The husband goes somewhere else, usually. According to the rules and regulations of different aid groups, married couples can't be together and receive aid. If you play the game of the system, you can use it to get off the street, but it's a tough game. It's a heartbreaker in many ways."

The *LA Times* reports that three out of four homeless people — 41,000 — live in cars, campers, tents, and lean-tos, by far the biggest single group of unsheltered people in any U.S. city. City officials have quadrupled homeless outreach teams, added 600 shelter beds, expanded winter shelter hours and ramped up hotel vouchers. Some 1,000 new employees are being hired at every level of homeless services, including support for people in the new housing projects. Everyone is trying to come up with ways to help.

Tom wasn't in favor of the attempt by the city of L.A. to subsidize the building of separate dwellings in residents' backyards to provide housing for the homeless.

"I don't think that's a good direction to go. There are enough empty buildings in the city of Los Angeles that the city could take, refit and make livable at a reasonable price for the taxpayer to provide mass housing – 400 to 500 beds instead of 100 or less at a shelter. There are warehouses downtown that are used for filming once or twice a year. The city could declare eminent domain and put [funds] into housing and give everybody a step up off the street, and an ability to have an address which gives you the ability to get a job, to get aid, to get help and food stamps. If you don't have an address, you can't get [on your feet.] Some get a PO box so they can receive mail. The homeless people that are skilled at being homeless, there are a few out there you can tell, that can be as smart as the guy who owns a bank across the street but they're begging for coins."

"I've been homeless three times. I'm homeless now," he states. "Nine months ago I lost my job, my home, my girlfriend all in the same month. Luckily, the part-time job I had gave me a place to park my van and a place to have my shop so I can try to rebuild my life and build my own company."

When asked if counseling is available, he said, "Not that I know of, unless you've been in jail. In jail, there are a few things available. It's just another game you've got to play to get a mere pittance from the state. It's never enough and always too hard to get. Most of [the homeless] don't even want to try. They'd rather stay in jail where they've got a cot, three meals a day and a TV. If they're smart and they're in jail, they know people, they've got something going on, there's always some sort of hustle, where they can be safer there than they are on the street."

Tom feels homelessness has changed him in positive ways. "It's made me stronger, more resourceful, more resilient, but it's all how you want to look at yourself as well. Having a roof over your head can be a temporary condition for anyone. I've known people, well-off people with $10,000-$15,000 savings in the bank, who lose everything and their savings are gone in a month or two because it wasn't enough to pay the rent or live on. They decide, 'I've got to sell this place.' They go to a motel, then that becomes too expensive, and they have no money to move into another place. Eventually, they end up in their car or, even worse, on the street pushing a cart. I've seen people who were well off who go to the street and never return. A lot do, but not everyone. It should not be a permanent place for anyone in today's society, but it is."

"You always feel kind of hopeless, but it's the fuel to the fire that gets that flame burning again to find something better, find a job, save a little money, get ahead. If you don't have a car, get a car. If you have a car, get a house or rent a room someplace, or storage shed. A lot of times that's the first AND the last stepping stone for a lot of people who lose their homes. Everything goes into storage, and if you carry it through, that's your stepping stone to getting out. Because you have a place to keep everything, you have your past and your future all in one place. If you lose your past, sometimes you lose your future.

"I'm not starving, and I still have change in my pocket to pass on to my homeless buddies I see on the street. We take care of each other. There's a sense of community and brotherhood. I earned my street cred when I was younger. It's an everyday struggle. When you're born in poverty, it's something you're never without. It's always been a part of my life. Always will be.

"After my mom and dad divorced, and my mom moved in with her parents, then got into her own place when we moved back down from Washington to the Bay area where I was born, she was a single mom and my sister and I were latchkey kids. There for a while both my mom and my sister were homeless; we were all homeless together for about three-four months at the beginning of the year. My mom got into a place now. My sister and her boyfriend have moved in with friends temporarily. They found a place they'll be moving into next month. "

Tom feels that both his circumstances of birth and the trajectory of his life brought him to this point. "With money, you can do anything. Without it, you're surviving. It's not like you're apt to do anything when whatever you want to do takes money away from your housing, your family, your food, your health . Certain priorities, if you took away one of them, could kill you. You don't want your family to suffer, you don't want to suffer. You get caught in this level of society that is very hard to get out without a helping hand, someone to say, 'I'm going to give you a place to stay for a month. You don't have to pay anything.' Some people take that month and get on a new road and never get back to the street. Others take it, and they're back 30 days later. I didn't want to stay on the streets, so I didn't. I don't want to stay on the streets now, so I won't. I've got people on the street who envy what I have. They would literally kill for it because they're sleeping on the rocks next to the tracks with a blanket. I have a van. I have electricity, portable AC in my van that keeps me cool during the 120-degree days inside the van most of the time. I'm so much better off than most, yet I'm still there. The homeless don't want to be there. A lot of people think he's there because he wants to be there. No. He's there because society has put him there and won't let him get up. There's a small population that doesn't care. They're content. They're healthy, they're fed and living life the way they want. It's not that they want to be there, but they don't see an option other than that. They've made the best of it.

"I need to go to the doctor, but thanks to the Republicans I don't have Obamacare anymore. I now have to pay for insurance and have no money to pay for it. According to them, I'm free to work so I should be able to work and get insurance, yet there are no jobs that can pay me a living wage that will hire me because I'm over-qualified, under-qualified or I don't have an address."

Poverty has not provided Tom with some life skills the more affluent take for granted, e.g., the belief in a safety net that has always been there, giving them the confidence to go out and fail because someone has always been there to catch them when they fall. In Tom's world and the world I came from, to fail is to fall hard, sometimes fatally, so it's better, *safer*, not to try at all.

Officials have quadrupled homeless outreach teams, added 600 shelter beds, expanded winter shelter hours and ramped up hotel vouchers. Some 1,000 new employees are being hired at every level of homeless services, including support for people in the new housing projects, according to the *LA Times*.

Chapter 24 Death and Taxes

Chapter 24

Death and Taxes

"They say death and taxes are the only things that are inevitable. The truth is, you can not pay your taxes. I've done it, and there's consequences, but it can be done. Death you're not going to get out of, and you kind of got to deal with it." Steve Earle

"The only difference between death and taxes is that death doesn't get worse every time Congress meets." Will Rogers

Death. It's a business.

When my mother died, we four siblings were embarrassed to admit we didn't have enough money to bury her. Mom had always wanted a burial plot, to have a gravesite we could always visit, but in her final days she realized what a financial burden those costs would be on us so she talked up the idea of cremation. We were for it for all the selfish reasons, but I had already decided that was how I was going to dispose of my own body someday.

Her surviving sisters and brother were incensed that we didn't consult with them, but our mother was gone and this body was merely her spent shell. The mortuary was kind in the extreme: before burning the body, they allowed us time to say goodbye. They never approached us about a bill.

What about those who don't live in a small town with a kind-hearted, caring local funeral director? I have seen families on street corners begging for donations to pay funeral expenses. My brother, who works in the business now, has seen families glow with pride as they shell out thousands of dollars for a top-of-the-line casket, an elaborate headstone, and a sumptuous feast after services. In retirement, I tried to sell life insurance to help families prepare for the inevitable, but death is "someday" and Netflix is now, or they just couldn't swing another payment for an event in some far, indeterminate future. Of course, many aren't able to provide the kind of funeral their loved one deserves because they are just one paycheck away from the street.

According to smartasset.com, "the average funeral costs $7,181. That includes viewing and burial, embalming, hearse, transfer of remains, service fee and more. It doesn't, however, include the cost of a catered luncheon with drinks after the memorial service, which can add hundreds if not thousands of dollars to the cost." The National Funeral Directors Association estimates the median cost of cremation to be $6,078, but other sources indicate the figure may be more in the $2,000-$4,000 range. In most cases, it will be a big check for most of us to sign, especially while stricken with grief and the grief of all those around you.

Sometimes a family who can't afford the associated costs never shows up at the morgue to claim the body. It's then the responsibility of local government and the taxpayers to either bury or cremate the indigent's remains. A small minority, according to my brother John, walk into the mortuary with a chip on their shoulder. "They think that they shouldn't have to pay for the funeral. After all, they just lost a loved one."

According to the Federal Trade Commission, the funeral director must provide an itemized list of costs, including a "good faith" estimate on goods and services that may be affected by inflation by the time the loved one dies. The cost of a casket alone can run from $2000-$10,000.

When dealing with funeral costs, family members may feel pressured to provide nothing but the best for their beloved family member. The funeral home will offer a broad range of products and services. It's important to make those plans. It's not morbid or bad juju to price the costs of bereavement for a loved one or even yourself. It is important to spend an amount that won't break the bank account, yet demonstrate how much the deceased meant to the family.

- Is it possible the deceased already made arrangements?
- Analyze the life insurance policy. Are burial and funeral costs covered?
- Consider low-cost burial options: cremation or a green burial with no casket or headstone.
- If costs look to skyrocket, consider getting a loan or asking other family members to chip in.
- Talk to your county coroner's office. Many times, if you sign a release, the country and state will pitch in to either bury or cremate the body. The ashes will be released to the family for a fee.

The Federal Trade Commission includes a checklist on their site to help guide the bereaved through a process that's emotional and wearying: https://www.consumer.ftc.gov/articles/0301-funeral-costs-and-pricing-checklist#Calculating.

Death tax

A lot of hand-wringing and complaints from the wealthy have brought the issue of an inheritance tax or estate taxes to the middle class as something we should all care about. Calling it an unfair "death tax," many of us were duped into believing we might somehow be affected. Unless your dear mom has passed along cash and property worth more than $11.18 million (up from $5.45 million pre-Trump), the middle class has nothing to worry about with a federal estate tax (40 percent, but the effective rate with loopholes and deductions brings that down to less than 17 percent). In fact, the passing of only two out of every 1,000 creates an additional tax burden for those who inherit.

However, 12 states and the District of Columbia have some sort of "death tax." Nebraska, Iowa, Kentucky, Pennsylvania, New Jersey, and Maryland have an inheritance tax. In fact, Maryland packs a double whammy with both an inheritance tax of up to ten percent and an estate tax of 16 percent on any amount of an estate worth over $4 million. Other states that tax estates include Maine, Vermont, Oregon, Minnesota, Illinois, Rhode Island, Hawaii, Connecticut, New York, Washington, D.C. and Washington state with the highest rate of 20 percent.

Taxes

In an article for the Institute for New Economic Thinking, contributor Lance Taylor suggests, "fundamental changes in income and wealth distribution will require equally fundamental changes in the way the economy generates and distributes pre-tax incomes." What is required, says Taylor, "are policies that go beyond the tax code to shift the very balance of power between workers and employers. Productivity has outpaced an equivalent rise in wages, contributing to income inequality."

According to Taylor, Robert Solow from MIT, the go-to guy on macroeconomics, points to labor's loss of leverage and power, the "explicit hardening" of business attitudes, the popularity of right-to-work laws that further undermined labor's voice, and that wages seemed to have flat-lined at the advent of the Reagan presidency. All of these begat income inequality.

Trump's Tax Plan aka the Republican Tax Act of 2017 passed in December 2017, promised the middle class would reap the greatest benefits, but the real recipients of Trump largesse were corporations and the wealthy. Big surprise, right?

He was, his supporters reported, fulfilling a campaign promise. He claimed back in 2015 that if his tax plan were adopted, 75 million taxpayers would no longer have to pony up income tax. They could keep those funds in their bank accounts, stimulating the economy through increased spending in the community.

President Trump also claimed and obsessed that corporate taxes were too high, that the federal corporate income tax rate of 35 percent, was higher than that imposed by other Organization for Economic Co-operation and Development (OECD) nations. That may be true technically, but, of course, loopholes in the federal tax code allowed many corporations to write off and pay a fraction of their tax bills. The Republican tax law cuts the corporate rate to 20 percent.

Why should that matter to us? These laws and loopholes shift the tax burden onto the backs of the middle class and turn us into mean-spirited citizens who wrongly blame income inequality on those less fortunate than us ($59 billion) rather than corporate welfare ($100 billion!) that make up a more significant amount of government subsidies.

Findings by the Institute on Taxation and Economic Policy (ITEP) show that the biggest and most profitable corporations have avoided taxes on nearly half of their profits. Between 2008 and 2015, 258 Fortune 500 corporations paid an average effective tax rate of 21.2 percent, and 100 of these companies didn't pay a dime of federal income taxes in at least one year during that time.

ITEP reports more than half of big, profitable multinationals paid a lower tax rate on their foreign profits than the rate they paid domestically. There are offsetting tax breaks that both encourage the development of fossil fuels and alternative energy sources. A tax code allows for accelerated depreciation that will enable companies to write off their capital investments faster than these investments wear out, but rewards companies for investments they would have made anyway.

In the previous tax plan, multinational corporations took advantage of a provision that allowed them to postpone taxes indefinitely on foreign profits until they land in a stateside bank. Corporations claimed 59 percent of those profits were earned in Bermuda and the Cayman Islands, among several other offshore tax shelters. What kind of interest were they collecting?

True rational corporate tax reform should include a transparent and thorough audit of corporate giveaways and loopholes and a plan to have companies pay their fair share without passing along their increased tax burden to us.

The *Washington Post* calculated a household living on $40,000 a year would average a $330 tax cut while the top 1 percent making $3.6

million, would receive $85,640. At the end of 2025 the low and middle class tax breaks would be gone, but corporations and the wealthy would keep theirs.

What about my taxes?

A lot of working folks bought into the hype when Trump's tax plan was revealed. The White House announced in April 2018, "Working Americans will see several tax benefits from the new law, including lower tax rates, a doubling of the child tax credit, and the standard deduction nearly doubled." It was passed by the US Senate on a 51-48 vote. Not exactly a mandate.

The conservative Tax Foundation expressed doubts about how much the new tax plan would boost the economy. Business Insider looked at savings for blue-collar workers and determined most would see a tax savings of about 20 percent. Electricians and other highly skilled workers would see an average of 11 percent. Aircraft mechanics would receive a savings of less than 9 percent. Power plant operators with an average wage of $74,000 would realize a savings of only approximately six percent. How do we pay for it? Here's the terrible news: The Senate Joint Committee on Taxation estimates the deficit could balloon over $1 trillion over the next ten years under Trump's plan. MSNBC's assessment: "If you earn less than $75,000, this tax cut is not for you."

One of the eye-opening discoveries I made when researching the impact of the 2017 tax plan was this statement on the FiveThirtyEight website: "...most people don't have a mortgage, most people don't own stocks." We've grown accustomed to 401(k)s in the corporate world and following our investments has become second nature for many of us. The tax code has always held its own share of mysteries, and the tax plan of 2017 doesn't clarify anything.

What does Uncle Sam do with our money?

According to usgovernmentspending.com, income taxes made up 56 percent of the federal budget in Fiscal Year 2018, the most significant percentage of revenue to the federal coffers by far. What did our government do with that 56 percent of $3.34 trillion in FY 2018? Budgeted federal income tax revenue for FY 2018 is **$1,878 billion**. What was our ROI (Return on Investment)? In other words, are we receiving value for those hard-earned funds we mail off every April?

First, a little history provided by the usgovernmentspending.com website:

> The federal income tax was initially paid only by corporations, but starting in World War I, it broke down about 50 percent between individuals and corporations.
>
> After World War II, the corporate income tax share began to shrink, going below 40 percent share in 1950, 30 percent share in 1968, and 20 percent share in 1980. By 1983 at the bottom of a recession, corporate income tax was down to 11 percent of total income tax collections.
>
> Since the mid-1980s, the corporate income tax has fluctuated along at about 20 percent of income tax collections.

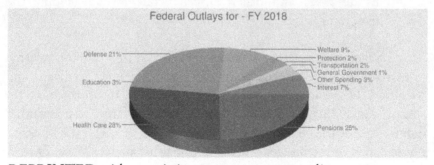

REPRINTED with permission usgovernmentspending.com

Total Spending	$4.2 trillion	Pensions	$1.0 trillion
Health Care	$1.2 trillion	Education	$0.1 trillion
Defense	$0.9 trillion	Welfare	$0.4 trillion

The percentages and numbers above reveal the most substantial federal budget expenditures and reflect the work of Congress as they attempt to oppose/support the president's agenda and includes input from lobbyists and colleagues, emails from constituents and individual biases, insight, and knowledge of the particular issue. How can we as folks at the bottom of the food chain influence congressional priorities? Attend town halls, learn the issues and follow the details you won't find on Fox News or CNN. These numbers also do not reflect so-called black budgets for NSA, CIA and other covert operations.*

The balance website breaks down federal tax revenues in the following manner:

- Income taxes contribute $1.622 trillion or 49 percent of total receipts.
- Social Security, Medicare, and other payroll taxes add $1.238 trillion or 36 percent.
- Corporate taxes supply $225 billion or 7 percent.
- Excise taxes and tariffs contribute $152 billion or 4 percent.
- Earnings from the Federal Reserve's holdings add $55 billion or 2 percent. Those are interest payments on the U.S. Treasury debt the Fed acquired.
- Estate taxes and other miscellaneous revenue supply the remaining 2 percent.

Most of the budget is already accounted for: $2.739 trillion, referred to as mandatory spending that pays for Social Security, Medicare, and Medicaid. Discretionary spending is $1.02 trillion and covers military spending including the Department of Veteran Affairs and every other domestic program. "There is an emergency fund of $111.4 billion that's not included in the budget process" reports thebalance. "Most of that, amounting to $88.9 billion, goes to Overseas Contingency Operations to pay for wars."

It is clear that 1) ALEC membership pays dividends and 2) corporations need to pay their fair share.

*The Washington Examiner reported that President Trump created another record in 2018 with the most massive black budget request in history. According to reporter Steven Nelson, "Trump is requesting $59.9 billion for non-military intelligence agencies and $21.2 billion for military intelligence in fiscal 2019."

The civilian spy request is 3.8 percent higher than what Trump requested last year, and the military figure is 2.4 percent higher than last year's request.

Evolution or Revolution?

Chapter 25

Evolution Or Revolution?

"Revolution is not a dinner party, not an essay, nor a painting, nor a piece of embroidery; it cannot be advanced softly, gradually, carefully, considerately, respectfully, politely, plainly and modestly. A revolution is an insurrection, an act of violence by which one class overthrows another." Mao Zedong

"You never change things by fighting the existing reality. To change something, build a new model that makes the existing model obsolete." Buckminster Fuller

"Within each of us exists the potential to contribute positively to society. Although one individual among so many on this planet may seem too insignificant, it is our personal efforts that will determine the direction our society is heading." Dalai Lama

Where are the solutions to the issues brought up in this book? The title suggests evolution or revolution? What happens, (as is happening now) when workers will no longer be able to afford the products American corporations and other Multinationals produce for distribution?

American citizens have been bombarded with advertisements from birth to death, brainwashed into believing we really MUST have that new Chevy, that bright smile, that home with the interest-only loan.

When workers are denied the "opportunity" to act on their consumer brainwashing, the level of frustration is palpable. In Los Angeles, where the divide between haves and have-nots is so apparent and observable, the have-nots act out with graffiti and a pretended disdain for all things commercial while wearing $200 sneakers.

Will society devolve as preordained by Engel and Marx into an uprising by the workers and blood in the streets? Or we will be so anesthetized by our technical gadgets that we are distracted into indifference?

Since the Industrial Revolution, the burgeoning middle class has emerged and played an ever-growing role in governance, culture, and commerce. Henry Ford understood our importance: He lowered the price of his cars so his workers could afford them and have money left over to contribute to society. "The highest use of capital is not to make more money," he stated. "But to make money do more for the betterment of life."

What do we do now? Do we, as the Declaration of Independence guides us, "throw off our shackles?"

If we are considering revolution, then the words of Bert Wolfe and the label of "plutocrat" for the rich and powerful may motivate us:

> Sadly, America has entered a stage of its history where the American plutocracy of the 1 percent has concluded that they no longer need the relative strength, stability, and safety of the American econo my to prosper. The plutocrats know that they can achieve a far greater return on investment overseas in the BRICSA countries (Brazil, Russia, India, China, South Africa) which are industrializing rapidly and have rising, prosperous middle classes. The plutocrats have also concluded that the United States of America has entered the stage of "imperial overstretch," is declining on the world stage and consider America has a has-been

economic superpower whose time has passed. Consequently the plutocrats, as cold-blooded, dry-eyed capitalists, have concluded that America is now economically expendable, and as "citizens of the world" in the worst sense of the term, with their ultimate loyalty not to the USA, but instead only to their own financial bottom line, are abandoning the American economy, which has been so good to them and where they first achieved their vast fortunes, by systematically dismantling, liquidating and offshoring the Great American Economic Patrimony (GAEP) – the accumulated wealth of the American economy built up by all previous generations of Americans and bequeathed, always enlarged and enriched, to the next generation of Americans for their use and enjoyment. The plutocrats are either depositing the cash in tax-free havens, like Switzerland or the Cayman Islands, or are investing it in the BRICSA countries.

The development is, of course, bad news for patriotic Americans of a progressive political bent, as the plutocrats are determined to not only vigorously milk the "cash cow" they view the American economy to be, but to also slaughter that cash cow for one final, massive feast of capital once it has been milked dry. Thus, the plutocrats have no incentive or interest in paying higher taxes in America or allowing the fiscal resources of American government at all levels to be invested in potentially popular and expensive progressive policies and programs. That would limit the amount of capital the plutocrats have to invest overseas.

The determination of the American plutocracy of the 1 percent to liquidate and abscond with the proceeds of the GAEP can be considered, at a minimum, unpatriotic economic ingratitude, and at the maximum, economic treason.

In any event, if this process is allowed to continue unimpeded, the average working people of America will be left to squabble and fight over the last few remaining crumbs of the GAEP, while the plutocrats flee the once wealthy, mighty United States of America, now reduced to third world status, with the lion's share of the GAEP. Sadly, the Democratic Party, once the party of the people, now in the back pocket of the plutocrats, is actively assisting in the destruction and robbery of the GAEP, the economic birthright of the American people.

Will the last plutocrat leaving America please turn out the lights?

Not all of us have succumbed to despair. There are those of us who are trying, and some who are succeeding, to move the Democratic Party to the left, to remind everyone of our traditional Democratic principles. At one point, Party officials were making moves to oust progressives from positions of leadership and the Party itself. Now, it appears the days of the corporate Dem may be numbered.

Move to Amend – A Realistic Solution?

Lately, there's been a groundswell of support for a change to the US Constitution. Bits and pieces that made up the eventual recognition of corporations as citizens with all the implied rights thereof have culminated in the Supreme Court decision in Citizens United v the United States. REAL citizens have become angry and frustrated over our inability to stop the onslaught of corporate money and influence in the political process. "What chance do we have as ordinary citizens to affect change?" we ask ourselves and each other.

In the past, we have had the sincere endeavors of the Clean Money movement attempt to bring public financing into politics. Some form of Clean Money legislation has been adopted in Arizona, Connecticut, Maine, Massachusetts, New Mexico, North Carolina, Vermont, and Wisconsin. In Albuquerque, New Mexico, Portland, Oregon and, now, Los Angeles, Clean Money has been adopted at the municipal level. In L.A., Measure H, passed in March 2011, banned those who bid on city contracts and their executive-level employees from giving to candidates for city office. (Registered lobbyists were already prohibited from doing so.)

Measure H also raised the cap on city matching funds. The L.A. Ethics Commission has proposed raising contribution limits from $500 to $1,100 for city council candidates and $1,000 to $2,200 for citywide candidates. "Regular voters can't afford to give the current contribution limit of $500 for city council candidates as it is," says Trent Lange of the California Clean Money Campaign, "which is why fewer than .1 percent of voters do." The proposal clearly favors incumbents unless a candidate has well-to-do friends. As the costs of elections rise higher, it becomes more difficult for anyone to raise "real" money, exorbitant funds that make a public statement to those in the know about a candidate's viability. This assessment, of course, also favors incumbents and makes an election a self-fulfilling prophecy. Just as businesses are more likely to get loans if they don't need it, so too, is a well-funded candidate even more well funded – a phenomenon sometimes referred to as the "bandwagon" effect. After all, doesn't everybody want to back a winner? It's an investment in a shared vision on bills that I may want the good City Council member to sponsor in the near future. Clean Money could take hold in L.A. The question is, though, will it make a difference in who gets elected?

Where does all that money go that candidates raise? A lot of it, especially for a first-timer, goes to building name recognition. How many of us have cursed the mailman every election cycle when our home is inundated with stacks of campaign literature? Our phone constantly rings with robo-calls. It's the candidate's voice, but not the candidate. In our electronic age, campaign consultants are always finding new ways to reach prospective voters. Consultants say that social media – Facebook and Twitter, especially – are currently winning hearts and minds. President Trump seems to think so. His 3 a.m. tweets are analyzed and critiqued by pundits and the public alike.

After the election is over, more often than not, any money left over in a winning candidate's war chest goes to the Party to be routed to other races where fundraising has been a bit more anemic. The leadership in the state capitol and Washington take note of how much a candidate has raised and often hand out plum committee assignments and leadership positions based on how much the candidate "worked." That's a clear indication that elected officials are fine with the system the way it is.

California is not resting on its laurels when it comes to transparency. There is a bill, the Disclose Act, passed by the state legislature and signed into law by the governor in 2017, that will force those groups that fly under the radar with names like, "Citizens for Decent Campaigns," and "Gunboat Veterans for Truth," etc., to walk into the daylight. We'll finally see who's behind those hit ads and, I hope, vote accordingly.

Clean money has not been warmly embraced. The laws in Massachusetts and Portland were later repealed, while Vermont's was struck down by the U.S. Supreme Court on First Amendment grounds. The Court argued that if a wealthy candidate wants to spend money on his campaign, it's his First Amendment right to spend as much as he wants. Money was determined to be a form of free speech. The Court has also declared Arizona's provision for matching funds to be unconstitutional, undermining similar provisions in Wisconsin and Maine.

Pretty soon, it won't matter what country you're in. We'll all be subsidiaries of Banc of the World. The President of the United States will have to go to the Grand Caymans or Geneva, hat in hand, to beg for our allotment of funds for what the CEO has predetermined for our region.

To paraphrase Pogo, we have seen the enemy and he is NOT us! That's a smokescreen; the enemy is THEM, the faceless corporations whose leaders are elected by a small elite cabal within the Multinationals.

That is what many multinational mega-corporations are now: not loyal to any country, just churning out capitalist democracy (or is it Democratic Capitalism?) that allows them to sell everything from jeans to genes. Indeed, there is recent Court precedent that genetically modified organisms, though organic, can now be patented. They won't stop till they can price and sell the very air that we breathe.

THAT is the lesson we must take from the Occupy Movement: Trust no one, no single party or Party. NOBODY has all the answers, but we must take the reins and control as much of our destiny as we can. Both major political parties have sold us out to the Multinationals (formerly known as Corporate America.)

What about the Next Generation? Will they have it so good or will the wheels of "progress" continue to grind them down?

Two-tiered wages and benefits point to leaner times for younger workers. In a bargaining strategy with labor of either the quick-fix or I've-got-mine-too-bad-about-you, younger workers, already unsure that Social Security will be there for them in their golden years, have had to bear the brunt of contract negotiations that represent lower wages and a move from defined benefit plans to defined contributions. In an effort to shore up Baby Boomers' gentle passing into retirement, have we forsaken those who follow? Would the previous generation, the folks that built the Labor Movement, have done the same? I was proud of CWA's bargaining team in 1989 when they said, "We'll bargain for active employees as soon as AT&T takes care of its retirees."

Maybe the Depression felt like rock bottom and workers knew there was only one direction for things to go: up. But having talked to some of the old-timers and read of their daring escapades, I know they were planting the seeds of economic prosperity for ALL of us.

Frankly, I'm worried about my stepdaughter Mikaela with her MBA and her student loans in the thousands, staring at a very different economic social contract between Corporation and Employee. She and her 20-something and 30-something friends and husband will have to take what they can get.

Looking ahead

What about the much-touted "jobs of the future?" The future looks rosiest in clean energy, biotech, and, unfortunately, war technology. The growth of automation and consolidation of corporations and industries threatens to darken that rosy outlook.

The price of clean energy continues to come down to within grasp of the Working Class. A system in California can be purchased or leased which, after government subsidies and rebates, comes to between $10,000 and $20,000. Solar in states such as California or Arizona makes sense and many a hopeful Generation Y graduate in Renewable

Energy is knocking on doors. Many of those jobs – both sales and installation – are, for the most part, non-union with no built-in job security for future work. Solar, it seems, is virtually maintenance-free.

Biotech, medical and long-term care have been lumped together as the last line of defense between Baby Boomers and Death. Many younger workers don't see this arena as commercially viable or the road to personal fortune. And while death panels may be a Republican bugaboo, some attention will be focused on the bottom line, on costs. Many of these are union positions but still lack a living wage.

War technology has always been with us. Many of the inventions on the battlefield have found practical applications at home, courtesy of DARPA, the Defense Advanced Research Projects Agency, and other agencies. Now military technology may be used by law enforcement to patrol our borders and our cities from the air with the 7500 drones that have been built and operated in Iraq and Afghanistan. That may translate to fewer personnel on the ground, literally, when someone in a remote location at a video game-like console has oversight and the capability to take out "bad guys." The outcome may mean fewer border patrol and law enforcement positions, but maybe the pay will be decent. The contractors that build and maintain these aircraft on foreign soil pay their employees very well, much more than their military counterparts.

Individual Solutions

Buy local. You can be fairly certain that if you buy a meal at a local restaurant that money will be circulated within the local economy, whether it's for produce from the local market or wages for the staff who will, in turn, spend their paychecks near where they live and work.

Buy American. Studies have shown that buying American stimulates the economy, creating more jobs fueled by increased demand. More jobs mean more middle class consumers for American products and services. Stop buying cheap! Wal-mart used to brag that everything in their stores was "Made in America." My friend Charles Kernaghan from the union Unite HERE was instrumental in exposing their lie. It appears the policy changed and they forgot to tell us!

Buy union. Companies that employ union workers and honor their contracts are facing increased pressure from the marketplace to abandon these "selfish" employees who threaten strikes and should be grateful they even have a job! Buying products and services from unionized companies means consumers are getting quality goods by trained personnel. Our increased demand for quality gives leverage to employees who can negotiate better wages and benefits. A higher level of compensation and quality sets standards for a particular industry. Non-union companies don't seem to understand that unions aren't adversarial; they're advocates for their members in the fields of wages, hours and working conditions and union leadership would like nothing more than for a company that employs their members, that provides dignity and respect in the workplace, negotiates in good faith, and attributes some or all of their success to their employees, to prosper and to share some of that prosperity with their employees.

Vote. I know, I know. This book is rife with my negative takes on our present political system, but it's the system we have and we have to change it from within or risk it all on a revolution that, should we lose, would clamp the lid down even further on civil liberties and our basic rights. I would expand the two-party system, but in the current environment of money fueling and buying elections, nobody wants to invest in either creating a new Party or bolstering an existing one. Coalitions, we've seen in other countries, are often messy, unorganized alliances built on mutual distrust that accomplish little or nothing. Oh, wait! We already have that! There may come a day when we realize the futility of progress through our current system and the need for more vigorous rebellion, but I pray that day is far off.

We need educated, informed voters. We need to teach civics in the classroom. We need to train voters to give issues and candidates critical scrutiny. The devil, as we have found time and time again, is in the details. If we don't bother to look into the implications of our blanket approval of policies like the Trans-Pacific Partnership or court decisions like Citizens United or to look at a candidate's record or who has contributed to their campaign, d emocracy, as we know it, is lost. In California, there are attempts to expose the groups that fund ballot propositions that seem to contradict the will of the people (over $475 million in 2002).

We need to ignore the efforts of the rich and powerful to divide and conquer us. As we fight over the airwaves on issues where we have fundamental differences, the power our forbearers handed us is being stolen from right under our noses.

What can labor do?

According to Mark Dudzic and Katherine Isaac's article, "Labor Party time? Not yet":

> This is a time of tremendous opportunity. After years of economic crisis and political impotence, working people are questioning the legitimacy of the entire political system and exposing its corrupt domination by a wealthy oligarchy. The Occupy movement struck a chord with so many because its organizers understand that the system is rigged to generate inequality. No matter what individual activists may desire, the simple fact remains that you cannot build a party of labor when the labor movement itself is in disarray and retreat.

Dudzic and Isaac realize today's labor leaders may not remember how we got here. "Many current leaders and activists in the labor movement were not around when the Labor Party was at its heyday more than two decades ago. Many of the key participants in the Labor Party are nearing retirement and have valuable lessons to share with a new generation."

They also suggest building activists from the ground up: "Unions should ... educate members about a real working-class agenda, identify and develop new leadership, and build relationships with potential allies."

Reform the Democratic Party. Although an occasional progressive or pro-labor candidate has been elected on the Democratic ticket and a majority of progressives have infiltrated the California state Democratic Party and tweaked planks of the party's platform, these efforts have not yet led to the kind of major changes within the party to reorient itself toward a working-class political agenda. One reason is that the "big tent" Democratic Party defines itself as a multi-class party with room for a wide spectrum of beliefs that sometimes runs contrary to those universal Democratic principles like a woman's right to choose or its support of labor. Neither of the two major parties has a structure that holds them accountable. Instead of accountability to voters, both parties support corporate neoliberalism and global capitalism that ignores the plight of the working class. The emergence of "insurgent" candidates like Bernie Sanders pull those who have become frustrated and toy with the idea of deserting the Democratic Party back into the fold. The frustration and desperation we feel at an unaccountable and unresponsive national party have turned into rage in recent times, b ut even here this is hope: in California's state delegate elections in 2016, a Progressive majority emerged. Energized by the Bernie Sanders' presidential campaign and intent on political change, their candidates thumb their noses at the corrupting influence of money from Oil, Tobacco and other corporations that are considered morally bankrupt.

Organize first, build political power later. This speaks to the idea of building trust between the shop floor and the boardroom and ignores the fact that every significant advance for working families was achieved through political action, us against them. Several unions left the AFL-CIO and formed the Change to Win alliance in 2005, believing the AFL-CIO was spending too much on political activities rather than on organizing. After almost seven years of trying to build power through organizing, those unions have not met with any breakthrough successes. In fact, many of them are now expending a higher percentage of resources on political activities than many of the old AFL-CIO unions.

Green Party/Nader electoralism. The Greens preach that to build political power is to win elections. For over twenty years, they have won hundreds of nonpartisan local offices. In 2000, Green presidential candidate Ralph Nader garnered enough votes (2.7 percent) to be considered a spoiler in that race and the reason why GW Bush was elected president. "The party continues to promote candidacies that serve to protest the status quo." Instead of looking for candidates who meet all the progressive criteria, Dudzic and Isaac think we should be more practical, transforming the electoral landscape to match our ideals after we've gained the seat.

Fusion. Several states allow candidates to be endorsed by multiple political parties. In New York State, "fusion" is nothing new. Much like coalition building in nations that have more than two major parties, minor parties endorse major party candidates in an attempt to gain some leverage and influence in the major party's administration. It has worked well in New York, where the Working Families Party has parlayed these cross-endorsements into increases in the minimum wage and other benefits for working people. Rather than emerging as power players, these minor parties become part of the machine. In New York, the Working Families Party found themselves being forced to fall in line and endorse Andrew Cuomo for governor despite his anti-worker campaign rhetoric.

Seize the media! Bill Moyers has felt encouraged by the rise of Progressive outlets and consortiums. Though they operate on shoestrings, their audiences are growing. The program *Democracy Now!* is broadcast on more than 1400 radio and cable stations, on satellite via Link TV and Free Speech News and beamed into 34 million US households.

There are progressive magazines: *The Nation, In These Times, Mother Jones, Yes!,* and others that feed an active, questioning generation looking for change.

Labor As Champion?

When I started this book some three years ago, the last chapter was easy to visualize. I was going to take 20+ chapters to lead readers to the inevitable conclusion that a revitalized labor movement was the solution to rebuilding the working and middle class.

I still think that labor as the only collective voice of working folks offers hope, but major changes are needed. Despite my protestations to my friends on the right that cigar-chomping union bosses don't exist, they do. I've known them.

They surround themselves with sycophants who rush to do their bidding, worried that they'll be swatted aside like pesky flies for some minor oversight. Many times these minions will abuse those further down the food chain, wielding their limited power and privilege with impunity. This is what gives rise to Republican members of Congress with an ax to grind against unions because of some slight that occurred early in their work history. Here are a few of my ideas for strengthening the labor movement so we can flourish:

No More Top-Down Unions. I'm tempted to abandon this philosophy. When I was a union president, many felt I was weak for trying a more democratic approach to running the local. I had been elected on a promise to spend 2-3 days at my job to remain accessible to the rank-and-file on the shop floor. Management took that as an opportunity to limit my hours at the union office; other union officials felt I was undermining their time away from the job, but many had not reported to work for years. At my own local, they wondered aloud if I could be an effective union leader with my hands tied by the company and an earnest campaign promise.

I have seen many unions who profess that rank-and-file were the drivers in political endorsements, but ultimately those decisions were made at the top. Some union locals have grown so large that layers of bureaucracy and top-heavy management drive a wedge between the union and those they represent, threatening to topple the structure when key individuals are tempted by sweetheart deals with management, malfeasance, and negligence.

Unions need to be accountable. Officers become firmly ensconced in their positions, growing further and further from the fights on the shop floor. They get wrapped up in sustaining their positions, ever vigilant, even paranoid, about possible threats to their authority. Some unions hold elections for stewards within their workgroups. An election by their peers would go a long way to make them accountable, though there wouldn't be a guarantee. Terms of office would ensure turnover though the corporation could hold up negotiations to coincide with the election of new officers. Current bylaws of the United Auto Workers call for forced retirement of the international president at the age of 65, no matter how effective that individual has been. The practice also means more opportunity for emerging leaders.

Less is more. The smaller, more nimble unions, representing an overlooked or much-maligned industry or a heavily immigrant population, seem to have caught on with millennials. There has been some encouraging growth in union representation for writers. My own union, the National Writers Union, UAW Local 1981, though we're outside the purview of the National Labor Relations Act and can't negotiate contracts with employers, has been moderately successful in negotiating freelance agreements with pro-labor publishers and leveraging settlements with publishers who have failed to pay up on money they owe writers.

Other unions have an undercurrent of discord from factions within. Sometimes those beefs aren't warranted; it's a group intent on regime change in the next election or making one particular officer (usually the president) look bad. Other times, the dissatisfaction comes from members who feel disenfranchised. Ignore disgruntled members at your peril. If we are to succeed as an element of market forces, we need to appear united. Pattern bargaining in the automotive industry and with supermarkets has stabilized industries by setting standards with one automaker or one supermarket, with the promise of comparable wage and benefit demands with the rest. The labor movement has a slogan: United we bargain, divided we beg.

Fixing Social Security

The Urban Institute and other have offered alternative solutions to a reduction in services:

- Reducing the cost of living adjustments (COLA) by one percentage point.
- Increasing the full retirement age to 68.
- Indexing the COLA to prices rather than wages, except for bottom one-third of income earner.
- Raising the payroll tax cap (currently at $106,800) to cover 90 percent instead of 84 percent of earnings.
- Increasing the payroll tax r ate by one percentage point.

Create Employee-owned Businesses. Earlier I mentioned the success of employee ownership at Harley-Davidson. Even though tariffs have driven some of their work overseas, the idea of employee-owned businesses and co-ops are an innovative solution to involve workers in the products and services they offer.

Create a Business that gives a damn about employees. Business was looking great at Lawrence, Massachusetts-based Malden Mills: revenues and employment were up, up, up after they emerged from bankruptcy in 1982. But then there was a fire at Malden Mills in December 1995, that put the company's loyal union workforce of three thousand, and Christmas, at risk.

Two days after the fire, Malden Mills' CEO Aaron Feuerstein announced he would rebuild his factory on the very site where his family had made textiles since 1906. He told employees they would get full wages for 30 days. He later paid wages for 90 days and benefits for 180 days, a decision that cost Malden Mills $25 million.

Feuerstein said, "I did it because it was the right thing to do."

Several years later, the plant was rebuilt and all the workers who wanted to come back were rehired. Business boomed once again, and productivity soared. According to a report:

- The company grew 40 percent from pre-fire levels.
- Customer and employee retention reached 95 percent.
- Quality control reported defects had dropped to just 2 percent.

Drowning in $140 million in debt, Feuerstein filed for bankruptcy in 2001 and was forced to relinquish his position as CEO. The company filed for bankruptcy again in 2007, a shadow of its former self, and was sold for $44 million.

Robert Gaskill and actor Morgan Freeman started Motev, a livery service in 2016 with a fleet of Teslas, electric vehicles that don't pollute. The company's headquarters are located in Southcentral Los Angeles and provide some of the best paying jobs to locals in the area.

"The average chauffeur job pays about $12 an hour plus gratuities," said Gaskill. "We pay $21 an hour and health benefits and gratuities."

Gaskill had been a Teamster, ferrying actors to the set and related events. He worked with actor Morgan Freeman for 23 years before they teamed up on Motev. They found local programs and incentives that offered tax credits and welcomed them into the community. "At the state and federal level, it's the complete opposite," said Gaskill. "I don't understand that."

Think outside the box. Economist Dr. Farid Khavari thinks the entire present structure of capitalism helps widen the disparity of income. Though his book focuses on his neighbors in Florida, Khavari has envisioned and written about a "zero cost economy" that could be implemented locally or globally.

> To realize a zero-cost economy, we must use environmentally safe energy technologies, increase productivity by implementing the ultimate productivity speed, and make financing not just consumer friendly but purposeful. Finally, anything an individual or a household owns should reflect true ownership–that is, ownership without future or recurring costs attached. In a zero-cost economy, once a property is paid off, the person will own it outright with no future or recurring costs attached.

Economy is based on more than business. Some costs include the environment, energy, raw materials, agriculture, politics, social issues, and natural disasters. In the book, Dr. Khavari compares these and other factors within the framework of various economic systems: capitalism, socialism, and his system that he has entitled "carefreeism," defined as "general economic security and true prosperity, reflected by less need to work."

Not surprisingly, he finds the benefits of living in a zero cost economy outweigh those in other systems. A "carefree" healthcare system promises, "high-quality services ... provided at relatively low cost due to manipulation of productivity, including technologies and efficient service delivery facilities," he patiently explains. "Preventive medicine, physical fitness, and proper nutrition are promoted."

His plan unfolds with low or no-cost energy that is readily available through self-sustaining technologies that could operate independently of a national power grid. By freezing costs, reducing or eliminating them he believes we could have a "healthy, booming economy. By freezing costs, we can maintain our purchasing power, by reducing costs we can increase our purchasing power. And by eliminating costs altogether, we can accumulate true wealth without fearing the future loss of its purchasing power."

Many of Dr. Khavari's ideas aren't conventional and would require a society-wide reboot or a "course correction" of priorities and policies, but they reflect a lot of intelligent thought.

These are just some of the innovative, thought-provoking ideas I have found during my research. There are more every day. I have created a Facebook page named after this book; I encourage you, the reader, to look at some of the articles I have posted there. I also encourage you to share those you have found. We're all in this together.

References

A special thank you goes out to Wikipedia which often provided a jumping-off point for further in-depth research. Some of the articles, websites, interviews, papers and books listed here may not have made it into the final version of the book, but still lead to insights or bolstered my arguments. I would also like to take this opportunity to recommend anything written by Dr. Noam Chomsky.

"5 Things You Should Know About the Capital Gains Tax." *Turbotax.* Turbotax.intuit.com. March 13, 2017.

Alperovitz, Gar. *America Beyond Capitalism: Reclaiming our Wealth, our Liberty, & our Democracy.* Second edition published by Democracy Collaborative Press, Takoma Park, Maryland and Dollars and Sense, Boston, Massachusetts. 2005, 2011.

Amadeo, Kimberly. "14 Obamacare Myths: What's the Truth Behind Them?" *the balance.* November 5, 2013. https://www.thebalance.com/the-truth-about-obamacare-3306075

Amadeo, Kimberly. "U.S. Federal Budget Breakdown: The Budget Components and Impact on the US Economy." https://www.thebalance.com/u-s-federal-budget-breakdown-3305789 August 14, 2018.

Anrig, Greg. "Twelve Reasons Why Privatizing Social Security is a Bad Idea." *The Century Foundation.* December 14, 2004. https://tcf.org/

content/commentary/twelve-reasons-why-privatizing-social-security-is-a-bad-idea/?agreed=1

Appleby, Joyce. *The Relentless Revolution: A History of Capitalism.* W. W. Norton & Company New York, London. 2010.

Archer, Robin. *Why is There No Labor Party in the United States?* Princeton University Press 2007.

Atkinson, Khorri. "California becomes first state to fully abolish cash bail." *Axios.com* August 29, 2018.

Arnold, Thurman W. *The Folklore of Capitalism.* Yale University Press 1937.

Barlett, Donald L. and James B. Steele. *America: What Went Wrong?* Andrews and McMeel Kansas City 1992.

Barlett, Donald L. and James B. Steele. *The Betrayal of the American Dream.* Andrews and McMeel Kansas City 2012.

Black, Conrad. *Franklin Delano Roosevelt: Champion of Freedom.* pub. in the US by Public Affairs, Perseus Books Group 2003.

Brooks David. *The Road to Character* Random House, LLC, a Penguin Random House Company 2015.

Burns. James MacGregor. *Roosevelt: The Lion and the Fox (1882-1940).* Open Road Integrated Media. New York 2012.

Campbell, Kevin. "Obamacare widened the health gap between the haves and have-nots -- will the American Health Care Act make it any better? *Washington Examiner* May 23, 2017.

Childs, John Brown. *Transcommunality: From The Politics of Conversion.* Temple University Press Philadelphia 2003.

China Uncensored. "Five Things You Don't Know About the Tiananmen Square Massacre." www.youtube.com

Cingano, F. "Trends in Income Inequality and its Impact on Economic Growth", *OECD Social, Employment and Migration Working Papers*, No. 163, OECD Publishing, Paris. 2014.

Clardy, Alan. "Kroning at Pac Bell" www.pages.towson.edu Towson University Human Resources Development Program

Close, Kerry.. "LinkedIn's CEO Is Giving His Entire $14 Million Bonus to Employees." *Time*. Time.com March 3, 2016.

Cohen, Michael. "How for-proit prisons have become the biggest lobby no one is talking about." *Washington Post*. www.washingtonpost.com April 28, 2015.

Cohler, Anne M. *Rousseau & Nationalism* Basic Books, Inc. 1970.

Cole, Harold L. and Lee E. Ohanian. "New Deal Policies and the Persistence of the Great Depression: A General Equilibrium Analysis." *Journal of Political Economy*. Accessed through http://mises.org. August, 2004.

"Comrade Milt Rosen, 1926-2011 Founding chairperson of PLP." Great 20th Century Revolutionary Encyclopedia of Anti-Revisionism. http://www.Marxists.orgOn-Line July, 2017.

"Consumer Response Annual Report January 1—December 31, 2017." *Consumer Financial Protection Bureau*. March 2018. S3.amazonaws.com

Cook, Blanche Wiesen. *Eleanor Roosevelt: Volume 2 The Defining Years* Penguin Books, Ltd. Harmondsworth, Middlesex, England 2000.

Corrections to College. "Don't Stop Now." www.correctionstocollegeca.org March, 2018.

Corsi, Jerome R. Ph.D. *The Late Great USA: The Coming Merger with Mexico and Canada*. Midpoint Trade Books New York, NY 2007.

DiLorenzo, Thomas. *How Capitalism Saved America: The Untold History of Our Country, From the Pilgrims to the Present*. Crown Forum/ Random House, 2004.

Dollard, John. *Caste and Class in a Southern Town*. The University of Wisconsin Press. 1937. 1949. 1964. 1988.

Dovere, Edward-Isaac."Can This Millennial Mayor Make Universal Basic Income a Reality?" www.politico.com April 24, 2018.

Dowd, Douglas editor. *"Understanding Capitalism: Critical Analysis from Karl Marx to Amartya Sen."* Pluto Press, London, Sterling, VA 2002.

Ehrenreich, Barbara. *Bait and Switch: the Futile Pursuit of the American Dream*. Metropolitan Books, Henry Holt and Company LLC New York, NY. 2006.

Eidelson, Josh. "Gig Firms Ask California to Rescue Them From Court Ruling." Bloomberg August 5, 2018. https://www.bloomberg.com/news/articles/2018-08-05/gig-firms-ask-california-dems-to-rescue-them-from-court-ruling

"Eleanor Roosevelt and Labor Law Reform." Accessed through http://www.nextnewdeal.net/eleanor-roosevelt-and-labor-law-reform The blog of the Roosevelt Institute July, 2017.

"End H-1B visa program's abuse." *The Times Editorial*. www.latimes.com. February 16, 2015.

Evolllution.com. "Newly Released Student Loan Data Bust Several Myths about Student Loan Repayment." May 9, 2018. www.evolllutiono.com.

"Fatal Occupational Injuries in 2015." https://www.bls.gov/iif/oshwc/cfoi/cfch0015.pdf

Faux, Jeff. "NAFTA's Impact on U.S. Workers" accessed through http://www.epi.org/blog/naftas-impact-workers/ Economic Policy Institute Posted 12/9/13.

Fishman, Charles. *The Wal-mart Effect* Penguin Press, New York 2006.

Pope Francis. "Apostolic Exhortation Evangelii Gaudium of the Holy Father

Francis to the Bishops, Clergy, Consecrated Persons and the Lay Faithful on the Proclamation of the Gospel in Today's World" Vatican Press, Rome 2015.

Frank, Thomas. "Listen, Liberal." Metropolitan Books New York, NY 2016.

Frank, Thomas. "What's the Matter with Kansas? How Conservatives Won the Heart of America." Metropolitan Books New York, NY 2007.

Freeland, Chrystia. *Plutocrats: The Rise of the New Global Super-Rich and the Fall of Everyone Else.* Penguin Press October, 2012.

Freeman, Jr., Chas W. "The End of the American Empire" accessed through http://rightweb.irc-online.org/the-end-of-the-american-empire/ last updated: April 5, 2016.

Gardner, Matt. "The Two Biggest Lies in Donald Trump's Tax Plan." *The American Prospect.* June 28, 2018. http://prospect.org/article/two-biggest-lies-donald-trumps-tax-plan

Gaskill, Robert interview with author. August 14, 2017.

Gearan, Anne and Fenit Nirappil. "New VP pick Kaine getting in line in opposition to Pacific trade deal" *The Washington Post* July 23, 2016

Glass, Andrew. "Reagan fires 11,000 striking air traffic controllers Aug. 5, 1981" www.politico.com August 5, 2018.

Grant, R.G.. *Ideas of the Modern World: Capitalism*. Raintree Steck-Vaughn Publishers, a Harcourt Company, Austin, New York 2001.

Gross, Larry interview with the author. August 20, 2018.

Grossman, Jonathan. "Fair Labor Standards Act of 1938: Maximum Struggle for a Minimum Wage" accessed at http://www.dol.gov/dol/aboutdol/history/flsa1938.htm

Gwilliam, Ivary, Chiosso, Cavalli & Brewer. "California's Tort Reform Puts Injuried Patients at a Disadvantage." www.giccb.com

H.R.610 - To distribute Federal funds for elementary and secondary education in the form of vouchers for eligible students and to repeal a certain rule relating to nutrition standards in schools. 115th Congress. www.congress.gov.

Hagerty, James R. "Why U.S. Manufacturing Is Poised for a Comeback (Maybe)" *Wall Street Journal* May 13, 2015.

Harrington, Michael. *Toward a Democratic Left: A Radical Program for a New Majority*. Penguin Books, Baltimore. Maryland 1969

Hausman, LJ. The Politics of a Guaranteed Income: The Nixon Administration and the Family Assistance Plan: A Review Article. *The Journal of Human Resources*. https://www.jstor.org/stable/144853 Autumn, 1973.

Heller, Nathan. "Who Really Stands to Win From Universal Basic Income?" *New Yorker* www.newyorker.com October 11, 1999.

Holland, Gale. "L.A.'s homelessness surged 75% in six years. Here's why the crisis has been decades in the making." *Los Angeles Times*. February 1, 2018.

Holtz, Colin. "The Panama Papers prove it: America can afford a universal basic income." www.theguardian.com April 11, 2017.

Howe, Irving. *Socialism and America*. New York: Harcourt Brace Jovanovich, 1985; pp. 54-55.

In the Public Interest. *Buying Influence: How Private Prison Companies Expand Their Control of America's Criminal Justice System.* https://www.inthepublicinterest.org/wp-content/uploads/ITPI_BuyingInfluence_Oct2016.pdf

Institute for New Economic Thinking www.ineteconomics.org

International Labour Office Bureau for Workers' Activities. "Trade Union Actions to Promote Environmentally Sustainable Development." from Geneva 22 Switzerland. Accessed April, 2018.

Johnson, Adam. "'Perseverance Porn' Bolsters System by Celebrating Survivors of Its Cruelties." *Fairness & Accuracy in Reporting (FAIR)* September, 2017.

Jones, Jeffrey M. "Democratic Edge in Party Affiliation Up to Seven Points" http://news.gallup.com/poll/211817/democratic-edge-party-affiliation-seven-points.aspx
June 6, 2017.

Justice Policy Institute. *Gaming the System: How the Political Strategies of Private Prison Companies Promote Ineffective Incarceration Policies.* October, 2011.

Karvelis, Noah. Internet interview with author. July, 22, 2018.

Kastrenakes, Jacob. "California passes strongest net neutrality law in the country." *The Verge*. August 31, 2018. https://www.theverge.com/2018/8/31/17805892/california-sb822-net-neutrality-law-vote

Kearney, James R. *Anna Eleanor Roosevelt*. Houghton Mifflin Company, Boston 1968.

Khavari, Dr. Farid telephone interview with the author. December, 30, 2017.

Klein, Aaron. "The real problem with credit reports is the astounding number of errors."

Brookings. September 27, 2017. www.brookings.edu

Kohler, Brian Director - Health, Safety and Sustainability, IndustriALL Global Union, interview by email June 21, 2017.

Kohn, Alfie. *No Contest: The Case Against Competition.* Houghton Mifflin Company 1986, 1992.

Korten, David C. *The Post-Corporate World: Life After Capitalism.* Kumarian Press, Inc. and Berrett-Koehler Publishers, Inc. San Francisco, CA and West Hartford, CT 1999.

Krugman, Paul. "The Conscience of a Liberal" W. W. Norton & Company, Inc. New York, NY 2007.

Krugman, Paul. "End This Depression Now!" W. W. Norton and Company New York, NY 2012.

Lawler, Edward E. III and Susan A. Mohrman. "Quality Circles After the Fad."
Harvard Business Review, January, 1985.

Levitin, Audrey. "How Rodney Roberts' Case Exposes the Injustice of Guilty Please." www.innoncenceproject.org September 13, 2018.

Lindsay. Tom. "New Report: The U.S. Student-Loan Debt Crisis Is Even Worse Than We Thought." *Forbes.com* May 24, 2018. https://www.forbes.com/sites/tomlindsay/2018/05/24/new-report-the-u-s-student-loan-debt-crisis-is-even-worse-than-we-thought/#76523a80e438

McLaren, John, and Shushanik Hakobyan. "Looking for Local Labor Market Effects of NAFTA." National Bureau of Economic Research Working Paper 16535. 2010.

Macleod, David. "What is Employee Engagement?" *Engage for Success.* http://engageforsuccess.org/what-is-employee-engagement

McGlynn, Adam and Lavariega Monforti, Jessica, The Poverty Draft? Exploring the Role of Socioeconomic Status in U.S. Military Recruitment of Hispanic Students (2010). APSA 2010 Annual Meeting Paper. Available at SSRN: https://ssrn.com/abstract=1643790

Miller, Michelle. "The Union of the Future." Accessed through https://www.forbes.com/sites/tomlindsay/2018/05/24/new-report-the-u-s-student-loan-debt-crisis-is-even-worse-than-we-thought/#76523a80e438 https://issuu.com/rooseveltinstitute Roosevelt Institute 2015.

Millhiser, Ian Justice Editor, ThinkProgress. "Why Black Lives Matter Protesters Are Targeting Democrats And Mostly Ignoring Republicans." Accessed through https://thinkprogress.org May, 2018.

Money.cnn.com "Facebook cofounder Chris Hughes: US need universal basic income."
March 15, 2018.

Qiu, Linda. "Did George W. Bush 'borrow' from Social Security to fund the war in Iraq and tax cuts?" *Politifact.* www.politifact.com August 3, 2015.

Panzner, Michael J.. *When Giants Fall: An Economic Roadmap for the End of the American Era.* John Wiley & Sons, Inc. Hoboken, NJ 2009.

Phillips, Kevin. "The Politics of Rich and Poor: Wealth and the American Electorate in the Reagan Aftermath" Random House New York, NY 1990.

Phillips, Kevin. *Wealth and Democracy: a Political History of the American Rich.* Broadway Books New York 2002.

Pickard, Victor. "Media Activism from Above and Below: Lessons from the 1940s American Reform Movement." *Journal of Information Policy*, vol. 5, 2015, pp. 109–128. *JSTOR*, JSTOR, www.jstor.org/stable/10.5325/jinfopoli.5.2015.0109.

Pierce, Sarah and Julia Gelatt, *Evolution of the H-1B: Latest Trends in a Program on the Brink of Reform* (Washington, DC: Migration Policy Institute, 2018), https://www.migrationpolicy.org/research/evolution-h-1b-latest-trends-program-brink-reform.

Raphelson, Samantha. "As the Gig Economy Grows, Advocates Raise Concerns About Workers' Safety." *NPR* December 4, 2017. www.npr.com.

Reich, Robert B. *Locked in the Cabinet*. Alfred A. Knopf New York, NY 1997.

"Right Web: tracking militarists' efforts to influence U.S. foreign policy."

Accessed through http://rightweb.irc-online.org/profile/Marshall_Will/

Roosevelt, Eleanor. *On My Own*. Harper & Brothers Publishers New York 1958.

Roosevelt, Eleanor. *Public Papers*, II (July 24 and 27, 1933).

Sanders, Bernie. "Corporate Greed Must End" *Boston Globe* June 24, 2015.

Schneiderman. Rose with Lucy Goldthwaite. *All for One*. Paul S. Erikson, Inc. New York 1967.

Schwartz, Nelson D. "The Doctor is in. Co-pay? $40,000." *The New York Times*. June 3, 2017.

Seidman, Derek. "What Happened to the Labor Party?" *Jacobin Magazine*. www.jacobinmag.com *May, 2018*.

Shankar, Subramanian. "Just like India, America has its own caste system." *Quartz India*. January 28, 2018.

Sinn, Mike P. "Government Spends More on Corporate Welfare Subsidies than Social Welfare Programs." ThinkbyNumbers.org March 6, 2011.

Solomon, Joel. *The Clean Money Revolution*. New Society Publishers, Limited, 2017.

Soros, George. *The Age of Fallibility: Consequences of the War on Terror.*".Public Affairs New York, NY 2006

Speri, Alice. "How the High Cost of Justice Pushes the Poor Into Prison." theintercept.com May 13, 2016.

Speth, Gus and Joe Uehlein. "Labor-Environmnetal Leaders and Activists Move Beyond Differences to a Common Vision about a New Economy." Labor Network for Sustainability accessed through www.labor4sustainability.com 2018.

Stern, Andrew. *Raising the Floor: How a Universal Basic Income Can Renew Our Economy and Rebuild the American Dream*. PublicAffairs, an imprint. of Perseus Books, division of PBG Publishing, LLC, a subsidiary of Hachette Book Group, Inc. 2016.

Stiglitz, Joseph E. *The Price of Inequality: How Today's Divided Society Endangers our Future*. W.W. Norton & Company New York London 2012.

Stockman, David. "How American Capitalism Died: The Age of Credit Finance." Accessed through http://davidstockmanscontracorner.com June, 2018.

Temin, Peter. *The vanishing middle class: prejudice and power in a dual economy*. MIT Press, Cambridge, MA 2017.

"The Dismal Future of Trump's Least Favorite Agency." *The Atlantic.* www.theatlantic.com November 20, 2017.

Von Drehle, David. "The Death of the death penalty." Accessed at http://time.com/deathpenalty/ August, 2018.

Wagner, Peter. And Bernadette Rabuy. "Following the Money of Mass Incarceration." *Prison Policy Initiative.* January 25, 2017. https://www.prisonpolicy.org/reports/money.html

Wagner, Peter and Wendy Sawyer. "Mass Incarceration: The Whole Pie 2018." *Prison Policy Initiative.* March 14, 2018. https://www.prisonpolicy.org/reports/pie2018.html?

Weiner, Tim. "The Dark Secret of the Black Budget." *Washington Monthly.* May, 1987. https://www.cia.gov/library/readingroom/docs/CIA-RDP90-00965R000707040013-3.pdf

Williams, Sean. "Bernie Sanders Just Proposed a Massive Overhaul of Social Security." *The Motley Fool.* Feb. 26, 2017. https://www.fool.com/retirement/2017/02/26/bernie-sanders-just-proposed-a-massive-overhaul-of.aspx

Wolfe, Bert comments used by permission. March 7, 2018.

Yellesetty, Leela. "How the racial caste system got restored." *International Socialist Review.* https://isreview.org/issue/73/how-racial-caste-system-got-restored. February. 2017.

Younkins, Edward W. *Michael Novak's Vision of Democratic Capitalism.* Quebecois Libre 3 Feb 2001. http://www.quebecoislibre.org/010203-10.htm

Biography

Gary Huck draws labor and political cartoons. From 1986-2015 he was the only full-time political cartoonist employed by a labor union in the US working with the independent progressive UE.

He continues to draw and syndicate cartoons with Mike Konopacki, huckkonopackicartoons.com. Their 7th collection of cartoons, **Torn**, was published in 2018.

He lives in Baltimore with the artist and professor Tavia La Follette and their twin 9yr. old sons Calder and Max.

CPSIA information can be obtained
at www.ICGtesting.com
Printed in the USA
FSHW010508060521
81190FS